PÈRE MARIE-BENOÎT
AND JEWISH RESCUE

Photograph courtesy of Rachel Hallman Schutz

PÈRE MARIE-BENOÎT AND JEWISH RESCUE

How a French Priest
Together with Jewish Friends
Saved Thousands during the Holocaust

Susan Zuccotti

INDIANA UNIVERSITY PRESS   *Bloomington & Indianapolis*

This book is a publication of

INDIANA UNIVERSITY PRESS
Office of Scholarly Publishing
Herman B Wells Library 350
1320 East 10th Street
Bloomington, Indiana 47405 USA

iupress.indiana.edu

Telephone orders 800-842-6796
Fax orders 812-855-7931

♾ The paper used in this publication
meets the minimum requirements of
the American National Standard for
Information Sciences–Permanence of
Paper for Printed Library Materials,
ANSI Z39.48–1992.

Manufactured in the
United States of America

Library of Congress
Cataloging-in-Publication Data

Zuccotti, Susan, [date]
    Père Marie-Benoît and Jewish rescue :
how a French priest together with Jewish
friends saved thousands during the
Holocaust / Susan Zuccotti.
    pages cm
  Includes bibliographical references and
index.
    ISBN 978-0-253-00853-4 (cloth : alkaline
paper) – ISBN 978-0-253-00866-4 (ebook)
 1. Marie-Benoît, le Bourg d'Iré, 1895–1990.
2. Righteous Gentiles in the Holocaust –
France – Marseille – Biography. 3. Capuchins – France – Marseille – Biography.
4. Priests – France – Marseille – Biography.
5. Holocaust, Jewish (1939–1945) – France
– Marseille. 6. World War, 1939–1945 –
Jews – Rescue – France – Marseille. 7. Jews
– France – Marseille – History – 20th
century. 8. Marseille (France) – History
– 20th century. 9. Marseille (France) –
Biography. I. Title.
  D804.66.M337Z82 2013
  940.53'18350944912 – dc23

                                2012047187

1 2 3 4 5   18 17 16 15 14 13

To

NICK, EMMA, SOPHIE, ROBBY, CASSIE, *and* NOAH

The heroic and fabulous feats of Father Marie-Benoît in rescuing Jews from the Gestapo during the Nazi occupation of Rome should inspire us in the United States to protect and respect the civil rights of all people regardless of how they may differ from us in race, color, or creed. Father Benoît saw the human dignity in the persecuted Jews and repeatedly risked his life to rescue them from the Gestapo and the incineration camps awaiting them. He blazed a trail for all of us to follow in protecting the civil and human rights of our fellow citizens and in thus respecting their dignity as fellow human beings.

PRESIDENT LYNDON B. JOHNSON
Pageant, November 1964

I have a tree planted in the alley of the Righteous at Yad Vashem in Jerusalem. This tree does not only represent me, it also represents the courageous Jews with whom I fought and without whom I would not have achieved a great deal.

PÈRE MARIE-BENOÎT
1975

Contents

Acknowledgments

MY LIST OF ACKNOWLEDGMENTS OF ASSISTANCE KINDLY GIVEN and gratefully received must necessarily begin with Père Marie-Benoît himself. I met this remarkable Capuchin priest on April 25, 1988, at the monastery in the rue Boissonade in Paris, where he spent the last three decades of his life. He was ninety-three years old at the time of my interview, a large man but frail and hard of hearing. Yet he was still willing to give time and attention to a stranger. Under the circumstances, not all of my questions could be answered, but the impression I received of a kind and gentle man has stayed with me ever since. When we met I did not know how ill he was, or that he would be leaving the monastery within a year for the rest home for elderly Capuchins in Angers, where he would pass away on February 5, 1990.

As I was leaving the monastery, a slightly younger man who also had an appointment with Père Marie-Benoît arrived. He introduced himself as Stefan Schwamm, the Jewish lawyer from Vienna with whom Père Marie-Benoît had worked in Rome during the Second World War to rescue thousands of refugees. The two men had remained close friends for the rest of their lives. My acquaintance with Stefan Schwamm was brief, but I was grateful for it; the other Jewish friends with whom Père Marie-Benoît had cooperated in rescue operations were all deceased. Mr. Schwamm appeared to me then exactly as he seemed in the documents I later studied: lively and curious; charming where Père Marie-Benoît was reserved; loquacious where Père Marie-Benoît was reticent. He must have wondered who I was and why Père Marie-Benoît had agreed to see me. After I left, Père Marie-Benoît would have explained my presence to him, adding, "How could I say no?" He said the same about the thousands of Jewish refugees who knocked on his doors between 1940 and 1944.

Stefan Schwamm died six years later, on February 9, 1994. When I examined his personal archives in Frankfurt am Main, Germany, in 2010, it appeared that his visit to Père Marie-Benoît when I saw him may have been his last. Previously he had visited often. Time was running out for these two elderly gentlemen that day in 1988, but both were willing to share their memories. Perhaps they were eager to do so, lest the most important events of their lives be forgotten. I wish I could tell them in person how grateful I am.

Years later, when I began to seriously study the life and times of Père Marie-Benoît, I had several technical concerns. From prior research I knew that I would have little difficulty finding material about that Capuchin priest's wartime rescue activities. I had already worked in two comprehensive Jewish archives – the Centre de documentation juive contemporaine (CDJC) at the Mémorial de la Shoah in Paris and the Centro de documentazione ebraica contemporania (CDEC) in Milan – and I was aware that there was ample material about Père Marie-Benoît in those two vast collections of documents. But I was much less certain about whether I would be able to unearth information about the priest's childhood and early education, or his military service and religious training. Equally daunting, would I be able to learn anything about how he spent the many postwar years of his long life?

I need not have worried. Beginning at the beginning, I traveled to the tiny village of Le Bourg d'Iré, in western France not far from Angers, where Père Marie-Benoît was born in 1895. There I had the good fortune to meet Jean-Pierre and Jocelyn Legourgeois. Jean-Pierre, the author of several volumes of the history of Le Bourg d'Iré from the Middle Ages to the present, seemed to know the genealogies of every resident of the village. He knew all about the family of Pierre Péteul, the boy who, upon ordination, would take the name Père Marie-Benoît. Not only did he share that family's genealogy with me, but he also drove me around the village, showing me the ruins of the mill and house where Pierre Péteul/Père Marie-Benoît was born and explaining the social and economic structure of a French region at the end of the nineteenth century. And then he invited me home for lunch. I was deeply impressed by this example of French hospitality. My gratitude to Jean-Pierre and Jocelyn is beyond words.

Through Jean-Pierre Legourgeois, I was able to meet three of the children of Père Marie-Benoît's brothers, now living in Angers. These included another Pierre Péteul, the son of Père Marie-Benoît's brother Louis, with his wife Christiane; Françoise Péteul Huel, the daughter of Louis; and Marie-Joseph Péteul Zenit, one of the four children of another brother, Joseph. These individuals remembered the priest well and were delighted to talk about his many visits. They proudly shared photographs, military records, certificates of honors received, and other mementos of the life of Père Marie-Benoît. I thank them for their great kindness.

The search for records of Père Marie-Benoît's military service and religious training took me back to the same Capuchin monastery in Paris where I had met him in 1988 and where he had spent the last thirty years of his life. His personal papers are in the Archives des Capucins de France (ACF), maintained at the monastery along with the Bibliothèque franciscaine des capucins. Carefully preserved are letters he wrote from the trenches during the First World War to his spiritual mentor in Holland, and the tiny notebook where he jotted down appointments and meetings, with some gaps, from the time of his arrival as a student in Rome in 1921 until 1961. Other documents include letters to and from other priests, religious superiors, and friends, mostly Jews; newspaper clippings about items of interest to him, mostly regarding Jews; reviews of books of similar interest; greeting cards and notes from grateful survivors whom he had helped; and much, much more. Through this material I was able to decipher the life and times of Père Marie-Benoît. Making it all available, often with explanations, were Marie-Hélène de Bengy, Cécile de Cacqueray, Pierre Moracchini, Frère Dominique Mouly, Anne le Bastard, and Monika Bem. Without their assistance this book would not have been possible. I am very grateful.

As it turned out, many other archives have material concerning Père Marie-Benoît and his friends, as well as archivists who are eager to be helpful. I am pleased to thank Frate Luigi Martignani at the Capuchin archives in Rome; Céline Hirsch at the archives of the Sisters of Notre Dame de Sion in Paris; Dominique Paquier-Galliard at the archives of the archdiocese of Marseille; Claude Floreal Herrera at the departmental archives in Marseille; Johan Ickx at the archives of Santa Maria dell'Anima in Rome; Luigi Allena at the Pontifical Gregorian University in Rome; Antonio Parisella at the archives of the Historic Museum of the Liberation of Rome in Rome; Diane Afoumado, Sandra Nagel, Lior Smadja, and others on the helpful staff at the CDJC in Paris; Liliana Picciotto, Michele Sarfatti, and other staff members at the CDEC in Milan; Shelley Helfand and Misha Mitsel at the archives of the American Jewish Joint Distribution Committee in New York City; Amy Schmidt at the National Archives in Washington, D.C.; Jane Stoeffler at the archives of the Catholic University of America in Washington, D.C.; and too many even to begin to list at Yad Vashem in Jerusalem and the New York Public Library.

Among the many others who kindly answered questions, supplied information, and offered explanations and observations were Professors Kevin Spicer, C.S.C., at Stonehill College, Michael Phayer from Marquette University, Vicki Caron at Cornell University, Gerald Steinacher at the University of Nebraska, and Donna Ryan at Gallaudet University; Judah Gribetz and John Barone in New York City; Pierre Sauvage in Los Angeles; Serge Klarsfeld and Olga Tarcali in Paris; Père Robert Levet in Marseille; Sergio Minerbi, Mordecai Paldiel, and Ed Greenstein from Israel; Frère Bruno-Marie in Oka, Quebec; Brother Roger Deguerre in White Plains, New York; Paul O'Shea in Sydney, Australia; Alberto Cavaglion in Turin; Carlo Badala, Padre Rinaldo Cordovani, Giorgio Fabre, Lutz Klinkhammer, and Monsignor Elio Venier in Rome; Thérèse Trévidic in Le Bourg d'Iré, and David Cesarani in London. Kevin Spicer and Michael Phayer also read the manuscript and made me the grateful beneficiary of their knowledge and expertise. They saved me from many errors. Needless to say, any that remain are my own. I thank these individuals profusely. Time is precious, and they all gave it generously.

Also invaluable are the testimonies of those who knew Père Marie-Benoît either because they worked with him or were saved by him. Among these I want to thank Samuel Berlin, Denise Caraco Siekierski, Lea Di Nola, Abraham Dresdner, Rachel Fallmann Schutz and her sister Esther Fallmann Kichelmacher, Miriam Löwenwirth Reuveni, Hermine Orsi, Hanna Rawicz Keselman, Charles Roman, Claude S. (who prefers to remain anonymous), Jacques Samson and his sister Paulette Samson Grunberg, Frieda Schnabel Semmelman and her son Jacques Semmelman, and Sedonie (Sidie) Templer Shytoltz, the latter name later changed to Sharon. Personal testimonies clarify and confirm the documents and make them come alive. The documents, in turn, validate the testimonies. I am grateful to have the benefit of this interaction.

In my quest for information about Père Marie-Benoît and his friends, I also focused on the friends. Here, except for that regarding Angelo Donati, material is scarce and more difficult to find. I would have despaired but for the kindness of descendants of Joseph Bass, Angelo Donati, and Stefan Schwamm. Joseph Bass's son Henri-Pierre and Angelo Donati's daughter Marianne Spier-Donati, both in Paris, shared memories with me and provided real and mental pictures of their exceptional fathers. Xavier Sarras Schwamm in Frankfurt did the same, and more. Stefan Schwamm's son gave me full access to his father's large personal archives of memoirs, letters, and documents. Père Marie-Benoît and Stefan Schwamm exchanged lively, amusing, nostalgic, often bittersweet letters until the death of the priest in 1990. They reminded each other of past triumphs and honors, chuckled over crazy mishaps, and mourned serious losses. They were remembering the difficult but exhilarating days of their youth. Their letters make them come alive. I hope that as an expression of my gratitude this book will do the same.

I would also like to thank my agent, Georges Borchardt, whose commitment to my work has been invaluable. He read my manuscript with his usual unerring eye and helped me make it more concise and, I hope, more immediate and moving. And finally I thank my family: my husband, John Zuccotti, without whom this book would never have been possible, and our children, Gianna Zuccotti and David Weinstock, Andrew and Margaret Mauran Zuccotti, and Milena Zuccotti and Jason Merwin. This book is dedicated to our children's children: Sophie and Noah Weinstock; Nicholas, Emma, and Robert Zuccotti; and Cassandra Merwin, with all my love.

PÈRE MARIE-BENOÎT
AND JEWISH RESCUE

Introduction

ON THE EVENING OF APRIL 17, 1944, PÈRE MARIE-BENOÎT, A
French Capuchin priest, and Stefan Schwamm, a Jewish lawyer from
Vienna, were preparing for a frugal meal in a small trattoria in Milan.
The two deeply committed rescuers of Jews had just completed a most
unusual, even zany, trip from Rome to Milan in an official German car
with an Italian Fascist driver and travel permits from the International
Red Cross. In Florence, with recommendations from their driver, they
had dined and rested at the posh Grand Hotel Baglioni, where most of
the other guests were German officers and diplomats – occupiers of the
country they both loved. Now in northern Italy, they hoped to obtain
from a clandestine Jewish organization the funds necessary to continue
their rescue operations in Rome, along with information about possible
escape routes to Switzerland for their Jewish protégés. With this in mind,
Schwamm phoned a local contact at her apartment. The woman told
them to stay where they were; she would join them at the trattoria.

Outwardly the two travelers looked harmless enough. Forty-nine-
year-old Père Marie-Benoît was a big, burly man with a bushy, slightly
gray beard and the brown cassock, ample pointed hood, rope belt, and
sandals of a Capuchin friar. Stefan Schwamm, then thirty-four, tall, lean,
and scholarly, looked every bit the lawyer and, critically at that time, not
noticeably Jewish. Both men spoke Italian with only slight accents. Père
Marie-Benoît's foreignness would have provoked no questions in Italy.
Priests in that country came from all over the world. As for Schwamm,
his excellent, if false, documents, fabricated by himself with great skill,
identified him as a citizen of France and a social worker for the Red Cross,

an activity that was acceptable in German-occupied Italy. Schwamm's slight accent when speaking Italian was more French than German, confirming his identification documents. His Austrian origins would not have been suspected. With some degree of comfort, then, they ordered dinner.

Half an hour later, a man in a sinister-looking raincoat – the familiar costume of the Gestapo – appeared at the entrance of the trattoria and summoned Stefan Schwamm to the door. After conferring with the stranger, Schwamm, stooped and ashen, returned to the table, picked up his coat, and whispered, "I am under arrest." After his friend disappeared with the stranger, Père Marie-Benoît did not waste a minute. Returning to the hotel, he gathered up their things and left, telling the doorman that he was returning to Rome. Instead he made his way to the local Capuchin monastery. Sure enough, police agents came for him at the hotel a short time later and then went to the railroad station. They did not find him. A few days later Père Marie-Benoît coolly traveled to Genoa and secured the one million lire that kept at least 2,532 Jewish protégés safely in their hiding places for another month, until the liberation of the Eternal City on June 4, 1944.

Equally resourceful, Stefan Schwamm survived deportation to a satellite camp of Auschwitz. Miraculously, his false papers stood up under scrutiny and his Jewishness was never discovered. In the camp his talent for languages – in addition to German, French, and Italian, he spoke English, Romanian, and some Russian and Hebrew – secured him a life-saving indoor job, and his experience with false documents for Jewish protégés in Rome enabled him to shuffle papers and help some fellow prisoners escape the attention of their persecutors. Liberated by the Russians in January 1945, Schwamm wandered through Poland, the Soviet Union, Romania, Hungary, Austria, and Yugoslavia before returning to Rome in September.

Who was this unusual priest, Père Marie-Benoît, ostensibly so unworldly yet so adept at hiding Jews, supplying them with false papers, and eluding their persecutors? How had he come to do what he was doing? And why? Père Marie-Benoît had a long and fascinating history. Obliged by the French laws of separation of the churches and the state to go to Belgium in 1907, at the age of twelve, to begin his studies to become a Capuchin priest, this young man from a tiny village in western France nevertheless returned to his country of birth in 1914 to spend four years in deadly combat, much of it at Verdun, during the First World War. After that horror, while completing his doctorate in philosophy and theology at Rome's prestigious Gregorian University, he witnessed the rise to highest office of both Achille Ratti as Pope Pius XI in February 1922 and Benito Mussolini as head of the Italian government the following October. Eighteen years later, after a successful if uneventful career as a teacher of young Capuchin priests or prospective priests in Rome, he was repatriated when Italy declared war on France and Britain in June 1940. Back in France, he established himself at a Capuchin monastery in Marseille and embarked on an extraordinary Jewish rescue operation. Why and how was he able to do this, and what did he accomplish? And what factors led to his famous audience with Pope Pius XII in Rome on July 16, 1943, just a few days before King Vittorio Emanuele III dismissed Mussolini and replaced him with Marshal Pietro Badoglio? The Capuchin priest went to the pope to plead for the Jews. What did he achieve?

Père Marie-Benoît's audience with the pope neatly marked the division of his wartime experiences between rescue activities in Marseille and his subsequent, still more dramatic assistance to thousands of Jewish refugees in Rome during the German occupation of Italy. But in neither case did he act alone. Unlike most non-Jewish rescuers of Jews during the Holocaust, this Capuchin priest almost always worked in cooperation with courageous Jewish men and women who were risking their lives to save their people. In Marseille in 1942, for example, he became part of a rescue network created by Joseph Bass, a brilliant Russian Jewish lawyer. Then in Nice and Rome in mid-1943, he worked on an imaginative and daring plan created by Angelo Donati, an equally brilliant Italian Jewish banker and diplomat, to bring Jewish refugees hiding in southeastern France to safety in North Africa – and almost succeeded. Finally, in Rome from September 1943 until that city's liberation nine months later, he acted as the virtual leader of the local chapter of Delasem, an Italian Jewish rescue organization whose formal directors and original activists had to maintain a low profile because they were Jewish. There he worked closely with Stefan Schwamm and other Jewish rescuers, especially Settimio Sorani and Aron Kasztersztein, to hide Jewish refugees in small hotels, boardinghouses, apartments, and institutions of the Church.

The Jews with whom Père Marie-Benoît worked remembered him with great affection and admiration. Settimio Sorani, acting director of Delasem in Rome during the war, paid tribute to him in 1962, writing, "Padre Benedetto [Père Marie-Benoît's name in Italian], a charming and really superior human being, is one of the noblest characters I have ever met. He was my most valued fellow-worker."[1] Four years later, Sorani again wrote of the priest's wartime work and referred to "the merits that Padre Benedetto acquired through his goodness, for his high moral qualities, for his enlightened, precious, courageous assistance for which everyone must be extremely grateful . . . also because he never tried to make conversions. His actions were always pure, crystalline, admirable."[2] A few years after that, Elio Toaff, the chief rabbi of Rome at the time, echoed Sorani's words, telling an Italian prelate, "I believe that in all of Europe [during the war] there was no one who did what Padre Benedetto was able to do. And then with a broadness of vision, totally disinterested, even with scorn for the danger, [he was] truly exceptional."[3] Indeed, he was exceptional in his courage but also in his close cooperation with Jewish rescue organizations.

In turn, Père Marie-Benoît never failed to pay tribute to those brave Jewish men and women with whom he had worked in rescue. In 1984, for example, he wrote to Stefan Schwamm's wife, "Dear Simone, I do not hide from you that [the honors I have received] . . . I owe in large measure to assistance from your husband."[4] To Schwamm himself he wrote of his rescue activities in Rome, "For my part I was far from being an effective director, I had rather to learn from you many things of an administrative and juridical nature. Courage, sang froid, the clear view of the situation . . . that is owed principally to you."[5] Père Marie-Benoît was equally generous in tributes to other rescuers with whom he had worked.

At least three of the Jewish rescuers with whom Père Marie-Benoît worked – Joseph Bass, Angelo Donati, and Stefan Schwamm – became close friends with whom he maintained contact throughout his life. But he also remained in contact with many of those he saved, especially the women – Miriam Löwenwirth, Esther and Rachel Fallmann, Clara and Frieda Schnabel, and others. These grateful women sent him photographs of their families and greetings at Christmas and New Year's, and they visited him in the monastery in Paris where he spent the last years of his life. In part because of those friendships, the priest dedicated himself to the promotion of Jewish-Christian understanding after the war, to the detriment of his career. For in the years before the Second Vatican Council that began in October 1962, Pope Pius XII and many of the ecclesiastics around him did not look favorably on social contact between Catholics and Jews.

This book tells the story of an extraordinary priest and his Jewish friends. Naturally it emphasizes the years of Jewish rescue during the Holocaust. To that end, it describes in some detail the development of the persecutions of the Jews, from the first racial laws in Italy and France to the onset of arrests and deportations. Such background material is essential to an understanding of what Père Marie-Benoît and his friends were able to accomplish. The book also looks at Père Marie-Benoît's Jewish friends, insofar as information about them is available. Joseph Bass, Angelo Donati, and Stefan Schwamm emerge most clearly from the mists of time. In addition, we shall meet several of the men and women whom Père Marie-Benoît and his friends saved, including Miriam, Esther, Rachel, and Clara, mentioned above, as well as Hanna Rawicz, Sedonie Templer, Abraham Dresdner, Samuel Berlin, and others. Theirs are the stories of lives saved by Père Marie-Benoît and his friends.

But this book has another dimension. Saddled around the tale of rescue, occurring before and after it, is the story of the formation and development of a French country priest. This Capuchin was exceptional in many ways, from his early brilliance in his studies of philosophy and theology to his dedication to Jewish rescue in the Second World War and the promotion of Jewish-Christian reconciliation afterward. But Père Marie-Benoît was also typical in several respects. His life demonstrates the manner in which the Church offered talented boys from humble backgrounds a higher education and an opportunity to excel. His experience in the First World War is not dissimilar to that of thousands of courageous young French Catholic priests and seminarians who loyally served and often died for a country that had persecuted Catholics, both during the French Revolution and a century later, at the time of the laic laws and the separation of the churches from the state. And his years in

Rome between the two wars were replicated in the lives of hundreds of other priests from many countries who shared the excitement of life in the city of popes and the anxiety of existence in the shadow of Fascism. These priests are rarely remembered in historical treatises. Through Père Marie-Benoît we can catch a glimpse of the lives of many earnest young men whose personal sacrifices and dedication to the salvation of souls have long been forgotten.

One word of caution: Pierre Péteul, Père Marie-Benoît, and Padre Maria Benedetto are one and the same person. Our Capuchin priest was born Pierre Péteul, and he retained that name throughout his secular life, including his years of military service in the First and Second World Wars. In his religious life he first assumed the name Frère, or Brother, Marie-Benoît, and then, after his ordination as a priest in 1923, Père Marie-Benoît. That latter name translated into Italian as Padre Maria Benedetto, although "Maria" was often omitted in informal references. Throughout this book, he will be referred to as Pierre Péteul when acting in a secular capacity, including his military service; as Père Marie-Benoît when he was a priest in France; and as Padre Maria Benedetto or just Padre Benedetto during his years in Italy. An imperfect solution, perhaps, but one that may help in our attempt to perceive him as his friends and confreres saw him.

ONE

Pierre Péteul

PIERRE PÉTEUL WAS BORN ON MARCH 30, 1895, IN THE VILLAGE of Le Bourg d'Iré, about fifty kilometers north of Angers. His father leased and operated the large local water mill of Pommeraye, which his ancestors had run since the eighteenth century.[1] When Pierre was little more than five years old, his father, also named Pierre, gave up or lost the lease to the mill for reasons that are unclear (fig. 1). The family, which now included two more sons, René Gabriel (1896–1916) and Louis (1898–1983), moved first to nearby Segré and then to Angers. Despite this early move to the city, however, the younger Pierre seems to have been stamped by the traditions of his ancestors. Years later, as a priest, he always referred to himself proudly as Pierre Péteul "of Le Bourg d'Iré" when required to give his secular name. Others writing of him used the same description.

The departure from Le Bourg d'Iré must have been wrenching, for the Péteul family seems to have suffered from hard times in Angers. The elder Pierre's job in a factory making ecclesiastical candles brought in much less than he had earned as a miller, even while the birth of a fourth son, Joseph (1901–1982), increased the family's expenses. Whether because of economic circumstances, personal stress, or other reasons, the elder Pierre's wife (our Pierre's mother) suffered an extreme mental breakdown and had to be hospitalized for most of the rest of her life. There is no evidence of the impact of this terrible event on her oldest son, except that he continued to visit his mother's relatives as long as he and they lived. But normal family life was over.

Within a few years after his move to Angers, the elder Pierre's position had deteriorated from modestly successful village businessman to head of a family in need. Through all of these troubles, the Catholic Church offered great consolation. The elder Pierre served with enthusiasm and dedication as choirmaster in the local parish church, while his son Pierre was an eager member of the choir. Somehow the father sent Pierre and, presumably, his three younger brothers to the local Catholic school. When his sons were older, he participated in several extended retreats at a nearby monastery. All of this contributed to the younger Pierre's formation and outlook on life. The Church came to represent, for him, shelter, security, and compassion. At the same time, he remembered Le Bourg d'Iré as a warm and happy place that offered stability and continuity through its connection to the past.

A brief look at the geography and history of Angers and Le Bourg d'Iré is essential if we are to understand the formation of Pierre Péteul. Before the French Revolution, the region in which Le Bourg d'Iré and Angers were located was known as the province of Anjou. Divided by the Loire River, flowing from east to west to empty into the Atlantic Ocean fifty kilometers west of Nantes, Anjou was bordered on the west by Brittany, on the southwest by the Vendée, and on the south by Poitou. The province became part of the royal domain of France temporarily at the beginning of the thirteenth century and definitively in 1584. Its capital was Angers, a lovely medieval city on the Maine River near where it flows into the Loire from the north. Like so many cities and small towns near the Loire, Angers boasted a huge thirteenth-century fortress and château, built by King Louis IX (Saint Louis) to protect the province from enemy incursions from Brittany or Aquitaine. In the fifteenth century the château served as the brilliant court of Duke René d'Anjou, regent of Sicily and Jerusalem.

During the French Revolution most of the province of Anjou became the department of Maine-et-Loire. The department was divided into several districts. Le Bourg d'Iré, with a population of 1,265 in 1891, four years before Pierre Péteul was born, was in the district of Segré, in the department's remote northwestern corner.[2] Equally important as far as Pierre is concerned, Le Bourg d'Iré was on the small Verzée River, which flows into the larger Oudon at Segré. The Verzée supplied the power for Pierre's father's mill.

Like most of the rest of Maine-et-Loire when Pierre was born, the area around Le Bourg d'Iré was predominantly agricultural. Wheat, corn, dairy cows, horses, and sheep were raised in gently rolling fields amply watered by meandering streams and rivers. While those same streams supplied power for water mills, there were in addition more than nine hundred windmills in the department during the nineteenth century. Pierre's father also leased and operated a windmill in Le Bourg d'Iré for a time. Millers were viewed with respect as economically indispensable businessmen in their villages, for every local family had to bring its grain to the nearest mill to be ground into flour. Bread was then baked at home. Earning a decent living, millers tended to marry their children to the offspring of other millers in order to keep the business in the family. This was true for our Pierre Péteul, whose father, Pierre (1866–1950), married Agnès Royer, daughter of the miller at nearby Le Tremblay, in 1894.[3]

Many inhabitants of Maine-et-Loire were handicapped by isolation from the rest of France. That isolation was dramatized by the fact that, as in Brittany, women wore distinctive headgear until well into the twentieth century. The problem was not rooted in geography – in deserts, canyons, or mountain ranges – but rather in an almost nonexistent infrastructure. Angers and cities on the Loire enjoyed an obvious water route to the outside world, an advantage compounded by the arrival of the railroad in the late 1840s. The interior of the department, however, suffered from the lack of decent roads, canals, and navigable rivers. The poor quality of the roads was articulated as a major issue in March 1789 when King Louis XVI invited his countrymen to articulate their grievances in the Cahiers de Doléances for consideration by the upcoming Estates General. It remained an issue for decades afterward.

As might be expected in a traditional French agricultural community where outside influences were scarce, most of the 513,490 inhabitants of the department of Maine-et-Loire in 1906 were fervent Roman Catholics. There were only 550 Protestants and about a dozen Jews in the department at the time, and agnosticism and atheism were rare. Everyone else was Catholic, and usually highly observant. Catholics in Angers were pleased to have a Catholic university in the city, founded in 1875.

Although there were 1,046 public elementary schools throughout the department at the beginning of the twentieth century, many parents, especially those from rural areas, preferred to send their children to Catholic schools. The teachers in such schools were priests, friars, and nuns who included religious subjects in the curriculum and prepared their pupils for the sacraments of First Holy Communion, Penance, and Confirmation. In Le Bourg d'Iré around 1900, an estimated nine out of ten families chose Catholic schools. The local public school eventually had to close because of a lack of pupils.[4]

Another indication of the fervent Catholicism of residents of Maine-et-Loire is the high number of religious vocations – that is, of men and women who became priests, friars, monks, and nuns. Precise statistics are elusive, but impressionistic evidence is revealing. Around 1907, when Pierre Péteul expressed his desire to attend the Catholic seminary in Angers to become a diocesan priest, he was told there was no place for him. One reason for the rejection was that after the separation of the churches from the state and the loss of state subsidies, as will be described below, the seminary could no longer afford the expense of training the high number of applicants. Pierre therefore joined the Capuchin order of priests and brothers.[5]

A look at Pierre's family history also confirms the impression of a high number of vocations, at least within one family in Maine-et-Loire. One of Pierre's three brothers, René Gabriel, also joined a religious order, the Frères de Saint Gabriel, before he was killed on the Somme in 1916. Pierre's uncle René Péteul (1854–1886), a brother of his father, was a Cistercian priest in Canada, where he died before Pierre was born. Of the twelve other siblings of the senior Pierre and René, three more chose a religious vocation. These three – Marie-Angèle, Célestine, and Dorothée – were daughters who became nuns.[6] There were also three nuns in the family of the younger Pierre Péteul's mother.

It was not unusual for individual French families to contribute more than one child to the Church in a single generation. Studies of the backgrounds of candidates for the priesthood elsewhere in France have indicated that religiously observant parents, trusted advisors, and good Catholic schools often influenced more than one young person in a family. According to a historian of Le Bourg d'Iré, however, the pattern was particularly prevalent in the area around that village during the end of the nineteenth century and the first decades of the twentieth.[7]

Despite its small size, Le Bourg d'Iré, when Pierre Péteul came into the world, had a long and proud history that left an indelible imprint on its residents. Its main claim to fame, and the historical calamity known to every man, woman, and child in the village, involved its role in the armed struggle against the French Revolution in 1793 and 1794. The story began harmlessly enough. Locals were eager to petition the king for redress of grievances in 1789. Among the nineteen signers of the Cahiers de Doléances from Le Bourg d'Iré was a miller named René Péteul.[8] The requests concerned not only dreadful roads but also obstructed rivers; inequitable land distribution; the unjust legal system; onerous feudal dues and labor service; the lack of schools, teachers, hospitals, and doctors; desperate poverty in the countryside; and high and arbitrary taxes, especially the *gabelle,* the heavy tax levied on the salt that was essential for the preservation of meat. Citizens also sought a greater voice in the selection of municipal and provincial representatives, especially those who determined the allocation of taxes.

Perhaps inevitably the Cahiers de Doléances raised expectations to impossible levels, and within two or three years of the storming of the Bastille on July 14, 1789, severe popular disenchantment with the new revolutionary regime set in. Although feudal dues and labor service were eliminated in August 1789, taxes seemed only to increase. Even worse, the nationwide conscription of three hundred thousand young men announced in February 1793 infuriated locals who lived in safety, far from invading armies of Prussians, Austrians, and French exiles threatening France from the east. Meanwhile, requisitions of food and livestock to feed soldiers and city folk left peasants hungrier than ever, angry, and desperate. Roads continued to deteriorate as bureaucrats struggled to organize themselves and address more urgent issues. Even the elimination of the gabelle provoked unrest in some quarters, for local peasants had long made extra money during the winter months by smuggling salt from Brittany, where it was not taxed, into Anjou, where it was, and selling it below the official price.

In highly Catholic and conservative Le Bourg d'Iré and its environs, however, all these grievances paled when compared to the issue of deteriorating Church-state relations. Tensions rose in 1789 and 1790 as the new government in Paris emancipated Protestants and Jews, eliminated tithes, nationalized large ecclesiastical properties, and abolished most religious orders. Especially in western France, a precarious situation escalated into a violent confrontation with the Civil Constitution of the Clergy, which decreed on July 12, 1790, among other measures, that parish priests and bishops were to be elected by parishioners, that French bishops must not act without consulting a permanent council of vicars, and that all clergy must sign an oath of loyalty to the state. Although these and other measures constituted a direct challenge to the Vatican, most prelates and priests throughout the country, bending to political realities, reluctantly signed the oath initially.[9] In the Vendée, however, 70 percent of all parish priests refused to sign from the very beginning, even before Pope Pius VI ordered that response in the spring of 1791. In the southwestern corner of Maine-et-Loire known as the Mauges the figure was 90 percent, and in the area around Le Bourg d'Iré it was 53 percent.[10] In Le Bourg d'Iré itself both the parish priest and the vicar refused the loyalty oath.

As these "refractory" priests went into hiding, and as parishioners refused to accept their official oath-taking, "constitutional" replacements, fanatic delegates from the revolutionary regime in Paris, began to comb the countryside, arresting thousands. Catholic dissenters, including priests, were imprisoned, deported, and often executed. As a result, large counterrevolutionary armies sprouted up in Brittany, the northern half of the Vendée, and the western corners of Maine-et-Loire, and a brutal civil war ensued. Temporarily victorious counterrevolutionary armies committed atrocities, which in turn led to massive reprisals as government troops gained the upper hand. Now revolutionary agents shot, drowned, or guillotined women, children, and the elderly; destroyed entire families; exposed severed heads and hands in public places; systematically raped women; burned fields; killed livestock; forcibly evacuated entire populations; and razed whole villages to the ground. In Nantes alone as many as ten thousand prisoners, including many women and children, were executed, often by being tied to barges and sunk in the Loire.[11] Tens of thousands are estimated to have been killed throughout the region in bitter fighting that contin-

ued off and on for years. Many villages bear the scars of the violence to
this day.

Throughout the terrible years of civil war, Le Bourg d'Iré, with a
population of about one thousand, was torn apart by numerous tragedies. Just one of many was Yves Bouvier, a local boy born in 1719 and
orphaned at the age of nine who nevertheless succeeded in becoming a
priest. Refusing the oath of loyalty to the state in 1791, he hid with local
farmers by day and roamed the countryside by night, visiting the sick and
celebrating mass. Caught at the home of his brother-in-law in 1794, he
was shot on the spot, but only after a soldier severed his hand with a saber
as he was attempting to give absolution to his equally doomed protector.
In another case, six counterrevolutionary insurgents, including a priest,
were caught in the village and shot, and the couple sheltering them was
imprisoned in Angers. In revenge the insurgents captured and shot five
local municipal republicans who had denounced them. Reprisals on both
sides soon followed. As the war evolved from regular battles to guerrilla
operations in the late summer of 1794, elusive bands of insurgents attacked National Guard posts in Le Bourg d'Iré, burned the church that
was being used by the republicans for storage, looted republican homes,
and murdered republican officials whenever they could catch them. Altogether thirty-seven insurgents, including twenty-one women, and eleven
republicans were killed in Le Bourg d'Iré during the civil war.[12]

The name Péteul is often found in records of the conflict in Le Bourg
d'Iré, always on the side of the traditionalists or insurgents. Seven people
bearing that name, for example, were among the sixty-nine signers of
a petition to the French minister of the interior on November 18, 1791,
complaining that "three quarters of the parish [of Le Bourg d'Iré] have
been deprived of the sacraments, religious instruction, and all spiritual
assistance, including even the last rites, because they remain faithful to
the voice of their conscience," and begging to be allowed to keep the services of their non-oath-taking priest, so long as he said nothing against
the laws of the state. More tragically, forty-eight-year-old Angélique Péteul, one of the signers of the petition, was arrested in the village a year
or so later, accused of helping non-oath-taking priests, and imprisoned
in the seminary in Angers. Taken before a revolutionary committee, she
was sentenced to death and shot. Louis Péteul, a cousin of Angélique and

also a signer of the petition, was more fortunate. Louis was the miller at Pommeraye, where his great-great-grandson, our Pierre Péteul, was born a century later. Age thirty-three in 1793, Louis hid the vicar Paizot in his mill, disguising him as a miller's assistant. With other disguises, as a peasant, worker, or traveling salesman, the vicar wandered through the region, saying mass and administering the sacraments. Among those he baptized on November 9, 1795, were the four children of a René Péteul who had also signed the 1791 petition. One of the four, René's eldest child, Marie, had already been baptized by the official oath-taking priest, Père Richard, at Le Bourg d'Iré on October 19, 1791, but her parents clearly considered that baptism invalid.[13]

Although somewhat subdued, counterrevolutionary violence in western France continued until at least the end of the eighteenth century. It gradually dissipated, however, after the concordat between Napoleon and Pope Pius VII in 1801. Among other things, that agreement resolved the issue of the appointment of bishops by declaring that they would be nominated by the secular French state but consecrated by the pope. Bishops, in turn, would appoint parish priests, but only if they were acceptable to the secular authorities.[14]

For the seven decades following the concordat, relations between the Catholic Church and the state were surprisingly peaceful, at least on the surface, and the scars of the civil war seemed to be healing. Particularly during the Bourbon Restoration after Napoleon, a religious revival flourished throughout the country. Thousands of churches reopened, and the government authorized the return of several male religious orders and more than two hundred female orders, especially those devoted to nursing, teaching, and social work. Even the Jesuits, suppressed well before the French Revolution, returned and flourished after 1814. With time, many more religious orders returned to France without official authorization.

Despite Napoleon's efforts to secure a healthy balance between constitutional and refractory clergy, however, the latter came to dominate the Catholic Church in France during the age of Romanticism. This was true in part because the restored Bourbon kings Louis XVIII and Charles X enlarged the number of dioceses and appointed many new bishops. Those bishops and the young priests they and the government agreed upon inevitably shared the attitudes of the Restoration authorities. Unlike clergymen of the ancien régime, who were often interested in Enlightenment ideas and political reform, the new men, usually from the nobility, were invariably counterrevolutionary, royalist, and conservative. This did not bode well for future relations with those French secular leaders who were increasingly liberal and anticlerical in their politics and rationalist, materialist, and positivist in their intellectual orientations.

The inevitable conflict between two cultures was not immediately apparent. Between 1815 and 1848, Bourbon and, after 1830, Orleanist government authorities instituted other changes that were pleasing to the Church in France and to the pope in Rome. Sunday was again declared an obligatory day of rest. The possibility of divorce was removed from the Napoleonic Code. Then in a new step toward the brewing battle for education, a law in 1833 declared that elementary schools were to include moral and religious instruction in their curriculums and that Catholic clergymen could operate such schools. This cordiality did not decline after the Revolution of 1848 and the establishment of the Second Republic. On the contrary, the new government, anxious to avoid a confrontation with the Church, offered more concessions. The most significant of these was the Falloux law of March 1850. The law was named for the minister of education at the time, who, coincidentally, maintained a family château in Le Bourg d'Iré.

The Falloux law permitted Catholic secondary schools, suppressed during the French Revolution, to operate and compete with state schools. Because the law did not specifically mention unauthorized religious orders, the Jesuits and others, both authorized and not, were able to establish secondary schools for boys. So many did so that within two or three decades nearly half of all male secondary school students in France were in Catholic schools. The law also promoted the creation of schools for girls, and by the same logic, religious orders of nuns could now establish those institutions. The Falloux law also required some religious education in the public schools, allowed members of Catholic religious orders to teach in the public schools, and established joint boards of priests and local secular officials to supervise elementary schools. The concessions embodied in the Falloux law profoundly alienated many republicans, anticlerical heirs of the French Revolution. But their time had not yet come.

During his period of authoritarian rule from 1851 to 1870, Louis Napoleon Bonaparte, soon to be Emperor Napoleon III, was able to keep the lid on the incipient confrontation. After the demoralizing Franco-Prussian War of 1870, however, followed by the immensely destructive Paris Commune in 1871 and the political struggles from which the Third Republic emerged, the Church-state conflict became a defining issue. Conservatives, royalists, and Catholic spokesmen, concerned that a republican regime would result in socialism, anticlericalism, and a restriction of Church prerogatives, vehemently opposed the fragile new constitution of 1875. Worried by that opposition, republicans in turn endorsed some of the very positions their antagonists most feared and set about to limit the influence of the Church in France. And because that influence seemed to operate especially in the schools, the conflict degenerated into a battle for education.

The result was a series of laic laws and measures between 1880 and 1889 and again between 1900 and 1906 that profoundly affected the lives of the young Pierre Péteul and millions like him. During the first period, the so-called Ferry laws prohibited Catholic priests and members of religious orders from teaching and working in public primary and secondary schools and outlawed religious education in those same state institutions.[15] These measures were not always enforced, however, and many members of religious orders, especially if they were willing to wear secular garb and distract attention from their vocations, continued to teach in public schools where they had been banned. Religious orders not specifically authorized by the state were again banished at this time, but here, too, enforcement was sometimes lax. In fact, some orders seemed to be flourishing. By one estimate there were 1,200 religious orders in the country in 1900, involving 30,000 men and 150,000 women, who were teaching about two million children.[16]

If enforcement was lax, however, it may not have seemed so to the parents of the yet unborn Pierre Péteul. Pierre's father's brother René Péteul was a twenty-six-year-old Cistercian priest at the nearby Abbey of Bellefontaine in Bégrolles-en-Mauges, in the department of Maine-et-Loire, when it was seized by the French army in November 1880. Priests and monks at the abbey were expelled from the country. Eight of them moved to Canada in April 1881 to found the Abbey of Notre-Dame-du-Lac at Oka in the province of Quebec. René Péteul joined them a year later. True to the family tradition, he was, among other things, a choirmaster there. He never saw his parents again. For him, his country's laic laws were cruel indeed. In 1886 he died of meningitis and was the first person buried in the cemetery of the new abbey.[17] This René had taken the name Père Marie-Benoît when he became a priest. In the 1920s, his nephew Pierre assumed that name to honor him.

While enforcement of laic laws regarding education was sometimes lax in the 1880s and 1890s, other measures affecting Catholics were more thoroughly enforced. These included laws ending Sunday as an obligatory day of rest in 1880, banning military chaplains and prohibiting army escorts for public religious processions in 1883, suppressing public prayers in 1884, reestablishing divorce the same year, and in 1889 requiring that all seminary students perform military service. These various measures rescinded the special recognition and privileges that Catholics had regained after the French Revolution and left them angered, embittered, and worried about the future.

In addition to being years of conflict between republicans and conservatives, including defenders of Church prerogatives, the 1880s and early 1890s witnessed severe economic depression, anarchist violence, and political scandals and corruption. Opponents of the Third Republic naturally blamed these problems on the regime itself. Needing a more visible scapegoat for their troubles, they also blamed the Jews. Arguing that the Jews had been emancipated by the French Revolution and were consequently fervent supporters of republican principles, conservatives, royalists, and many Catholics depicted them as beneficiaries of everything that they themselves despised. With much logical inconsistency, Catholics portrayed the Jews as responsible for extreme liberalism, heartless industrialization, individualism, internationalism, materialism, anticlericalism, and socialism – in short, with all the perceived ills of modern life. Such ideas appealed to many who were suffering from unemployment, bank failures, and economic dislocation, and antisemitism soared.

The worst, however, was yet to come. France's most devastating culture clash began in 1894 with the Dreyfus Affair and continued for more than ten dreary years. During that period, French conservatives, including many priests, members of religious orders, and Catholic laymen, clung to their conviction that French Jewish army officer Alfred Dreyfus was guilty of espionage long after the evidence indicated otherwise. Priests and members of religious orders who printed vicious antisemitic and antirepublican newspapers and pamphlets did much to polarize public opinion. The Dreyfus Affair brought disgrace to the right and electoral victory to the Radical Party, which was now more anticlerical than ever.

A new series of anti-Church measures ensued, and this time they were vigorously enforced. In July 1901, for example, in the context of a broader law on associations, all religious orders were required to request government authorization within a specified period. Authorization was rarely given, and in 1902 unauthorized orders were dissolved and their property reverted to the state. Some three thousand schools run by unauthorized religious orders were promptly closed, and, in a replay of 1793, thousands of priests, friars, monks and nuns who refused to give up their orders left the country.[18] Then in July 1904 a new law prohibited teaching by men and women in all religious orders, even if authorized, and more members of those orders departed. Those same men and women could continue teaching only if they abandoned all visible signs of living in religious orders, including the wearing of religious habits. Many, including those teaching at the local Catholic elementary school in Angers where nine-year-old Pierre Péteul was a pupil, chose that option. But the boy would have witnessed forcible school closings elsewhere, as well as priests, brothers, and nuns on their way into exile. Family stories of the persecutions of his ancestors took on new meaning.

The culmination of this process finally came with the government's unilateral revocation of the concordat of 1801 and declaration of the separation of all religious institutions, Catholic, Protestant, and Jewish, from the state in December 1905.[19] After announcing that the French Republic would assure "liberty of conscience" and guarantee "the free exercise of all religions," the law declared that the state "neither recognizes, nor pays salaries for, nor subsidizes any religious group." Then, to the horror of the faithful, the law stated that there must immediately be an inventory of all the movable and immovable property of religious institutions. Although not intended as a confiscatory measure, the mere idea that tainted, heathen nonbelievers would be pawing sacred objects,

PIERRE PÉTEUL   19

including even the tabernacles that housed the Blessed Sacrament, set off a popular furor in many parts of France. Within a month, at nearly a dozen important churches throughout Paris, doors were barricaded with logs, paving stones, church chairs, or living human bodies, and angry crowds assembled to insult and throw stones at state agents trying to enter. Those same agents were obliged to smash doors with axes, pull out window bars, shatter stained-glass windows, and disperse crowds with water from fire hoses. A dozen people were arrested and sentenced to prison terms.

In many dioceses outside Paris, parishioners were indifferent or their priests encouraged them to accept an unfortunate reality. In other dioceses, however, popular responses during the next two months echoed those seen in Paris. As might be expected, some of the worst incidents occurred in the west, the region of the counterrevolutionary uprisings more than one hundred years before.[20] There, scores of mayors and other local officials as well as army officers refused orders to facilitate the inventories and resigned or were fired or arrested as a result. Local residents, often armed with pitchforks, cattle prods, or clubs, guarded churches night and day. Huge crowds filled the streets, intimidating and occasionally beating up state agents conducting the inventories. Police occasionally responded with gunfire, while state agents slashed holes in the doors of churches and broke windows and furniture.

In the end a semblance of reason prevailed. After the death of a civilian in the department of the Nord on March 6, 1906, government agents postponed operations in the most difficult areas. Elsewhere, demonstrators simply grew tired and discouraged and went home. But the psychological damage from the inventories far outpaced the physical. Catholics wounded in spirit, if not in body, made a great effort to remember their outrage. They had physically resisted the anticlerical enemy, and they passed stories of their adventure down to subsequent generations. Nuns and teachers brought their pupils to watch the demonstrations in order to reinforce the memory. In an age before radio and television, many demonstrators photographed the crowds, printed the scenes as postcards, and sent them throughout the country, thus spreading the news visually. Those cards make up much of the historical record today. Many originated in the area around Angers.

As a final visual reminder of what was considered a heinous anticlerical government assault on religion, the damage to church buildings was often not fully repaired when the troubles ceased. Many churches bear scars to this day, with signs informing the public of the cause. Typical is the church of Saint Serge in Angers, where the young Pierre Péteul lived. On a side door on the rue de Jussieu, a huge gash, more than four feet high and one foot across, has been carefully boarded up from inside but not otherwise repaired (fig. 2). The gash was made by the French army on March 2, 1906. A nearby sign says, "This is the last visible testimony in Angers of the intense confrontations that marked the Inventories of Church property, in 1906."

Pierre Péteul was not quite eleven years old on March 2, 1906. He had received the sacraments of First Communion and Confirmation the year before and was still a star pupil in a Catholic school in Angers. We do not know if his teachers brought him to watch the demonstrations at Saint Serge or if perhaps his father did. But the boy must have witnessed the angry crowds and shared the pain of the faithful. He would not have been surprised, as he had been raised on tales of counterrevolution and the government repression of his ancestors. But his youthful sense of belonging to a persecuted minority within a hostile state could only have been reinforced. One year later, in 1907, he decided to become a priest.

The separation of the churches from the state also directly affected the education of young Pierre Péteul. Deeply disappointed by his rejection at the seminary in Angers, where he hoped to be trained as a priest, Pierre met and was greatly influenced by a dynamic Capuchin named Père Paulin de Ceton (1872–1933). Ordained in 1900, Père Paulin had been driven out of his monastery in Angers in 1904 with his confreres amid fierce demonstrations by supporters and detractors alike. Reestablished in a tiny room in the same city, he founded a Franciscan association of laymen the following year, dedicated to attracting the populace to the Church by means of public conferences. Occasionally harassed by the police, the association nevertheless grew and thrived. How Pierre Pèteul met Père Paulin is unknown, but the older man directed the boy toward his own religious order.[21] But as we have seen, unauthorized religious orders had been dissolved in 1902, while in 1904 all members of religious orders, whether authorized or not, were prohibited from teaching. As a result, Pierre Péteul could not undertake formation to become a Capuchin in France. Although he was only twelve years old, he was obliged to leave the country to pursue his goal.

What was this Capuchin order that attracted Pierre Péteul when he was still only a boy and to which he devoted his entire adult life? In the first years of the sixteenth century in the regions of Umbria and the Marches in Italy, a group of Franciscan friars came to desire a simpler lifestyle. A greater emphasis on poverty, austerity, and eremitical life, they believed, would be more in keeping with the intentions of Saint Francis three hundred years earlier. The friars received papal permission in 1528 to live in the manner they wished, more cloistered from the public than was then the case for Franciscans. Officially known as Capuchin Friars Minor, they became a branch of the Franciscan order.[22] They were allowed to beg and to wear their distinctive brown habits with great pointed hoods, cord belts, sandals, and long beards. Not all Capuchin friars are priests. Some take the three vows of poverty, chastity, and obedience to their religious superiors and to the pope but do not study for the priesthood and are not ordained. But all Capuchins place great emphasis on personal prayer, fraternity within the order, and a life of service to others, especially those with special needs. They work as missionaries, nurses, or teachers and attempt to serve prison populations, immigrants, workers, people with financial problems, or individuals harassed by hostility or racial prejudice.

All of this suited Pierre Péteul perfectly. Because of the French laic laws, however, he was obliged to travel to the village of Spy, near Namur in Belgium, where Capuchins exiled from France had established themselves. At Spy on September 23, 1907, he enrolled at the École séraphique des Capucins, a private secondary school for Catholic boys. His home was now among the Capuchins; he would never live with his parents again. The academic program at Spy was rigorous; Pierre studied Latin, Greek, French, rhetoric, philosophy, theology, and other subjects under conditions of strict discipline. But the school also offered some sports, hiking, and even amateur dramatics. Pierre's teachers and peers were supportive, and the boy did well.

An old photograph records that Père Paulin visited Pierre and other students at Spy in 1911 (fig. 3). In the photograph Père Paulin wears a floor-length cloak with small buttons down the front from collar to hem – a clerical overcoat used in France by Capuchin priests and friars to hide their banned brown monastic habits from public view. To Pierre's right is his friend René Bériot, also born in 1895, who, like Pierre, went to war in December 1914. Unlike Pierre, René was killed on the Marne on September 8, 1918, just two months before the end of the war, after volunteering for a liaison mission with another unit. Hit in the hip by a shell, he bled to death while awaiting help. In a biography of René written after the war, a devastated Père Paulin wrote, "According to his most ardent wishes, his blood flowed, to the last drop, for God and for the *Patrie*."[23] René's Médaille Militaire, awarded posthumously in October 1919, was signed by Marshal Henri Philippe Pétain, French commander at Verdun in 1916, commander in chief after April 1917, and head of state during the Vichy regime after June 1940.

Sometime in 1912 or 1913, Pierre Péteul moved to the small city of Breust-Eysden, in the province of Limburg in the Netherlands, to continue his studies. With some sixty other boys from several countries at the Capuchin school at Breust, he began the advanced study of philosophy, theology, and other subjects. He also embarked upon a strict program of formation as a Capuchin. A Capuchin candidate must first undergo a probationary period as a postulant. During this period he is introduced to liturgy, methods of prayer, religious instruction, and experience of apostolic work. His background is checked for impediments, moral or practical, that might prevent him from entering the order, and he is subjected to a spiritual examination to test the nature of his vocation. If accepted, the postulant becomes a novice and begins his novitiate, a period of more intense initiation. For a period of twelve months that must be spent in the novitiate community itself, he undergoes strict training in prayer, discipline, spiritual exercises, and examination of conscience. He also receives a modified Capuchin habit at this time.

If the candidate successfully completes his novitiate, he makes a simple or temporary profession of faith and takes the three vows of poverty, chastity, and obedience. At that point he is considered a brother in temporary vows. His vows, however, are not binding. During a period arranged with the Capuchin provincial minister at the time of his first temporary profession and consisting generally of no less than three years and no more than six, he is free to return to the secular world.[24] His order during these years also has the right to dismiss him if he has not been deemed worthy. During that trial period the candidate continues his spiritual formation and regularly renews his vows. At the end of the trial period, if he is successful, he makes his perpetual, solemn, or definitive profession of faith, which is binding for life. He is now permanently incorporated into the Capuchin order, with all its rights and obligations.

Pierre Péteul began his novitiate on April 28, 1913, and donned the "Holy Habit," or modified Capuchin robe, on September 8 of the same year. He made his first temporary profession of faith exactly one year later, on September 8, 1914, at the age of nineteen. As a professed brother, he assumed the religious name Frère Marie-Benoît at this time. He now looked forward to pursuing the standard three-year course of religious formation until he could make his binding perpetual profession as a Capuchin. He also hoped to pursue his studies for the priesthood. But that peaceful spiritual program was to be grievously interrupted by the First World War.

After declaring war on Russia on August 1 and on France on August 3, 1914, the German army invaded Belgium. By the time Pierre made his first temporary profession as a Capuchin on September 8, the Germans had defeated the Allies in the Battle of the Frontiers, occupied most of Belgium, and advanced to within thirty miles of Paris. The German army had made its fatal mistake by wheeling southeast before Paris and had been stopped on the banks of the Marne River by French and British troops. The German retreat and eventual installation in fixed positions began on September 9. It was soon clear that the war would continue for many months, or perhaps even longer; unfortunately, it was to last for years. Pierre Péteul's next four years were to be spent outside a monastery and very much in the secular world, focused on the most worldly of preoccupations – keeping alive in the midst of brutality and violent death on the Western Front.

What are we to make of the impact of the French Revolution in the eighteenth century and the anticlerical laws a hundred years later on the young Pierre Péteul? Of course we cannot assume that he was sympathetic to conservative Catholic positions and opposed to the anticlerical measures of the government in Paris simply because he was born in Le Bourg d'Iré. Most villagers took those positions, but not all. But for Pierre Péteul the legacy was one of family, and it must have been inescapable. The fact that during the French Revolution his great-great-grandfather hid a refractory priest in the very mill and house where he was born and spent the first years of his life must have captured his imagination. The fact that a female cousin of that great-great-grandfather was shot for harboring a priest must have done the same. Vivid memories of the counterrevolution lingered in the area around Le Bourg d'Iré for at least a century and a half. Houses bore scars; churches built obvious additions to replace sections that had been destroyed; cemeteries and public squares had monuments to those who had died in the civil war.

As for the government's anticlerical measures a hundred years later, the impact on an impressionable boy was direct and immediate. Pierre knew that his uncle had been obliged by the initial French laic laws to leave France in order to continue his life as a priest and had died in Canada. In early 1906 in Angers he must have seen soldiers forcing their way into churches. He certainly witnessed the anger and despair of his father, relatives, and teachers. Then in September 1907, while still only twelve, the anticlerical laws obliged him to leave home forever if he was to become a Capuchin. And while he was away, his beloved mentor visited him wearing a special overcoat, necessary to disguise his Capuchin habit. The burden of young Pierre Péteul's personal history lay heavily upon him. He must have looked on the modern world with some suspicion and found comfort in the society of the Catholic faithful. At the same time, he also must have felt himself to be something of an outsider, different from the majority. For while most Frenchmen and women were Catholics, only a minority felt grievously and personally persecuted by the separation of the churches from the state. But Pierre Péteul grew up in one of the regions of France where that minority prevailed.

Equally intriguing is the question of whether Pierre Péteul's historical legacy encouraged his obvious later sympathy for the underdog. From his earliest childhood, he had heard stories of the French government's persecution of the group to which his ancestors belonged. As a ten-year-old he had witnessed that persecution firsthand. Years later, as Père Marie-Benoît during the Second World War, he witnessed another French government persecution of a different minority, but this time the minority was not his. This time the oppressive government was the Vichy regime, installed in June 1940 at the time of the fall of France to the German invaders, and the minority was the nation's Jewish community. To further complicate matters, the Vichy regime was conservative, extremely nationalist, and approved by the Roman Catholic hierarchy and most French royalists – groups with which Père Marie-Benoît personally identified, at least as a young man.[25] Yet he never hesitated. The man whose ancestors had hidden priests now hid Jews, and he hid thousands of them.

Did Père Marie-Benoît occasionally think of his ancestors in Le Bourg d'Iré as he resisted? Unfortunately we shall never know. But in 1940 and 1941 in Marseille, as Vichy anti-Jewish measures intensified, he began his solitary resistance with exactly the same technique that his mentor Père Paulin had used in Angers nearly forty years before. Just as that priest had brought small numbers of people together to talk about the meaning of Catholicism, Père Marie-Benoît spoke to groups in Marseille about the evils of antisemitism. Then after the Second World War, when Père Marie-Benoît began his personal, solitary campaign to improve Jewish-Catholic relations in Rome, he organized conferences and spoke incessantly to group after group. Like Père Paulin, he believed in the power of the spoken word, and he believed that the ripples created by his lectures would reach out to ever larger numbers. He believed, finally, that one man can make a great difference, and he proved it throughout his life.

TWO

Pierre Péteul and the
First World War

WHEN THE FIRST WORLD WAR BROKE OUT IN AUGUST 1914,
Pierre Péteul was living in the Netherlands. French priests, friars, monks,
and seminary students, however, were not exempt from conscription.
As one French priest and historian has remarked wryly, "The French
Republic that had expelled [priests, friars, and monks] . . . was happy to
see them come back to France to put themselves in the service of their
country."[1] A member of the military class of 1915, Pierre was not liable for
service that first autumn of the war, but he knew he would be called up in
January. The neutral Netherlands was surrounded by German-occupied
territory at the time. On January 5, 1915, therefore, Pierre managed to
escape to England.[2] From there it was not difficult to proceed to France,
where he was mobilized on January 12 and began his training with the
77th Infantry Regiment. Unfortunately, nothing is known of any dangers
or difficulties he might have encountered in leaving the Netherlands. It
appears, however, that he might have sat out the war in a neutral country,
although he would have risked punishment if he returned to France after
the conflict. His military service involved an element of choice.

On April 28, 1915, Pierre was assigned to the 135th Infantry Regiment
as a stretcher bearer. He continued in that position, one of the more dangerous at the front, for most of his military career, with occasional bouts
as orderly and medic. The young soldier seems to have gone into action
fairly quickly. His first military citation for valor involved his conduct
on August 12–13, 1915. At that time, according to the commanding officer
who wrote the citation, he continuously carried wounded soldiers out
of an area under heavy fire for an entire day and night. On October 10,

1915, he was transferred to the 44th Infantry Regiment, with which he continued to find himself in the front lines for months, enduring bloody trench warfare during the fighting at Verdun and coping with mud, rats, filth, and unremitting fear (fig. 4).

With the 44th, Pierre received four more citations, for actions on February 25, 1916; September 14, 1916; April 17, 1917; and September 7, 1917.[3] The official language of the first three of these citations was similar, if rather dry and vague: he transported two wounded officers, about to become prisoners, to safety; he threw himself into an area of heavy artillery fire to save an officer; and he approached enemy trenches under heavy fire to reach the wounded. Writing years later, Pierre provided details about the February 25 event. Sheltered with his battalion in the cellars of the château of Bezonvaux, near Fort Douaumont at the Verdun front, he heard rumors that the Germans were about to surround the village. It was nighttime and snowing. Then from the top of the cellar stairs came a cry for volunteers to retrieve an officer who had been badly wounded. "I presented myself with two others and we set out," Pierre recalled rather blandly under the circumstances. "We did not take our supplies or our packs, because we expected to return to our post, as was our duty."

The three stretcher bearers picked up the officer and, uncertain where to go, headed toward Fort Douaumont. They barely escaped the Germans, who, attempting to capture the fort, seized Bezonvaux and everyone in it. Nearly all the French defenders from the 44th and other units were killed in the vicious hand-to-hand fighting that ensued. Fort Douaumont fell to the Germans the same day. Separated from their unit and with nowhere to go, the three French stretcher bearers finally found a recovery station and delivered the wounded officer. They then wandered around the vicinity of the fort for about ten days, looking for the remains of their regiment and living off a ham that Pierre had thought to take with him when they set out. Looking back years later, the by-then Père Marie-Benoît remembered his great regret at the loss of his pack of books, including a volume of the philosophy of Lévesque that his Capuchin spiritual director had sent him. "I often wondered what became of that book," he mused, "and what the Germans thought when they found it in the basement of the château. Was the château destroyed in the bombardment? Does it still exist? I never returned to that region."[4]

In fact, the entire village of Bezonvaux, which had a population of about two hundred before the war, was wiped out in the fighting. The French army recaptured its smoldering ruins in December 1916.

Pierre Péteul's final citation, on September 7, 1917, referred to a leg wound he received while rescuing other wounded soldiers, still in the Verdun sector. As a result of that wound, he was obliged to spend the next eight or nine months in hospitals and recovery centers. That respite kept him out of other battles and increased his chances of survival. Because of these citations, Pierre Péteul was awarded the Médaille Militaire and the Croix de Guerre after the war.

On June 28, 1918, Pierre returned to active duty with a different infantry regiment, the 288th, just in time to be caught up in the final battles of the 1918 German offensive. Returning to the front must have been a nightmare. For seven or eight nights in a row, he shared the job of guarding a particular trench that accessed the enemy lines. He did not record the location, but a German attack was imminent. His partner in the ordeal was a soldier from Brittany, practically his home region. The two men were ordered to sleep in the daytime and guard the trench at night. They argued a bit, because the Breton insisted on smoking and Pierre feared that the light from the cigarette would reveal their position. The Breton prevailed, but they became friends and survived the guard duty for a time. When the bombardment preceding a German attack finally began, however, the two heard a shell coming in their direction. They leaped into a nearby hole, but Pierre arrived seconds before his friend. The other man landed on top of him. The explosion tore through the friend's groin, and he died almost immediately. "I unquestionably owe my life to the fact that he was lying above me and his body protected me," the priest wrote in 1970 with characteristic reticence. "If he had not been there it would have been I who received the explosion of the shell. A tragic ending of a wartime friendship!"[5]

Even after the fighting stopped on November 11, 1918, Pierre Péteul was not demobilized. Instead, on November 21 he was transferred to the 7th Régiment de Tirailleurs Algériens and sent to Poitiers for further training. He was made a sergeant on March 20, 1919, and selected for an officer-candidate program. After preparing for and successfully taking a special exam, he was promoted to *aspirant,* the lowest rank of a French commissioned officer, in the army reserve a month later. On June 1, 1919, he left Bordeaux for Casablanca in French Morocco. From there he was sent with his regiment to Meknès, in the interior of the country, where he supervised the building of roads and fortifications. He was finally demobilized in September of that same year.

Thus far in our examination of the life of the young Pierre Péteul, we have found little that reveals his personality and inner life. We do not know if he was a kind boy, or mischievous, or unruly. We can guess but not be certain about the effects of his family heritage – the repression of Catholics during the French Revolution and at the time of the anticlerical laws and the separation of the churches and the state. We know little about his family dynamics or about why he chose a religious vocation. We do not know if he was lonely when, at the age of twelve, he left his family forever and moved to a foreign country to prepare to become a Capuchin. His parents and three brothers are now dead. If he wrote letters to them, they have not survived. Because he was a priest, he had no wife or children to testify to his personal life. His several nieces and nephews, the two children of his younger brother Louis and the four of his brother Joseph, remember him in his later years, but they did not know him when he was young.

During his military service, however, young Pierre wrote frequent letters to his Capuchin spiritual director at Breust in the Netherlands. The older man saved many of the letters and apparently returned them to Père Marie-Benoît when the latter was living at the Capuchin monastery in Paris toward the end of his life. They can be found today in that monastery's archives.[6] However, they have certain limitations. They are always short, confined to both sides of a single flimsy page. They reached Breust via London and must have passed the scrutiny of several military censors. Pierre never said precisely where he was in combat, or how many men were in his unit, or how many were sick or wounded. Indeed, he provided little information about actual military engagements. Also, the young man was expected to account for his use of his meager soldier's wages – at one point, nineteen sous, or less than one franc a day – and send any surplus to his order. In most letters, therefore, he dedicated much limited space to his few simple expenses. Despite these limitations, however, Pierre's letters are fresh, lively, informative, and sincere. He was clearly a modest and restrained young man who rarely alluded to his personal emotions. But despite his restraint, his personality and personal views burst forth in his own words.

Most immediately clear from the letters is the fact that Pierre Péteul was a firm patriot who ardently endorsed the French position in the war and desired a French victory. He frequently referred to the Germans with the pejorative French slang word *Boches* and sometimes seemed not to like them much, at least during this period of his life.[7] Never a blind chauvinist, however, he directed intelligent and observant criticism to some of his French compatriots as well. He was not duped by wartime propaganda. He often criticized incompetent, pompous French officers and worried about low morale among the men. At one point, for example, probably on July 26, 1917, just after the French army mutinies, he reflected, "The collapse of the morale of the men is considerable, and very difficult to raise up again. Good officers are very rare. The incapable and the bunglers abound, and if we put our confidence in tanks and horses, in solely human forces, without invoking the name of the Lord, we will be too weak to triumph."[8]

For all his contempt for incompetent officers, Pierre never maligned the common soldiers. He could have had few illusions about them, for, although he may have been sheltered as a child, a student, and a Capuchin candidate, he was certainly not sheltered now. In the trenches he saw shirkers, cowards, cheats, thieves, and worse, as well as simple good men and a few heroes. But he had nothing but sympathy for what he called "the poor *poilu*," the common French infantryman. For example, on January 2, probably in 1917, in one of his rare lyrical passages, he wrote,

> The war weighs heavily on the poor soldiers. What devastating scenes they sometimes have before their eyes! . . . It is difficult to comprehend the mentality at the front now. The poilu, fierce, made irascible by every kind of fatigue and pain, separated from everyone he loves, exposed to danger continually for reasons he does not understand, always busy, always in movement, leaves an impression of sadness; it seems that among the majority the war has uprooted the last remnants of faith, and implanted the bestial life.

Pierre did not give up on these soldiers, however. In the same letter of January 2, he wrote, "It seems to me that the war, despite appearances to the contrary, pursues its work in secret. In effect, once peace has been reestablished, I believe not in splendid and sudden conversions but in good serious dispositions profoundly from the heart and spirit working to clarify and direct [these men] to the good path." He then continued along these same lines, writing, "Everything will return little by little when the war is over, when the poilus, having returned home and found calm again, review what they have seen and done and reflect on it. The blood generously flowing from so many victims fallen for God and for France is a certain sign of the good condition of the land that the priests ... will have to sow."

Like all good candidates for the clerical and monastic life, Pierre Péteul was an idealistic young man, ready to believe in the best qualities of human beings. But he was also realistic and not naïve. He was fully aware of what he called the "bestial life." And he was not fooled by hypocrisy, pomposity, and pretense. While convalescing in a hospital at the foot of the Pyrenees, for example, he wrote on October 20, 1917, with gentle irony and irreverent humor, "The [hospital] directors are Catholics; a stout monsieur of L'Action française is president; immediately, like a good Camelot du Roi, he proposed that I read Maurras, Daudet and other royalist big-wigs." L'Action française was a right-wing, royalist, chauvinist, and antisemitic organization; Camelots du Roi translates as "Hucksters" or "Street-hawkers of the king" and refers to L'Action française's youth group but more broadly to all who propagandized for the organization. Charles Maurras (1868–1952) and Léon Daudet (1867–1942) were important novelists, journalists, and cofounders of the newspaper *L'Action française*. Pierre here was poking fun at comfortable members of the bourgeoisie who try to impress priests. Similarly, in a letter from Morocco on July 11, 1919, he wrote, "As for the Europeans here, they are all businessmen who only go to church because they can get together and meet their friends easily." This young man had few illusions and was not easily fooled.

Although Pierre Péteul loved his country and strongly desired a French victory in the war, he was not much interested in politics. "Politics is the science of the relative," he wrote in his letter of October 20, 1917. "Until I came here, no one has been able to convince me to be royalist or republican; I suppose that I am a monarchist, according to the etymology of the word, but religion comes before everything else; politics comes after." It is predictable that this young Catholic from western France, from a region devastated by republican troops in 1793 and harassed again by republican gendarmes in 1906, would flavor his patriotism with monarchism. What is surprising is that he spoke of politics so little. In only one letter (with no clear date but during the war itself) did he mention that he had read an article by the nationalist Maurice Barrès (1862–1923) in the conservative daily *L'Echo de Paris*. After the war, on December 14, 1918, as the Paris Peace Conference was about to begin, he mentioned just once that he had been reading *L'Action française*. He explained, "I find it important to follow the broad lines of the struggle of political ideas," but one senses that he was not riveted by the subject.

Although reading about politics was not Pierre's favorite occupation, his letters were full of comments about reading in general. At the front, apart from the mud and the frequent impossibility of attending mass, his only complaint concerned the lack of books. The only supplies he ever asked for were books. In one letter he wrote that he had been in the trenches for two days and begged for books. From a hospital on January 3, 1918, he wrote that his leg was getting better and he could walk a little with a cane, but "I am a bit lonely in spite of everything [a rare confession], and I lack reading material." By April 29, 1918, he was in a little village in the Jura Mountains of eastern France, retraining to return to active service. Again he complained of the scarcity of books and the lack of time to read them, writing, "The absence of substantive nourishment is a penance for the intelligence; what emptiness, what a gaping hollow sometimes in our poor soldier brains!"

The plea for books is natural in letters written to one's spiritual director and teacher, but Pierre's comments sound perfectly sincere. Much less clear is what exactly he preferred to read if given a choice. From a hospital on February 1, 1918, he wrote with some satisfaction that he had been studying English, but that was surely not what he meant by reading material. In his wartime letters to his spiritual director, he mentioned J. K. Huysmans (1848–1907), a novelist who converted to Catholicism as an adult and wrote several works about monastic life, but whose style, witty, perverse, and sensuous, is a prime example of the French Decadents. On January 3, 1918, Pierre commented about Huysmans that although his position regarding the Church was acceptable, "despite what he says, his bad taste makes him unsupportable, not to be imitated, disrespectful sometimes." The only other specific literary reference in these letters was to Ernest Psichari (1883–1914), also a novelist and Catholic convert, who was influenced by L'Action française and killed in action in the first year of the war. If Pierre Péteul was reading high-quality republican literature like that of Victor Hugo, Honoré Balzac, or Gustav Flaubert, he did not mention it to his superior.

In addition to books, Pierre Péteul loved music, or at least church music. Astonishingly, he spent time in the trenches composing a Gregorian chant in Latin. One wonders what his companions thought of that. "But there was no question of singing," he remembered years later.[9] He sent the written chant to another Capuchin brother, who returned it to him after the war. It is in the archives of his monastery in Paris today.

While the young Pierre Péteul longed for books, his letters to his spiritual director emphasized that he missed his religious life even more. This was a predominant theme in his letters. It was also a natural theme, for his mentor would have wanted to know that the young soldier was able to hear mass and remain faithful to his religious commitment. At times all was well. On April 28, probably in 1915, Pierre wrote that he was leaving for the front but had been assured that he would have "all possible facilities and permission to fulfill my religious duties." In another letter, dated June 11 but without a year, he explained that he had no complaints about his religious life, for he was able to attend mass every day. But on other occasions the situation was not so favorable. He once wrote that he had been in the trenches for two days, sometimes only seven or eight meters from "the Boches," and announced that his religious life was not all it could be. Predictably, that was often the case.

But although Pierre could not always attend mass, he wrote often of other religious matters. If he saw a particular priest or friar he knew, he reported it. He asked for news from his monastery in the Netherlands. He remembered holy days and birthdays, and he commiserated if a priest or brother lost a family member. His letters convey a strong sense of how much his religious life meant to him. On July 11, 1919, for example, not long after the death of his mother, he wrote about how grateful he was for "my religious vocation that has given me a new family."

Pierre Péteul was an idealistic young man, then, but also realistic, perceptive, reserved, and conservative, with a love of books and a deep commitment to his religious vocation. He also seems to have been basically cheerful. He had a healthy sense of humor and was able to laugh at himself. In one letter early in the war, for example, he wrote of getting lost in Paris during a brief leave, taking a bus in the wrong direction and losing so much time that when he discovered his error it was time to return to his unit. This was the country bumpkin who, during the next war, would spend much of his time deftly conducting Jewish fugitives through the streets of Marseille and Rome. Then on December 25, probably in 1915, he wrote: "It seems that I look older than I am. I surprise everyone when I say I am only 20 and a half. They take me for 28, 30, 32, they go up to 38! What will they say when I am 40?" In 1915, of course, it was far from certain that he would live to be forty. But his sense of humor continued. On October 20, 1917, after being wounded, he wrote from a hospital of "a badly lodged wound [that] forces me to drag myself painfully around like an old man of 95." And in a postwar letter with no date, he wrote to his spiritual director about the officer-candidate exam he took: "I have had the opportunity in an exam of general instruction to shine in French; I have been good in history, mediocre in geography, and almost null in math. I have come to realize that I am rather rusty."

Unless it was a question of his religion, Pierre did not take himself or government propaganda too seriously. From Morocco he wrote on August 4, 1919, "Thus I can flatter myself that I am overseeing the building of several hundred meters of roads to transport French civilization to the savages." Despite his self-deprecating irony, however, Pierre was unquestionably moved by Morocco. In the same letter he continued, "I have seen Moroccan Africa with its mosques and kasbahs, the Arab cities and the *douars* of the bled; I have seen how we try to civilize the local people; I have seen the mountains so severe and so hard bathed in brilliant sunlight; perhaps someday I will be nostalgic."

Such statements of heartfelt emotion often come as a surprise, for they were rare. Pierre rarely mentioned his family in his letters to his spiritual director, for example. His brother René Gabriel, like him in a religious congregation, was killed in action at Morval, during the battle of the Somme, on October 12, 1916. Of this, Pierre wrote, not in the first paragraph of a letter on November 13, 1916, but close to the end and almost in passing: "I have learned from home that my brother René, in the 66th infantry, has been reported missing from his company since October 9. Someone saw him wounded and lying near a trench that the Boches had seized." He said nothing more. His remarks about his mother's death were equally restrained. On the third page of a letter in early June 1919, soon after his arrival in Casablanca, after describing the heat, some Franciscan friars who had been kind to him, and his monthly expenses, he wrote: "Before leaving France, terrible news reached me: that of the death of my poor mother. I was able to get a special three-day leave, but I arrived too late to see her at her last moments; I refer her to your prayers and to those of the community." About a month later, on July 11, he wrote more from Meknès. In the same letter in which he referred to the Capuchins as his new family, he thanked his spiritual director for his letter of sympathy and for his prayers for his mother. He then explained, "As you thought, I was not able to be present for my mother's last moments; I was still in France, but I was traveling continually and my father, not having my address, was not able to advise me in time." Nothing more.

Pierre's restraint in describing family tragedies must not be mistaken for coldness and indifference. We know little about his relationships with his mother or with René Gabriel, only a year younger than he, but his personal notebook for later years reveals that he visited his father and his brothers Louis and Joseph in Angers regularly.[10] After he became a professor of theology in Rome, he went to see them during his summer vacations almost every year, except during the Second World War (fig. 5). He also went regularly to Le Tremblay, his mother's hometown, not far from Le Bourg d'Iré, to visit women identified as Aunt Célestine and cousin Claire, or simply C. Royer, his mother's maiden name. His nieces and nephews testify that he was often present at family events, such as weddings, christenings, and funerals. He had a way with youngsters, and the children and grandchildren of his brothers adored him. Given this warmth, the deaths of his soldier-brother and his mother must have touched him deeply. René Gabriel, after all, was a member of a religious congregation. The two young men had much in common. His mother had been hospitalized for years with incapacitating mental depression, a condition that must have been greatly aggravated by the death of her second-oldest son and the absence of the other three for the final years of her life. For not only was Pierre in the army during the First World War, but Louis and Joseph were stranded in German-occupied Belgium, where they had been going to school, and were unable to get home. This sorrow must have gnawed at Pierre's heart, but he never complained.

Pierre Péteul's wartime letters to his spiritual director also reveal him to have been a selfless, generous young man without worldly ambition or a great ego. On September 27, 1916, he wrote that he was going up to the front soon and added: "I am now . . . the 'old man' of the medics at the first aid station, and I prefer to finish the war here; I will profit more completely from the harsh lessons. When one passes whole days between life and death, one learns unforgettable things." Then in a letter dated November 27 he wrote that he had given up his position as medic to a newly arrived priest who could serve as a chaplain better than he. He was now simply a stretcher bearer. Still later, on August 31, 1918, he reported that he had been made a corporal. "I am surprised by this; I was accustomed during nearly four years of war and service to living as a simple soldier; that has its charm."

Also an indication of his modesty and restraint was Pierre's reticence about the extreme danger that he faced during the war. He was often in the trenches, but he rarely mentioned it. In a letter dated April 22, but with no clear year, he wrote: "I am writing these lines to you from a miserable muddy hole . . . Here we can't move a step during the day; all the Boches who occupy the shell holes can see us. All the work is done at night; we can only go to the wounded with the help of darkness. We are swimming in mud." And then on November 18, also with no year given, he declared: "One night I go with nine stretcher bearers to search for some wounded and one dead man at an advanced listening post. We are on our knees in front of the dead man. It is necessary to avoid making the least noise. Suddenly a movement of air – attention! A shell falls on the dead man and, fortunately for us, it does not explode." On August 9, 1918, he stated that "we remain the sole tenants and owners of houses precipitously evacuated under the blows of preceding advances of the Boches." Three weeks later, on August 31, he wrote: "The Holy Virgin has protected me as always during the hard period of more than two weeks that we have passed; many of my comrades have been killed or wounded around me and I have had nothing; we have dislodged the Boches from strong positions guarded with machine guns."

In his letters to his spiritual director, Pierre mentioned one other battlefield experience, probably because of the devastating effect it must have had on him. His job as stretcher bearer required him to bring in dead bodies and bury them. "Some time ago," he wrote from the front on June 11, with no year given, "we found a *mi adjutant-chef* [a non-commissioned officer]; he was lying on his stomach. When we turned him over and pushed him to make him fall into a grave dug alongside, my 'gardeners' [slang for his assistants] backed off in horror and I was left alone, leaning over the poor cadaver, searching through his things, now rotten and in shreds, for some way to identify him." Pierre Péteul did not back away. Throughout all his future life, he would not back away from dangerous, difficult assignments.

The man who became Père Marie-Benoît did not speak or write much in later life about his military career in the First World War. However, those wartime years must have been as formative for him as his childhood experiences in Le Bourg d'Iré and Angers. We have seen that he grew up with a vivid awareness that secular governments were capable of harassing and opposing selected minorities. He undoubtedly had sympathy for the targets of such policies, as well as some suspicion of the modern world. Then the First World War thrust him, with no preparation, deep into the essence of that modern world – an arena of spiritual irreverence, struggle for survival, violence, and contempt for individual human life. That experience showed him the worst that man is capable of, but it also demonstrated the courage, tenacity, and occasional selflessness and heroism of the human spirit. Pierre Péteul's letters show him considering these multiple impressions and meditating on the condition of common soldiers, both French and German. He, a Capuchin friar, was different from the others, but he learned to understand them better than he could have done from the remoteness of a monastery. He did not lose his faith, but he came out of the war with an enhanced capacity for independent thinking. That independence would hold him in good stead when he came to consider a new persecution of another minority in 1940.

THREE

The Years between the Wars

1919 TO 1939

ACCORDING TO HIS LETTERS TO HIS SPIRITUAL DIRECTOR, Pierre Péteul was overjoyed to be demobilized at last in 1919 and able to return to the Capuchin monastery and school in Breust-Eysden in the Netherlands. By that time he had made his temporary profession as a Capuchin, but he still faced a minimum three-year trial period during which he could change his mind or be dismissed by his superiors before taking perpetual vows. During those years, he expected to continue his ongoing formation as a Capuchin at Breust. He did extremely well in his studies, however, and after only two years his superiors chose to transfer him to the International College of Saint Lawrence of Brindisi in Rome. Founded in 1908, this college was dedicated to the formation and higher education of the most intellectually gifted and spiritually committed young men in the Capuchin order throughout the world, preparing them for a lifetime of service as priests and teachers. While at the college, they would also have an opportunity to obtain graduate degrees from various pontifical institutions throughout Rome.

Pierre left Breust on August 11, 1921, visited his family in Angers and Le Bourg d'Iré as well as his mother's relatives in Le Tremblay, and departed for Italy on October 14. Three days later he arrived in Rome in time for the autumn term. He was housed at the Capuchin monastery at 159 via Sicilia, which was attached to the college and adjacent to the order's General Curia at 71 via Boncompagni. Twenty-two years later that same monastery would serve as his base for the rescue of thousands of Jewish refugees.

When he reached Rome, Pierre was a battle-hardened twenty-six-year old veteran of a horrendous war who had seen much of the worst that men are capable of. Nevertheless he was also a refreshingly eager and enthusiastic young man from the provinces. Rome was glamorous, exciting, and fraught with political tensions at the time, and his brief diary notations reflect his fascination with the city.[1] During the three weeks before his classes began on November 5, he visited Saint Peter's Basilica and Vatican City and toured Rome, admiring the Trevi Fountain, the forum of Trajan, the Capitoline Hill, and many important churches. November 4 was a holiday marking the third anniversary of the end of the First World War in Italy. Former combatant Pierre Péteul was moved by the ceremony for the interment of Italy's Unknown Soldier at the national monument to King Vittorio Emanuele II on that day.

After his classes began, Pierre continued to observe the ferment that was Rome in 1921 and make notes of what he saw. Much of the country was on the verge of civil war, with Fascists and Socialists provoking each other to violence, especially in the fertile agricultural areas of central Italy. A week after the ceremony for the Unknown Soldier, Pierre witnessed a Fascist manifestation in Rome. Fascist radicals were often anticlerical, especially in those early years. Pierre's superiors apparently thought the danger to their young students serious enough that they sent an older priest to escort them home after morning classes at the nearby Gregorian University. It is amusing to imagine the bulky, physically fit veteran of four years on the Western Front "protected" by a single elderly gentleman. For evening classes the students went out in pairs.

Pierre was equally impressed with the magnificent religious ceremonies, high masses, and church music that he witnessed in the Eternal City. On December 22 he was pleased to see a papal procession. On a more somber note, however, he wrote on January 22, 1922, "6 AM: death of [Pope] Benedict XV." The conclave of cardinals for the election of a new pope opened on February 2, and the eager young student followed it closely. He noted huge crowds in Saint Peter's Square every day, much excitement, and even a false alarm when observers imagined prematurely that they saw the puff of white smoke arising from the Vatican announcing a papal election. Finally on February 6, Pierre wrote, "Morning. Rain at midday, 11:00 *habemus Pontificius* Achille Ratti of Milan Pius XI." The papal coronation took place on February 12. Pierre noted, "An immense crowd. I am at the door [of Saint Peter's Basilica] at 7:30 A M."

In the months that followed, Pierre Péteul continued to record some events of religious and political significance. The former were of greater importance to him. On May 17, 1922, he noted that he had received communion directly from the hands of the pope. On March 18, 1923, he was thrilled to attend an audience granted by the pope to a group of priests and students. With a surge of emotion unusual in his writing, he declared, "This meeting is a great joy for me and a consolation: [the pope] records his time as a student . . . and makes a splendid speech." In the months that followed, Pierre continued to mention ceremonies, lectures, masses, and other special commemorations for feast and name days. His passion for music was clear in his appraisals of concerts and lectures on the subject. Like his father in the little church at home in Angers, Pierre Péteul loved to sing and had a booming voice.

On the subject of politics Pierre was more restrained. At the bottom of the page for late October 1922, he noted tersely, "Coup d'état by the Fascists in Rome. Mussolini president." In fact, Mussolini became prime minister, or president of the Council of Ministers, when King Vittorio Emanuele III, intimidated by thousands of Fascists marching on Rome, selected him to form a government. The new head of government had come to power legally, technically without what Pierre called a "coup d'état," but he was no democrat. More important in Pierre's eyes, he had not yet come to terms with the Church. The young Capuchin was decidedly unimpressed. He remained unimpressed with the Duce at the ceremony for the Unknown Soldier on November 4, 1922, noting simply that Mussolini and the king (who was also anticlerical) were there. A year and a half later he wrote in his notebook, "Visit to the zoo. There I see Mussolini in the lion cage, playing with a lion cub." Apparently this was not unusual behavior for the flamboyant leader. Pierre may have been more curious than he cared to admit, and gone to see him deliberately.

Although he did not mention it much in his notebook, the years between November 1921 and July 1925 were for Pierre Péteul a period of intense study and considerable academic achievement. In addition to training for the priesthood, he was working on a doctorate in theological studies in preparation for a career teaching talented Capuchins like himself. For much of that period he attended the prestigious Pontifical Gregorian University, where he studied with some of the most brilliant Catholic professors of his time. His fellow students were priests and aspiring priests from all over the world, members of many religious orders, and even laymen. His subjects included theology, ecclesiastical history, Christian archeology, philosophy, dogma, liturgy, ethics, and a number of languages, including Latin, Greek, Hebrew, and German. Occasionally he referred in his notebook to examinations: dogma and morals as well as Hebrew on June 16 and July 14 and 15, 1922; dogma again on July 10, 1923; and other unstated subjects on July 22, 1924.

With his customary modesty, Pierre did not record his grades in his notebook, but his record book from the Gregorian University reveals excellent results: summa cum laude in his examination in fundamental theology on July 14, 1922; summa cum laude in Hebrew on June 16, 1922; cum laude in biblical Greek on June 6, 1924; and a citation of "good" in dogmatic theology on July 22, 1924.[2] One highlight of his student years that he did record was a lecture given on November 19, 1923, by the prominent French Catholic philosopher Jacques Maritain on "Saint Thomas and the crisis of the modern spirit." Pierre would meet Maritain again after the Second World War when the latter served as the French ambassador to the Holy See from 1945 to 1948. Pierre received his doctorate in theology on July 18, 1925. In the meantime he made his perpetual profession as a Capuchin in December 1922 and was ordained as a priest the following year. He was now, fully and proudly, Père Marie-Benoît.

Our young Capuchin had enjoyed summer vacations at a Catholic retreat for students for the priesthood at Frascati, outside of Rome, after each academic year in 1922, 1923, and 1924. During one of these he noted, "*Solitude délicieuse.*" After receiving his doctorate, however, he was able to travel to Assisi, Florence, Genoa, Marseille, Lyon, and Paris. On this trip he also visited his father and brothers in Angers and his mother's relatives in Le Tremblay.

On June 26, 1925, a few weeks before receiving his doctorate, Père Marie-Benoît was appointed *répétiteur,* or assistant professor, of theology at the same International College of Saint Lawrence of Brindisi where he had been studying and living. This was a tremendous achievement, for, as his superior wrote at the time, only the very best became teachers there, chosen on the basis of their intellectual qualities as well as "the dignity of a totally exemplary life, the security and solidity of the doctrine and the clarity of the teaching."[3] Père Marie-Benoît's superior never suspected that by 1940 or 1941 the young priest would begin questioning one aspect of Church policy – that regarding Jewish-Catholic relations. But in 1925 all of that remained far in the future.

Père Marie-Benoît flourished at the college between the two wars, eventually becoming a full professor and a spiritual advisor to younger students. The life clearly suited him. He was an excellent teacher who got on well with young people. He liked them, and they reciprocated. Some of his students later testified that he had a deep, serious gaze, which he always focused attentively on whoever was addressing him. A big man, he walked slowly, "like an ox under the yoke," according to one student. He wrote out all of his speeches but then delivered them without looking at the paper and without allowing interruptions. If someone asked a question before the end of the speech, he barked, "This objection is premature!"[4]

In addition to his teaching, Père Marie-Benoît's notebooks indicate that he treasured the quiet, reflective life that gave him time for scholarly pursuits. During this period he was able to publish numerous articles, mostly on religious subjects, in *Études franciscaines,* a journal produced at the French Capuchin monastery in the rue Boissonade in Paris. He frequently communicated with the publisher of the journal, discussing the fine points of his contributions.[5] The work continued until the 1970s, by which time he had published some thirty complex and difficult philosophical articles.

Each July and August Père Marie-Benoît had a few weeks of vacation, which he often used to visit his family in France. His trips seem to have been important to him, for he generally recorded them in his notebook. In 1935, for example, he traveled to Angers and also visited a woman identified as C. Royer, a relative on his mother's side, in Le Tremblay. In June 1936 he traveled to Naples to give exams in theology, dogma, Greek, and Hebrew. He used the occasion to see a bit of the city, visiting the national museum, the port, and the Roman ruins in Pompeii. In July 1938 he recorded another trip to France. After arriving in Paris early on

July 21, he spent the afternoon wandering through the streets to see the decorations for the visit of King George V of England. He then went on to visit Angers, Le Tremblay, and Le Bourg d'Iré. In the latter village he noted with pleasure that he attended a mass with music. He was back in Rome by the first of September.

Père Marie-Benoît's notebook listing his daily activities rarely includes personal reactions or reflections, much less observations of the political events swirling around him. Thus there is no mention of the crisis in June 1924 that followed the murder in Rome by Mussolini's thugs of Giacomo Matteotti, a prominent Socialist deputy and critic of Fascism. The atrocity nearly brought down the government and led, in the long run, to an intensification of Mussolini's dictatorship. Of perhaps greater interest to Père Marie-Benoît, Pope Pius XI finalized the Lateran Accords with Mussolini on February 11, 1929. Thus the "Roman question" came to an end when the Church ceased its claims to the entire Eternal City, seized by the Italian army in 1870, but obtained in return, among other things, the Italian government's recognition of the inviolability of the 108.7 acres of the Vatican City State adjacent to Saint Peter's Basilica and the Holy See's additional properties scattered throughout the city.[6] Père Marie-Benoît's private opinion of this diplomatic treaty, religious concordat, and financial convention between the Holy See and the Fascist regime is unknown.

Nor are the devastating events of the 1930s that brought Europe to the brink of war covered in the surviving pages of Père Marie-Benoît's notebook. Adolf Hitler became chancellor of Germany on January 30, 1933. There followed Hitler's announcement of rearmament in March 1935, the Italian invasion of Ethiopia in October 1935, the German remilitarization of the Rhineland in March 1936, the Spanish Civil War in July 1936, and the Anschluss, or German absorption of Austria, in March 1938. Like all Europeans, Père Marie-Benoît would have followed these events with concern, but they did not alter his day-to-day life. It was different in September 1938, however, when Hitler announced his demand for the Sudetenland, the predominantly German-speaking region along Czechoslovakia's northern and western frontier. "*Menaces de guerre*," Père Marie-Benoît wrote in his notebook on September 26. Still in the army reserve, he expected to be mobilized for military service.[7] On September 29, as Hitler and Mussolini began their two-day meeting at Munich with the French and British prime ministers, Édouard Daladier and Neville Chamberlain, he left Rome with a group of French priests who were presumably in the same situation. His train entered Switzerland at Chiasso, near Como, and continued to Basel, Luxembourg, and Liège in Belgium. Near Liège he noted, "Soldiers everywhere: bridges mined." The war scare must have been a nightmare for a Frenchman who had fought the Germans just twenty years earlier.

In the end the French and British caved, Hitler occupied the Sudetenland on October 1, and war was postponed for a year. Père Marie-Benoît gratefully made his way from Belgium to the Netherlands, where he visited his old school at Breust. On October 10 he traveled to Paris. After arriving at 5:00 PM, he wrote, "In spite of the rain I go to the Italian consulate, which is closed. I am at the monastery by 6:00." He received his Italian visa the next day, left for Rome on an evening train, traveled all day on the twelfth, and arrived in Rome after midnight on the thirteenth. His entries for the next two days were terse: "October 13, 1938: Headache, I take aspirin and do not say mass," and "October 14, 1938: I say mass."

In the weeks immediately preceding and following the war scare of September 1938, another issue emerged in Italy that attracted less attention worldwide. On July 14 a pseudoscientific document titled "Manifesto of Racial Scientists" was published in the mass-circulation daily *Giornale d'Italia* and then in most other Italian newspapers. Claiming to be the creation of a group of Fascist scholars, the ten jumbled points of the manifesto in fact constituted Mussolini's endorsement of extreme biological racism. They stated that human races existed, that the racial composition of different nations varied, that there was a pure Italian race of "Aryan" origin, and that Jews did not belong to the Italian race. They declared clearly, "To say that human races exist does not mean a priori that superior or inferior races exist, but only that different human races exist." With a more sinister flourish, however, the manifesto announced, "It is time that Italians proclaim themselves to be frankly racist." It concluded, "The purely European physical and psychological characteristics of the Italians must not be altered by any means. Union [marriage or cohabitation] is admissible only in the context of the European races."[8] In August, just a few weeks after the manifesto was issued, the newly created government Office of Demography and Race conducted a census of all Jews in the nation and reported that there were roughly forty-seven thousand Jewish Italian citizens and ten thousand foreign Jews present.

The official government decrees presaged by the "Manifesto of Racial Scientists" and the Jewish census were not long in coming. On September 5, 1938, children all over Italy returning from vacations and gathering up their books for the new school year learned that the Jews among them were banned from public elementary and secondary schools. The law, which also applied to Jewish teachers at all educational levels, was immediately and thoroughly enforced. Two days later another decree announced that foreign Jews who had immigrated to Italy after January 1, 1919, must leave the country within six months or face expulsion. In addition, Jews who had been naturalized as Italians after January 1, 1919, lost their citizenship, were declared foreigners, and were subject to the same terms. Only in November were exceptions made for those over sixty-five or married to Italian citizens. Roughly ten thousand foreign Jews duly emigrated before the outbreak of war, although they were replaced in part by new Jewish immigrants from the Third Reich and Eastern Europe, accepted, ostensibly temporarily as tourists or travelers in transit, by the inconsistent Fascist regime.

A more comprehensive set of anti-Jewish decrees was announced on November 17. Now intermarriage between "Aryan" Italians and all other "races" was prohibited. Jews were banned from employment in the public sector, banks, private insurance companies, and the Fascist Party. They were prohibited from owning land, factories, or businesses of more than a certain value, as well as any enterprise involved in national defense. A host of additional proscriptions followed in the first six months of 1939. Overnight, thousands of people lost their jobs. Expropriation of property took a little longer, but it too was eventually enforced with devastating effectiveness.[9]

Unfortunately we do not know what Père Marie-Benoît thought of these new anti-Jewish laws, or if he thought much about them at all. What is virtually certain, however, is that he was aware of what Pope Pius XI did and said publicly during this period with regard to the laws. The pope's speeches were published in full in the Vatican daily newspaper

L'Osservatore Romano, which Père Marie-Benoît, like most priests in Rome and throughout the country, read regularly. Thus, he knew that in speeches on July 15, July 21, July 28, and August 21, Pius XI clearly condemned exaggerated nationalism while also declaring on two of the occasions that "Catholic means universal, not racist, nationalistic, separatist," and "human dignity is to be one single great family, the human type, the human race." The pope did not use the words "Jews" or "antisemitism."[10]

Although Père Marie-Benoît knew of the speeches, he did not know about behind-the-scenes Vatican diplomatic efforts between July and September to alter the content of the anti-Jewish decrees. In effect, on October 7, the day after Mussolini presented his comprehensive anti-Jewish program to the Fascist Grand Council, the Italian ambassador to the Holy See informed Foreign Minister Galeazzo Ciano of the Vatican's position. The ambassador wrote, "Vatican circles have adopted a cautious attitude towards the deliberations of the Grand Council regarding the defense of the race [the proposed anti-Jewish laws]. *Some positive points are noted* regarding the deliberations themselves, while there is some preoccupation with respect to the regulations on marriage." He added that the proposal to prohibit marriages between non-Jewish Catholics and converts from Judaism "is the only point of the Grand Council's proclamation that the Church would object to."[11] The ambassador was not quite accurate, for in their negotiations with Mussolini's government, the pope's diplomats focused on two, rather than one, objections to the new measures. All individuals with two Jewish parents, regardless of conversions, were considered Jewish. Representatives of the Church were unhappy that the definition made no exception for those who had converted even years before, and that the children of mixed marriages were to be considered Jewish unless they had been baptized before October 1, 1938, or within ten days of birth. Second and most important, however, as the Italian ambassador to the Holy See predicted, Vatican spokesmen objected to prohibitions on mixed marriage. By the terms of the concordat of 1929, the Church had the right to decide whom Catholics could marry. Interference with that right constituted a treaty violation. By limiting themselves to these two objections, Pius XI and his advisors revealed that for the most part they condemned racism that considered Jews who had converted to Catholicism as Jewish because of their biological heritage, but they did not object to laws that separated Jews who remained Jewish by religion from their Christian neighbors.

In fact, Pope Pius XI made one semi-public declaration that revealed a broader concern about Mussolini's anti-Jewish measures, but it is unclear whether Père Marie-Benoît knew about it. On September 6, the day after the government's original education decree barring Jews from the public schools, the pope granted an audience to a group of 120 Belgian pilgrims. "Listen carefully," he said, "Antisemitism is a hateful movement, with which we Christians must have nothing to do . . . [I]t is not licit for Christians to take part in manifestations of antisemitism . . . Spiritually, we are all Semites." There, indeed, was the line that might have been repeated over and over again from the very beginning as anti-Jewish persecutions intensified throughout Europe. But it was not to be. *L'Osservatore Romano*, which faithfully published all papal speeches, mentioned the Belgian pilgrims' audience with the pope but never printed the pope's reference to Jews. A Belgian prelate present among the pilgrims took the statement home with him for publication in lesser Catholic journals that were circulated unofficially and to an unclear extent.[12] It is not known whether the pope's words reached Père Marie-Benoît.

Although *L'Osservatore Romano* declined to publish the pope's remarks to the Belgian pilgrims, it did choose on January 15, 1939, to print a long homily on anti-Judaism by Bishop Giovanni Cazzani of Cremona. This was an unusual step, probably taken under pressure from Roberto Farinacci, the Fascist party boss of Cremona, who had recently publicly taunted the Church with the claim that Mussolini's new anti-Jewish laws were merely a reflection of traditional Catholic teaching and asked why the Church was not supporting them. Farinacci may have been disappointed with the result, for in his description of Catholic teaching on the subject, Cazzani neatly summed up the distinction between racism, which the Church opposed, and anti-Judaism, which it did not. Just weeks after the Italian government had banned Jews from public schools and many professions, the bishop declared:

> The Church has always regarded living side by side with Jews, as long as they remain Jews, as dangerous to the faith and tranquility of Christian people. It is for this reason that you find an old and long tradition of ecclesiastical legislation and discipline, intended to brake and limit the action and influence of the Jews in the

midst of Christians, and the contact of Christians with them, isolating the Jews and not allowing them the exercise of those offices and professions in which they could dominate or influence the spirit, the education, the customs of Christians.

After more along those lines, however, the bishop then explained, "The Church does not and cannot accept racist materialism." He added, "The Church has condemned the exaggerated German racism in the name of which Germany is harshly persecuting the Jews." He reminded listeners that "for the Church, sincere converts, whether from Judaism or paganism or apostasy or heresy, once baptized, are Christians like all the others."[13]

Pope Pius XI died on February 10, 1939, after a long illness. In contrast to his enthusiastic fascination with Vatican affairs in 1922 when Pius XI was elected, reflecting a young man's excitement at being close to the scene, Père Marie-Benoît did not mention that same pope's death in his notebook. Nor did he refer to the election on March 2 of Eugenio Pacelli, Pius XI's secretary of state since 1930, who became Pius XII. The new pope proved less willing than his predecessor to criticize the Fascist and Nazi regimes on points with which he disagreed. As was his right, he declined to release *Humani generis unitas,* the so-called hidden encyclical in which Pius XI had planned to condemn racism and antisemitism.[14] Instead, on October 20, 1939, eight weeks after the outbreak of war, he issued his own encyclical, *Summi Pontificatus,* in which he spoke of his anguish at the suffering caused by the conflict, reminded listeners that the Church sees "the human race in the unity of one common origin in God," and called for compassion and help for all victims of war, but did not specifically mention Jews.[15]

In March 1939 the German army, contrary to Hitler's promises at the time of the Munich conference, seized the rest of Czechoslovakia's Bohemian and Moravian regions and encouraged Slovakia to declare its independence. Then on August 21, 1939, the announcement of a nonaggression pact between the Third Reich and the Soviet Union startled the world. After the pact was signed two days later, Hitler's demands for Danzig and the Polish Corridor intensified. Because the British and French had been declaring since March that they would stand by Poland, war now seemed inevitable. On August 25 Hitler ordered a partial mobilization for the invasion of Poland. That same day Père Marie-Benoît, still eligible for military service, and some other priests went to the French embassy in the Palazzo Farnese in Rome. There they were instructed to return to France and immediately obeyed. They left Rome on an evening train for Turin, where they arrived early the next morning. After crossing the French border a few hours later, they left the train at Chambéry at 2:30 in the afternoon.[16] There they stayed to await events. Would this be another false alarm like their flight north the year before?

Unfortunately this time the threat was real. German troops invaded Poland in the early morning hours of September 1. Père Marie-Benoît's notebook for the next day reads, "September 2, 1939: general mobilization – departure from Chambéry for Paris." He arrived around 11:00 the following morning and promptly attended mass. The British, French, Australian, and New Zealand governments declared war on the Third Reich that same day, September 3, 1939. That afternoon Père Marie-Benoît wrote, "I presented myself at the Quartier Fontenoy, École militaire."[17] The forty-four-year-old priest, now again known as Pierre Péteul, was back in the army. He held the same rank of *aspirant* with which he had been demobilized in 1919.

After some uncertainty Pierre was assigned to the staff of General Gaston-Henri-Gustave Billotte and the 15th Infantry Division in southern France to serve as an interpreter. He was, after all, fluent in Italian, and Mussolini was expected to join his German ally before long. In the event of war with Italy, General Billotte intended to invade that country. As his contribution to the preparations, Pierre wrote that he was monitoring the radio in "a foreign language," certainly Italian, to help prepare a daily bulletin for the military staff.[18]

But Mussolini was not yet ready for war. When he made no move, Billotte was transferred north to command the First Army Group. Pierre Péteul's language skills were no longer needed, and he was too old to be assigned to a combat position. Besides, the French and British armies had failed to help Poland by attacking Germany on its western frontier, and the "phony war" – what the French called the *drôle de guerre* – had set in. Pierre received his orders for demobilization on December 20. "*Adieu au 2ème Bureau*," he confided to his notebook, referring to the Second Bureau of the French army General Staff, charged with collecting mili tary intelligence. He seems to have had a touch of regret. He certainly did not want war, but if it was to be, he wanted to contribute. A part of this scholarly and contemplative priest also seems to have relished the activity and risk involved. He had obviously enjoyed the assignment to General Billotte, writing on December 24, "I have a good memory of the last military staff where I was. I knew some excellent officers there."[19] His zest for adventure would become more evident during the years of war ahead.

Pierre Péteul left Nice that same afternoon and arrived in Paris the next morning. After attending mass he returned to the Quartier Fontenoy for his official demobilization. Now again known as Père Marie-Benoît, he began the quest for travel visas – the same problem that he would soon be helping Jewish refugees to solve. It was easier in 1939 than it would be in the years to come. On December 22 he obtained a French exit visa from the Paris Prefecture of Police, which was valid until the thirty-first. The next day he received an Italian entry visa at the Italian consulate. He was pleased to spend Christmas in Paris, attending several special masses with music. He took an evening train from the Gare de Lyon in Paris on December 26, waited for three hours at the Italian frontier the next morning, and arrived in Rome early on the twenty-eighth. He thought his war was over, but it was only just beginning.

FOUR

First Steps toward Jewish Rescue

MARSEILLE, MAY 1940 TO AUGUST 1942

BACK IN ROME AT THE END OF 1939, PÈRE MARIE-BENOÎT WAS to enjoy little more than four months of uneasy peace before his life changed forever. On May 10, 1940, following an extended period of inaction on the Western Front, the German army attacked Belgium, Luxembourg, and the Netherlands. Advancing rapidly, it reached the French border in a matter of days. On May 14 the Germans broke through the French lines at Sedan, and the Battle of France began. The following day French and British troops abandoned Belgian territory. The British withdrawal from Dunkirk began on May 26. Belgium surrendered to the Germans on May 28.

The fighting in Western Europe immediately affected Père Marie-Benoît in his monastery in Rome. For the third time in a year and a half, and still eligible for military service, he had to return to France. On May 19, just nine days after the beginning of the German offensive, he and two other French priests in Rome boarded a train headed north.[1] Looking back on that period years later, he wrote, "Being of French nationality and still liable to being mobilized, I left Rome, where I usually resided, because of the imminence of war between Italy and France . . . and, to await events, I went to the monastery of the Capuchins, 51 rue Croix-de-Régnier in Marseille, where I stayed for three years."[2] In an interview for a newspaper article after the war, he gave a slightly different reason for his departure, explaining, "The *gallophobie* [anti-French sentiment] of the Fascists had made the air of Rome unbreathable for all French men and women."[3]

Père Marie-Benoît was in Marseille when Italian prime minister Benito Mussolini, unable to resist grabbing a share of the spoils in what seemed to be an inevitable German victory, declared war on Britain and France on June 10. He was there four days later when the Germans entered Paris. He must have worried about his Capuchin confreres in Paris and at his old schools in Belgium and the Netherlands, not to mention his family in western France, but there is no record of that concern. He also must have been dismayed when his own former commander at Verdun, the newly appointed prime minister, Henri Philippe Pétain, informed the French people by radio on June 17 that his government must seek an armistice. Five days after that the armistice was signed and announced.

Père Marie-Benoît's country was now divided. An area consisting of about three-fifths of France north of the Loire River and extending south in a narrow strip along the Atlantic coast to the Spanish frontier was occupied by the Germans and cut off from the rest of the country by a strictly guarded demarcation line. Forty departments south of the line, including Bouches-du-Rhône, where Marseille was located, constituted "Free" or unoccupied France.[4] The French government, soon to be established in the spa town of Vichy and labeled the "Vichy regime," was to have full jurisdiction in the south and limited influence in the north, as long as it did not challenge the occupation forces there. For the French, at least, the war seemed to be over.

Despite the armistice and the apparent peace, Père Marie-Benoît in Marseille would have been distinctly aware of the enormous lingering problem posed by hundreds of thousands of war refugees in southern France – the issue to which he would soon dedicate his life. Already during the first week of the German offensive, some one million refugees from Belgium, Luxembourg, and the Netherlands, including ten thousand to forty thousand Jews, had fled into France, often without entry visas or even passports. Within a few days they had been joined by men, women, and children from invaded northeastern France, not illegal foreigners but nonetheless desperate people in need of food, shelter, and transportation. Then as the Germans approached Paris in early June, the civilian exodus heading south swelled to enormous proportions. It now numbered a staggering four million French and foreign men, women, and children, including hundreds of thousands of Parisians and some one hundred thousand to two hundred thousand Jews.[5]

With the signing of the armistice, refugees who were French could go home, at least if they were not Jewish. French Jews who had not yet returned to homes in the northern, German-occupied zone were prohibited from doing so by a German ordinance on September 27, 1940. Foreign refugees, especially those who were Jewish, faced even more difficult problems. Belgium, Luxembourg, and the Netherlands, now under German occupation, did not welcome the return of former residents who had revealed their anti-German sentiments by fleeing a few weeks before. They raised even greater objections to the return of Jews, many of whom had immigrated from the Third Reich or Eastern Europe in the 1930s and had temporary or even nonexistent legal status. Nor did most of the foreign refugees want to return. No matter how difficult conditions were in unoccupied France, they seemed better than in areas under direct German occupation – at least at first.

Soon, however, it became clear that appearances could be deceiving. Many of the trains that had carried refugees from the Low Countries across France had not stopped or allowed passengers to disembark along the way. Instead they had proceeded to small cities or towns in the south, designated somehow by harassed bureaucrats at the height of the chaos of the Battle of France. There they disgorged their passengers, who were promptly registered and assigned to local hotels, boardinghouses, homes, farms, or makeshift camps. The French Red Cross and other national and local social service agencies fed them and provided small daily subsidies as long as the refugees remained in their assigned residences. But it was a situation guaranteed to leave local officials uneasy and nervous. The foreign refugees, after all, were illegal aliens, often Jewish and often German-born or at least German-speaking. Never mind that they were anti-Nazis or that many had originally fled from the Third Reich to the Low Countries well before the war to escape Hitler's murderous regime. In Vichy France they were politically suspect as well as an economic burden, competing for jobs and resources in the communities to which they were assigned. Ominously, the Jews among the refugees were soon registered as such and assigned to separate residences. Some were actually interned, including about six thousand German, Austrian, and Polish wartime refugees from Belgium, not all of them Jewish, sent to Saint-Cyprien at the end of May.[6]

The recent refugees who arrived in France just ahead of the German army in May 1940 were not the only foreigners with problems just before and just after the armistice. Germans and Austrians who had immigrated to France legally before the war were, if anything, even more suspect to paranoid bureaucrats fearing a third column of spies and informers. Stefan Schwamm, whom Père Marie-Benoît would meet in Rome in September 1943 and who would become his close friend and associate in Jewish rescue there, was one of these. Born in 1910 and awarded a doctorate of law from the University of Vienna in 1934, Schwamm also studied at the École normale de musique and at the Institut de droit international in Paris before the war. He immigrated to France in the spring of 1938 after the Germans took over Austria in the Anschluss. Accompanying him were his non-Jewish wife, Gisela; their two-year-old daughter, Anita; and his parents, David Hersh Schwamm, a prestigious magistrate in Vienna, and Tipora, a talented pianist. When the German army invaded Poland in September 1939, Stefan and his father were among the twelve thousand German and five thousand Austrian men, along with some women, both Jewish and non-Jewish, arrested as enemy aliens and interned by the French government.

In the months following the German invasion of Poland, about half of these longtime resident aliens, including Stefan Schwamm's sixty-year-old father, were released. Younger men of military age had a more difficult time. Some were able to get out of the camps by joining the French Foreign Legion, the Czech or Polish Legions, or special companies of foreign workers called *prestataires* attached to the French army. Accordingly, Stefan Schwamm tried to join the Foreign Legion almost immediately after his arrest. He was refused on medical grounds – the result of an old ski injury – but was registered as a prestataire in February 1940. Transferred out of a foreign worker company and attached to the British Expeditionary Army just before the Battle of France because of his language skills, he was spared the new round of internments of legal longtime immigrants from the Third Reich that the French government initiated when the Germans attacked in May. Many less fortunate immigrants released in the autumn of 1939 were rearrested at that time, along with tens of thousands of others, including at least nine thousand women and children. Men and women without children were interned under dreadful conditions in camps such as Saint-Cyprien, Rivesaltes, Gurs, Rieucros, Le Vernet, and Les Milles. Women with children, when not interned, were placed in supervised residences in crowded, dirty, understaffed hotels, most notoriously the Bompard, Terminus, Atlantique, and Levant hotels in Marseille.[7] Père Marie-Benoît would have been acutely aware of these developments.

In the chaotic weeks following the Franco-German armistice of June 22, many internees escaped or were released by camp guards who either were indifferent or wanted to help keep their charges out of German hands. Once out of the camps, however, many lacked the documents necessary to live and work securely, especially the essential residence permits (*permis de séjour*) and ration cards; they and their families were liable to be arrested again at any time. Stefan Schwamm's situation was a bit different, for he was legally demobilized in Tarbes (Hautes-Pyrénées) on June 26, 1940. But despite his military service and the document to prove it, his legal status as an enemy national in Vichy France was far from secure.

At the end of June 1940, then, there were two basic categories of foreigners in southern France who were in serious trouble. Those who had entered the country from Belgium, Luxembourg, and the Netherlands just ahead of the German army were, for the most part, living in small towns in assigned residences, registered as non-Jews or Jews, as the case may be, and afraid to move for fear of breaking the law, living without identity papers, and losing the subsidies that were keeping them alive. Longtime resident aliens from the Third Reich usually had more economic resources, French acquaintances, the ability to speak French, and proof of legal entry into France before the war, but many either were still in internment camps or work groups or had escaped and were living illegally. To make matters worse, the Vichy French government agreed, in clause nineteen of the June armistice, to "surrender on demand" any immigrant from the Third Reich or its occupied territories whom the Germans wished to repatriate. Throughout the summer of 1940, German officials, many of them Gestapo agents, in what was called the Kundt Commission combed French internment camps and poked about in cities looking primarily for professed anti-Nazis. About eight hundred people, mostly political activists rather than Jews, were claimed and deported to Germany, the majority of them by the end of September.[8] The traditional right of asylum no longer existed in France.

This was the situation that Père Marie-Benoît was called upon to address – and the problems gradually grew worse. On July 9 and 10, 1940, what was left of the senators and deputies elected to the French Popular Front Parliament in 1936 voted by an overwhelming majority to revoke the 1875 constitution of the Third Republic and award Prime Minister Pétain full powers to promulgate a new one. Within a few hours Pétain declared that he was chief of the French state with a "totality of government power" and adjourned the Chamber of Deputies and Senate. Unoccupied France was now governed by an authoritarian and increasingly antiforeigner and antisemitic regime. Punitive decrees were initially aimed at foreigners in general. Laws in July, August, and September 1940 limited employment as civil servants, physicians, dentists, pharmacists, and lawyers to individuals born in France to French fathers, and called for a review and possible revocation of grants of French citizenship awarded since a liberalized law of August 10, 1927.[9] On September 3 a law directed departmental prefects to intern immigrants from the Third Reich who were considered "dangerous for the national defense and public security." Then on September 27, as government subsidies to recent refugees who were not French citizens were beginning to be terminated in many departments, another law authorized prefects to intern, at their own discretion, indigent male immigrants between the ages of eighteen and fifty-five regarded as "superfluous in the French economy" (*en surnombre dans l'Économie Nationale*). Alternatively, indigent male immigrants in that age bracket who could work could be forced into *groupements de travailleurs étrangers* (GTE), obligatory labor groups for foreign civilians.

The newly formed GTEs, now under the jurisdiction of the Ministry of Labor, were in fact a demilitarized version of the foreign labor companies formerly attached to military units, such as the one Stefan Schwamm had been in for a while. Those drafted for labor in the GTEs included some former French, Polish, and Czech soldiers who were unable to return to their homes; Indochinese workers; and foreigners formerly attached to the French army as prestataires or to units associated with the French Foreign Legion. Men in the latter had enrolled for the duration of the war and were now demobilized. All of these men worked on roads, construction, drainage projects, sewers, lumbering, mining, and other manual tasks for meager wages. They lived in miserable little camps throughout the country, while their women and children received small subsidies and were often crowded into strictly supervised shabby hotels in big cities. Only after a year of service did some workers receive a ten-day leave to visit their families. An estimated sixty thousand men, of whom about a third were Jewish, were laboring in the GTEs at the end of July 1941.[10]

Stefan Schwamm seems to have eluded the GTEs, but he still had to find work to avoid classification as "superfluous in the French economy," to obtain a *permis de séjour,* and merely to live. Ever foresighted and resourceful, he obtained letters of recommendation from a friendly priest in a village in the foothills of the Pyrenees and from a mayor in another village in Languedoc. Both letters testified to his French military career, his love for France, his Viennese legal training, and his good conduct without mentioning that he was Jewish. With those letters Stefan and his wife secured the necessary permits to live and work in the region, at least for a while. Both became involved in refugee assistance at this time.

Although these early Vichy measures were aimed at foreigners in general, several specific anti-Jewish measures soon followed. Already on August 27, 1940, the so-called Marchandeau decree of April 21, 1939, which prohibited attacks on individuals in the press based on race or religion, had been revoked, unleashing a flood of antisemitic publications. Then on October 3, 1940, the Vichy regime's first *Statut des juifs* defined who was to be considered Jewish and excluded Jews from the public service, the officer corps of the armed forces, teaching, journalism, theater, radio, and cinema. Unprompted by the Germans in the north, these anti-Jewish measures were applicable in both occupied and unoccupied France. A second Statut des juifs, issued on June 2, 1941, broadened the definition of who was to be considered Jewish, extended the list of prohibited occupations, and imposed a census on Jews in the unoccupied zone.[11] For reasons of pride as well as fear of the consequences of disobedience, some 140,000 Jews, representing perhaps as many as 80 or 90 percent of the total in "Free France," registered for the census.[12] In the German-occupied zone, another 149,734 Jews in Paris and the department of the Seine and some 20,000 others elsewhere had already registered in a German-decreed census applicable only in the north in October 1940.[13] The authorities now knew exactly who they were and where to find them.

Devastating as the Vichy regime's antisemitic legislation was for French Jews, the measures aimed exclusively at foreign Jews were worse. Most threatening was a law declared on October 4, 1940, that gave French prefects discretionary authority to send any foreigners "of the Jewish race" in their departments to internment camps, forced labor groups, or assigned residence without cause or justification and regardless of nationality. By the end of 1940 some twenty-eight thousand to thirty-five thousand Jewish immigrants and refugees had been interned in the unoccupied zone. The number increased to forty thousand by the end of February 1941.[14] It would drop significantly in the months that followed, as women and children were moved out of camps into supervised "welcoming centers" or Jewish children's homes and as thousands of men were transferred to forced labor units. But these individuals were not free to live where they chose. In addition, an order to the prefects from Vice Prime Minister Admiral François Darlan at the end of June 1941 specifically stipulated that "no foreigner of the Jewish race" who had not lived in France before May 10, 1940, should henceforth be freed from internment camps or forced labor groups.[15]

During the second half of 1941, Vichy decrees specified that all destitute male Jews (but not all destitute non-Jews) between the ages of eighteen and fifty-five who had entered the country after January 1, 1936, were to be put into forced labor groups. Many such groups that had previously included both Jews and non-Jews were reorganized at this time, with special so-called Palestinian units established for Jews. Even foreign Jews with jobs useful to the national economy were to register for forced labor, but they could be released under supervision. Other measures established obligatory professional training centers for foreign Jewish boys younger than eighteen. Jewish refugees and recent immigrants who were not in camps or forced labor units were also reminded that they must register for assigned residence.[16]

Even as early as 1941, then, foreign Jews, especially those from the Third Reich or countries it occupied, were the most endangered group living in France and the most in need of the help Père Marie-Benoît could offer. The priest could not do much if the foreign Jews stayed in their assigned residences, internment camps, or forced labor groups, but if they escaped and tried to live illegally, he could help them secure false documents, shelter, some funding, and routes to neutral Switzerland or Spain. All this he eagerly set out to do.

About his first weeks in Marseille in late May and early June 1940, Père Marie-Benoît later wrote, "A completely unexpected activity was reserved for me." It is not clear when the first refugees came to him, how they found him, or even who they were. Père Marie-Benoît himself remembered, "I had already been in contact with several Jews who had fled the zone occupied by the Germans when the Vichy government published the Statut des juifs. From that moment it was necessary to protect foreign Jewish refugees in France, which ceased to be a secure place and a land of liberty for them."[17] Thus, Père Marie-Benoît implied that his rescue activities began after and because of the first Statut des juifs in October 1940 or, at the very least, after the second Statut in June 1941. But this statement is confusing for two reasons. First, as discussed earlier, some longtime resident foreigners from the Third Reich in France who had been interned in September 1939 or May 1940 and had escaped needed help well before the anti-Jewish laws. Second, the two Statuts des juifs seriously penalized Jews who were French citizens, but they did not threaten them with arrest or oblige them to go into hiding and seek rescuers. The laws and decrees that drove Jewish and non-Jewish refugees to seek the assistance of individuals like Père Marie-Benoît were initially the measures against foreigners, beginning as early as September 1939 and escalating in the months and years that followed, as described above.

Père Marie-Benoît was clearer about the origins and nature of his rescue work in another postwar interview. He explained, "In the beginning at Marseille I began an action of propaganda when it was still possible to combat antisemitism by means of conferences and study circles as well as family meetings. On several occasions, I visited the camp of Les Milles to help the administrative internees, to bring their problems to the authorities in Marseille and to facilitate their departure abroad."[18] By late 1940, Les Milles, an internment camp near Aix-en-Provence and about thirty kilometers from Marseille, had become a holding center for mostly Jewish men who, because of personal connections and resources, had a possibility of emigrating. Though better off than those without such possibilities, these men still often needed assistance in negotiating for exit, entry, and transit visas at various consulates in Marseille. Père Marie-Benoît was able to help some of these men and their families. Through these perfectly legal activities, he met other Jewish and non-Jewish foreigners in need, and some, sensing his sympathy, came to him for other kinds of help.

In still another interview, Père Marie-Benoît recalled that his first protégé was introduced to him by a man who visited his monastery in Marseille to ask for help for a young Jewish girl in his family. The Capuchin priest agreed to help the girl, he said, because he welcomed all who came to him for help, and this family came. The rescue effort developed gradually from there as one case led to another. As word spread, Père Marie-Benoît also began to receive referrals from the Sisters of Notre Dame de Sion in Marseille. This was an order of nuns founded in 1843 expressly to pray for the conversion of the Jews. Making a fine distinction, the nuns were not to proselytize but were to be receptive to Jews who came to them. By the 1930s, however, the order had expanded its purpose to include delivering help to needy Jewish families, especially immigrants. Thus it developed into an institution known for its sympathies to Jews and its willingness to help them regardless of religious affiliation.[19] Jews in trouble trusted and turned to this particular order of nuns, and the sisters in turn referred the men among them to priests or friars whom they knew to be sympathetic.

The question then arises as to why Père Marie-Benoît was doing what he did to attract that first Jewish refugee. Why was this seemingly contemplative and scholarly priest holding public meetings to combat antisemitism in the first place, and why was he going to Les Milles to help foreign Jewish internees there? On the most basic level, he explained, "I had no particular responsibility [when he arrived at the monastery in Marseille], and could carve out my own role." After reflecting, he added, "I was, in a sense, a war refugee myself, and I felt a particular sympathy for the refugees."[20] All of this was undoubtedly true. He probably did have extra time on his hands. The break in monastic routine and the adventure, excitement, and psychological satisfaction of making a contribution outside the monastery may also have appealed to him. In his explanations Père Marie-Benoît did not dwell on his own humanitarianism and natural compassion for others, but they also were important factors. Clearly he had noticed fugitives in trouble with the Vichy authorities and resolved to help them.

The most important explanation for Père Marie-Benoît's activities in 1940, however, is that he had developed a loathing for antisemitism long before the war. As a newly ordained priest in Rome, if not earlier, he came to believe that anti-Judaism and antisemitism were not only evil but also theologically erroneous. He perceived the Jews as the Chosen People of God, creators of the Old Testament upon which both Judaism and Christianity are based, and the nation of people among whom Jesus was born. Rather than being rejected, the Jews merited admiration and respect, and both Christians and Jews could benefit from reconciliation and dialogue. Père Marie-Benoît may also have felt some guilt about Catholic anti-Judaism and the harsh treatment of Jews by Catholics in the past and present and hoped to atone for such evils. He never wrote much about his pre-1940 attitudes toward Jews, but in 1926 or 1927 he acted on them by joining a new Catholic group called Amici Israel (Friends of Israel). This organization of some 3,000 priests, 278 bishops and archbishops, and 19 cardinals was devoted to promoting mutual respect and dialogue between Jews and Catholics and, in the eyes of some but not all members, creating conditions favorable to the conversion of the Jews.[21]

As the number of members of Amici Israel suggests, Père Marie-Benoît was not alone among Catholics in his disapproval of antisemitism in the 1920s. Since the end of the First World War in France and elsewhere, small numbers of secular and regular priests and nuns, especially some Jesuits and members of the Fathers and the Sisters of Notre Dame de Sion, had been advocating better Jewish-Christian relations and sponsoring lectures, conferences, and publications on that subject.[22] Vatican authorities were wary of these attitudes, disapproving of contacts between Catholics and Jews unless they were directed exclusively to conversion. As will be seen, prelates in the Roman Curia convinced Pope Pius XI to ban Amici Israel in 1928. But as Nazi measures against Jews in

the Third Reich became increasingly evident in the 1930s, the numbers
of men and women of the Church who publicly opposed antisemitism
grew slowly but steadily.

During the years of persecution and deportation of Jews in France,
opposition to antisemitism sometimes developed into a commitment
to rescue. Unlike most wartime rescuers of Jews who were asked for
help by friends, neighbors, or purely by chance, a small handful of men
and women of the Church attracted fugitives because their prior opposition to antisemitism was well known. Those same men and women
of the Church, then, acted in large part because of that opposition. In
addition to Père Marie-Benoît, among French Catholic priests in this
category were Pères Roger Braun, Pierre Chaillet, and Théomir Devaux,
and Abbé Alexandre Glasberg. Catholic laypersons included Germaine
Ribière in France and Gertrude Luckner and Margarete Sommers in
Germany, to mention only a few. French Protestants who held strong
views in opposition to antisemitism before the war were even more numerous. Protestant pastors like André Trocmé, Édouard Theis, Marc
Donadille, Roland de Pury, and Pierre-Charles Toureille acted after
1940 on their prewar favorable conceptions of Jews as the "People of the
Book" and the elder brothers of Christians. Large numbers of Protestant
laypersons shared these views.[23]

The question remains as to why and how Père Marie-Benoît came to
be so opposed to antisemitism and anti-Judaism. The pressures pushing
him in the opposite direction, after all, were great. We know that he read
the literature of the viciously antisemitic Action française during the
First World War, for example, and he probably had done so before and
would do so again. He must have been aware of anti-Judaism within the
Catholic Church, whose spokespersons, when he was a boy, often taught
that Jews were to be condemned because of their responsibility for the
death of Jesus. Those same spokespersons, while perhaps rejecting racial
antisemitism, nevertheless taught that Jews were responsible for the ills
of the modern world and should be separated from Christians in their
residences and in the workplace. Given his roots and early education in
one of the most conservative and Catholic regions of France, why did
Père Marie-Benoît, a priest who was not otherwise radical, reject these
influences and take it upon himself to combat antisemitism?

Père Marie-Benoît himself never explained it. Perhaps a condemnation of antisemitism was first expressed to him by a respected mentor, teacher, or older priest in the Capuchin schools he attended in Belgium, the Netherlands, or Rome. Perhaps he met Jewish soldiers during the First World War and began to meditate on the injustice of religious and racial prejudice at that time. If either of these situations applied, however, he never mentioned it. Or perhaps his own legacy as a member of a Catholic minority persecuted by the secular state during the French Revolution and at the end of the nineteenth century and the beginning of the twentieth played a role. Historians generally agree that French Protestants' memories of government persecution in previous generations made them more sensitive and sympathetic to the sufferings of other minorities. French Catholics did not usually emerge from similar conflicts with the state in the same manner, but there were exceptions. Père Marie-Benoît was one of them.

One non-Jewish woman who knew Père Marie-Benoît well during the war had yet another explanation. She wrote, "His special affection for the people of Israel had been awakened as a young seminarian by his study of the Old Testament, and it had grown and been strengthened when, as a young man determined to master the Hebrew language, he had cultivated friendships among the Jewish community of Rome." During their rescue work together in Marseille, this woman may have asked Père Marie-Benoît why he was so concerned about Jews, and he may have offered that explanation. It certainly rings true. We have seen that he studied Hebrew for several terms during his graduate work at the Gregorian University, and that he received a designation of summa cum laude in that subject after an exam in 1922. We also know that he later administered exams in Hebrew to other students. Survivors who knew him in Israel after the war confirm that he spoke and read Hebrew, although not fluently.[24]

The theory that Père Marie-Benoît came to oppose antisemitism after actually meeting Jews in Rome suggests that he had a particular affinity for the people and their culture. Everything we shall see about his wartime work and postwar life confirms that social dimension. As Père Marie-Benoît came to know more Jews personally, he clearly liked them more and more. Perhaps he was attracted to their differentness – after all, most of the Jews he first met were foreigners, and his association with them evoked his intellectual curiosity and widened his horizons. He valued his relationships with individual refugees and continued to communicate all his life with many, including Denise Caraco Siekierski, Miriam Löwenwirth Reuveni, Frieda Schnabel Semmelman and her sister Clara Schnabel Mandel, and the Fallmann sisters and their mother. His special friendships with Joseph Bass, Angelo Donati, and Stefan Schwamm also strengthened his commitment. He clearly enjoyed the company of those energetic, bright, courageous, and irreverent men. All of these factors interacted to provide Père Marie-Benoît with an affinity for the Jewish people and made him particularly sensitive to the persecutions. His natural kindness, courage, and compassion did the rest.

A final question about motivation asks not why Père Marie-Benoît first came to oppose antisemitism but why he did not put aside that position in 1940 when the Vichy regime replaced the Third Republic and introduced anti-Jewish policies. After all, Marshal Henri Philippe Pétain, his revered commander during the First World War, headed the new regime. Did Père Marie-Benoît not feel loyal to him? Even more pressing, perhaps, most leaders of the Catholic Church welcomed Pétain with great enthusiasm. Just as they had in the 1880s and 1890s, those leaders still detested the Third Republic, with its separation of the churches from the state, its dissolution of religious orders, and its banning of religion in the public schools. Because they hoped the new Vichy regime would restore some of the privileges of the Church, particularly in the field of education, they were willing to overlook abuses.[25] Did Père Marie-Benoît not agree? The Capuchin priest never answered or even addressed these questions. He never recorded his opinion of Pétain and the Vichy regime. We do not know what he thought about the Third Republic that had preceded it, except that he fought and almost died for it. All of that was politics, and, as he wrote in a letter during the First World War, he never concerned himself much with politics. He did concern himself with ethics and morality, and for him, antisemitism was a moral offense.

For most of his life Père Marie-Benoît showed himself to be highly independent and individualistic. He did not necessarily demonstrate those characteristics as a boy, for in choosing his religious vocation he was not doing anything that would surprise his family, friends, or neighbors in his region of France. In the army during the First World War, however, his differentness because of his religious vocation became vividly apparent, but it never caused him to waver or pause. That independence, individualism, and willingness to operate out of the mainstream became most apparent in 1940 when he questioned particular policies of the popular Vichy regime and chose to act on his opinions. After the war those same qualities remained visible as he committed himself to Jewish-Catholic reconciliation, a cause that, as we shall see, was not endorsed by the Vatican hierarchy until the mid-1960s.

In her study of wartime rescuers of Jews in Poland, sociologist Nechama Tec found much variety of character and motivation. Some rescuers acted from specific compassion for Jews, while others were antisemitic. Some tended to the right in their politics, while others were left-wing. Among the rescuers there were upper-, middle-, and lower-class individuals; young and old; men and women; rich and poor; educated and illiterate; urban and rural; professionals and unemployed; practicing Catholics, Protestants, and atheists. But all or nearly all rescuers demonstrated extreme individualism, independent thinking, and a sense of being different from the majority.[26] Père Marie-Benoît fully shared these characteristics. He also shared with other rescuers certain explanations of his wartime work. "I just did what I had to do," he explained on many occasions. Or, "They came to me for help. What else could I have done?" Or again, "I just did my duty," or "I did what anyone would have done." That last, of course, was not true. His own personal values determined his actions. The expectations of the wider society did not.

What did Père Marie-Benoît actually do for his protégés, as he called them, in those early days of rescue? At first, and until early August 1942, he seems to have acted independently. As he recalled, "I received my protégés at the monastery, which was not without inconveniences or without [the danger of] attracting attention, because the public rooms [in the monastery] were almost continually full."[27] The mostly Jewish longtime resident immigrants who came to him had usually avoided or escaped from internment camps and needed false papers, above all, along with some money and a place to live. Recent Jewish refugees trying to avoid

assigned residences or, a bit later, internment as unregistered and destitute aliens had the same needs, and somehow Père Marie-Benoît was
able to address them.

Sister Gabriella Maria from Notre Dame de Sion, a nun who worked
outside her convent, confirmed in 1947 that most of Père Marie-Benoît's
protégés had been Jewish. She wrote that she had been assigned to work
among the poor in Marseille in December 1941, but that after a few
months she left that job to work "more actively and exclusively among the
Jews with a Franciscan father (in reality a Capuchin) whom Providence
had put in my path: the Reverend Père Marie-Benoît. With him, I was
fully in Israel. Home visits, rescue efforts, false papers, departures for
Spain and Switzerland, everything was tried to save these poor unhappy
people who came to us for help."[28]

Even in these early days of rescue, the securing of false documents
was of the highest priority. The systematic manufacture of documents
was not yet well organized, but Père Marie-Benoît managed to obtain
authentic blank forms from friendly parishioners working in government offices and from nascent resistance groups. The Sisters of Notre
Dame de Sion, who operated a lycée and boarding school for girls at
their premises at 232 rue Paradis in Marseille, also obtained blanks from
former students who worked for municipal or departmental authorities.
Such forms, filled in and completed with attached photographs of the
bearers, could be filed in the appropriate government office. They were
known as "real false papers," as opposed to the "false false papers" that
were later made from scratch.

Housing was also not too difficult to find at this early stage, for Père
Marie-Benoît could call upon colleagues in Church institutions in Marseille as well as in the countryside. In this respect, he specifically recorded
his work with the Sisters of Notre Dame de Sion, "who for their part were
very active in the same way, and I received from them a number of our
protégés." In addition, he contacted trusted parishioners, who put up
fugitives in their homes and apartments. Père Marie-Benoît also wrote
that, with time, "a very active cooperation was established between us,
the Catholics, and pastors from Protestant, Orthodox and other religious
groups."[29] It must be remembered that in these early days, before the Vichy regime began to deliver foreign Jews in the unoccupied zone to the

Germans in the north in August 1942 and before the Germans occupied the south of France in November 1942, levels of terror were not as high as they later became. The punishment for assisting illegal refugees might involve imprisonment but not yet deportation or execution.

Hiding places were often needed for only a few days or weeks, until the fugitives could be escorted to safety in Switzerland or Spain. Père Marie-Benoît recalled, "I entered into relations with organizations of smugglers and evasion networks for Spain and Switzerland; I even had some just for my own disposition."[30] While the idea of a gentle, ostensibly unworldly man of the cloth dealing with smugglers may make us smile, these operations were deadly serious and increasingly fraught with danger.

Rachel and Esther Fallmann, who had fled from Belgium to France in May 1940, well remember their own attempt to cross into Switzerland. The event occurred in January 1943, but it was typical of what had also occurred earlier. After their father, Heinrich, was arrested on August 26, 1942, and deported, their mother, Ida, who had two narrow escapes herself, somehow met Père Marie-Benoît in Marseille and asked for help. The Capuchin priest put Ida and her two daughters, then twelve and ten years old, on a train in Marseille headed for Annemasse, on the Swiss border. Ida, who spoke no French, posed as a deaf-mute, a ruse that would probably have fooled no one if she had been seriously questioned. In Annemasse, Ida and the children went to a café to meet a local woman, Père Marie-Benoît's contact. The woman directed them to a small brook where they could cross the border. Unfortunately they met Swiss guards at the border who informed them that Jewish refugees were not welcome. Parents with children under six would be accepted, but Rachel and Esther were too old to qualify.

The Swiss guards permitted the three exhausted refugees to sleep on the floor of a customs house near Saint-Julien-en-Genevois for two nights and then sent them back to France at 7:00 PM on a Sunday. They explained to Ida and her daughters that the French on the other side of the border changed their guards at that hour. The Swiss were kind enough to point out a French convent and hospital within view where the three refugees might find help. It was hard to run in wooden shoes, Rachel and Esther remember, but run they did. When they reached the

hospital, all three broke down and began to cry. The nuns agreed to no-
tify Père Marie-Benoît's contact in Annemasse, who came for them and
helped them return to Marseille. Père Marie-Benoît continued to help
them there, but they did not try again to reach Switzerland.[31]

Père Marie-Benoît was more successful with Joseph Aelion, whom
he helped escape to Spain. Once there, Aelion served in Barcelona to
assist other Jews and non-Jews referred to him by the priest. Père Marie-
Benoît instructed his protégés to approach his Barcelona contact with
the password "Suzanne" or, occasionally, "Valentine" or "Christiane."
Aelion housed them for one or two nights and then helped them travel to
Lisbon or Casablanca. Père Marie-Benoît noted after the war that these
refugees had included at least two Belgian airmen and several former
French army officers who hoped to join Gaullist forces in Africa, as well
as Jews from France, Belgium, Czechoslovakia, and Poland.[32]

In his postwar writing and speaking, Père Marie-Benoît specifically
evoked only two or three other protégés in Marseille and usually failed
to note dates and other details about the help he gave them. For example,
he wrote about a young girl who came to his monastery at 5:30 AM asking for help for her father, who had just been arrested. He gave her some
suggestions about what to do, but she returned at 10:00 PM to say that
nothing had worked. Unfortunately he did not relate the outcome of this
incident. Père Marie-Benoît also wrote with amusement about a Belgian
officer who came to his monastery at 10:00 PM asking for help. He had
been arrested and imprisoned in Marseille but had managed to escape
by convincing a guard to accompany him on what the priest described
as a *sortie galante,* a romantic rendezvous, that the Belgian officer was
willing to share. Once out of prison, the Belgian shook off the guard and
disappeared. Père Marie-Benoît put the man up for a night and then sent
him on his way.[33]

FIVE

With Joseph Bass in Marseille

IF PÈRE MARIE-BENOÎT'S LIFE CHANGED DRAMATICALLY WHEN he left his monastery in Rome and settled in Marseille in May 1940, it was equally altered during the tragic month of August 1942. Until that time Père Marie-Benoît was, as far as he knew, helping Jewish and non-Jewish foreigners as well as escaped Allied soldiers and others in trouble with the Vichy regime to avoid internment and imprisonment. He undoubtedly knew that in the German-occupied north of France, thousands of mostly foreign Jewish men in Paris had been arrested in May, August, and December 1941 and deported in the spring of 1942. He also knew about the appalling arrests and deportations of some 12,884 foreign Jewish men, women, and children in the same city in July 1942. But such horrors had yet not occurred in the Vichy-controlled southern zone. They must have seemed inconceivable.

Everything changed when officials from the Vichy regime agreed, in the summer of 1942, to deliver ten thousand foreign Jews in the south to the Germans in occupied Paris. The actual order from Vichy police headquarters to the regional prefects was issued on August 5.[1] According-ing to the order, individuals eligible for delivery were Jewish immigrants and refugees from the Third Reich, Poland, the Soviet Union, and the Baltic countries who had entered France after January 1, 1936. Specifically excluded initially were individuals over sixty; unaccompanied children under eighteen; parents with a child under five; pregnant women; sick people incapable of being moved; war veterans (but not *prestataires*) who had seen combat or served for at least three months with the French army or its former allies, and their families; men or women with French spouses or children, or with spouses from countries other than those eligible for expulsion; and adults with jobs in the national economic interest or with a record of special service to France. In addition, parents with children under eighteen could choose to leave them behind. The ultimate fate of the victims was not discussed in the order.

As a result of the order, about 3,436 recent immigrant and refugee Jews in the internment camps of Gurs, Récébédou, Noé, Rivesaltes, Le Vernet, and Les Milles were jammed into the filthy cattle cars of four different trains headed north. They arrived at Drancy, a makeshift camp in an unfinished housing project on the outskirts of Paris, between August 7 and August 14. Then it was the turn of Jewish men of similar nationalities and immigration dates who were dispersed in forced labor sites throughout southern France, along with their women and children being held in obligatory residence hotels. Assembled in mid-August, about 1,184 people in this category arrived at Drancy on August 25 on yet another wretched train. At least 4,394 of these 4,620 internees and forced laborers and their families were deported "to the east" within a few days.[2] For most, "the east" would be Auschwitz.

But the horrors of August 1942 had barely begun. To fulfill the Vichy authorities' agreement with the Germans, French police with carefully compiled lists of names and addresses of Jews of specific nationalities and recent immigration dates began raiding homes throughout the unoccupied zone in the early morning hours of August 26. In an effort to obtain more victims, the date of arrival in France for male bachelors between the ages of eighteen and forty was extended back from January 1, 1936, to January 1, 1933, unless they had served in the military or rendered special services to the country. For the same reason, parents were now exempted only if they had a child under two, rather than five; unaccompanied minors were exempted only if they were under sixteen, rather than eighteen; and parents lost the right to leave their children under eighteen in France. Also, in the name of the "non-separation of families," police were instructed to find children not living with their parents so that they could no longer be classified as exempted unaccompanied minors and could be sent north in family units. In the days that followed, thousands were arrested. In the terrifying eight days between August 29 and September 5, seven trains from the unoccupied zone arrived at Drancy with about 5,259 newly arrested immigrant and refugee Jews. Another 1,135 arrived on five more trains between September 15 and October 22. Deportation within a few days of arrival can be traced for at least 4,989 of these passengers. Of the total number of about 11,014 foreign Jewish men, women, and children expelled from unoccupied France to Drancy between August 7 and October 22, 1942, and the 9,383 known to have been deported from Drancy to Poland by November 6, roughly 200 to 300 survived.[3]

Until the late summer of 1942, Père Marie-Benoît must have been unhappy with the stance of his bishop on Jewish issues. On more than one occasion, Monsignor Jean Delay, a firm admirer of Pétain, had publicly attributed France's social and economic troubles to the immigrants in her midst, a reference that especially included foreign Jews, as was understood by all. In the autumn of 1941 and the spring and summer of 1942, he strongly disapproved of the *Cahiers de Témoignage Chrétien,* a clandestine journal published by a team of Catholic priests and Protestant pastors in and around Lyon, and discouraged its distribution in Marseille.[4] Among other things, the journal condemned antisemitism and the persecution of Jews in France, including the roundups of foreign Jews in Paris. As roundups began in the unoccupied zone in August 1942, however, Père Marie-Benoît received for the first time public assurance that some prelates of the Catholic Church in France were deeply troubled by the Vichy regime's policies. On Saturday, August 22, about two weeks after the expulsions of foreign Jews already in internment and forced labor camps but four days before the arrests of thousands of others still living freely, the frail and elderly Archbishop Jules-Gérard Saliège of Toulouse issued an anguished letter of protest to be read during masses in all the churches of his diocese the following day. The letter said:

> That children, women, fathers and mothers should be treated like animals, that family members should be separated and sent off to an unknown destination, it has been reserved for our time to witness this sad spectacle . . . Jews are men. Jewesses are women. Foreigners are men and women. All is not permitted against them, against these men, these women, these fathers and mothers. They are part of the human race. They are our brothers like so many others. A Christian cannot forget it.[5]

Within a few weeks at least four other French bishops in the unoccupied zone followed Saliège's example. The most forthright letter, read throughout his diocese on August 30, was from Bishop Pierre-Marie Théas of Montauban, who even referred to "an unknown destination" and declared, "The present antisemitic measures are a contemptible attack on human dignity, a violation of the most sacred rights of the individual and the family."[6]

Then on Sunday, September 6, letters from Cardinal Pierre Gerlier in Lyon and Père Marie-Benoît's own Bishop Delay of Marseille were also read at mass. These letters alluded to the right of the state to resolve "a problem" (Gerlier) and to "protect itself against those who, especially these last years, have hurt it so much" (Delay). But they condemned the persecutions of innocent men, women, and children simply because they were Jewish. And only Delay declared that Jews were being sent "perhaps to their deaths."[7] A few days after Bishop Delay's letter, his vicar wrote a letter of introduction for Père Marie-Benoît, authorizing him to have free regular access to Les Milles and to the Bompard, a supervised residence hotel in Marseille for the wives and children of internees.[8] Until then he had visited those places with more difficulty.

There is no evidence that the protests by French bishops were prompted by the Vatican. Indeed, Pope Pius XII's policy was that bishops throughout Europe should decide for themselves how to respond to the ongoing persecutions of the Jews. On April 30, 1943, he explained that policy to his friend Monsignor Konrad von Preysing, the bishop of Berlin, who had begged him to intercede on behalf of a group of Jews affected by a new wave of deportations in Germany. "Regarding pronouncements by the bishops," the pope wrote. "We leave it to local senior clergymen to decide if, and to what degree, the danger of reprisals and oppression, as well as, perhaps, other circumstances caused by the length and psychological climate of the war may make restraint advisable – despite the reasons for intervention – in order to avoid greater evils. This is one of the reasons why We limit ourselves in Our proclamations."[9] The pope's public proclamations were indeed limited; at the time of the expulsions of foreign Jews from unoccupied France, he had not yet referred specifically to men and women who were being persecuted because of their nationality or race. But while the French bishops' protests were not issued on instructions from Rome, they may have been encouraged by the general ideals of human brotherhood and the unity of the human race that the pope had articulated in a few of his encyclicals and speeches.[10]

If Père Marie-Benoît was reassured by the letters of protest of several French bishops, he was galvanized by conditions around him. His notebook indicates that he was at Les Milles on August 5 as Jewish refugees and recent immigrants began to be assembled for expulsion to the north "A Protestant pastor is here constantly," he wrote, probably alluding to Pastor Henri Manen, active in the camp since at least March 1941, and revealing his own concern that there should also be a sympathetic Catholic presence. He added tersely, "Lamentable cases."[11] This was a considerable understatement. Between August 4 and 10, internees struggled desperately with camp officials to establish some technical grounds for avoiding deportation. Age, the ages of children, state of health, country of origin, date of immigration to France, military or civilian service records, connections with non-Jewish families – all these conditions were carefully scrutinized to determine if they met the criteria for exemption. The most wrenching cases involved the children. Realizing that unaccompanied youngsters under the age of eighteen were not eligible for deportation, Jewish and non-Jewish religious leaders and social workers found themselves in the unenviable position of urging parents to give up their children.

On Monday morning, August 10, about 70 children from Les Milles were torn away from their parents and returned to Marseille. The parents had agreed to give them up, but the pain was unbearable. A French policeman on the scene told Pastor Manen the next day, "I have been in the colonies, I have been in China, I have seen massacres, war, famine. I have seen nothing as horrible as this." The devastated parents were among the approximately 260 Jews crammed into boxcars under the blazing Mediterranean sun and sent north on August 11 and the 538 others who left on August 13. Nearly all of these victims were deported to Auschwitz and did not return.[12]

After the roundups and expulsions of August 1942, most Jewish refugees and recent immigrants who were lucky enough to have escaped now realized that they could not remain in legally registered residences. Consequently, the trickle of prospective protégés knocking on Père Marie-Benoît's door and wishing to hide swelled into a flood. Suddenly there were not enough false documents, not enough hiding places, and not enough money. At the same time, police searches intensified. Père Marie-Benoît, the Sisters of Notre Dame de Sion, and others who were trying to hide Jewish fugitives needed help, and they needed it immediately. As Père Marie-Benoît later told an interviewer, "At this time I met André."[13] André was one of several noms de guerre of the brilliant Russian Jewish engineer and lawyer Joseph Bass, who, like Stefan Schwamm later, became Père Marie-Benoît's great friend and associate in rescue (fig. 6).

In memoirs of his wartime rescue activities in southern France, the prominent historian Léon Poliakov fondly recalled Joseph Bass, with whom he had closely collaborated.

> Joseph Bass, called "Hippopotamus," alias Monsieur André, alias Gart, Georges, Bourgeois, Roure, Rocca. I am not sure that I ever knew all his names. André, as he chose to be called at that time, was undeniably what the English call "conspicuous." Tall and bulky, he seemed taller and more bulky than life. He had a special capacity for invading by his very presence the place where he found himself. Impossible not to notice him. It is difficult to explain; those who knew André will understand me: warm and noisy, he was imposing.[14]

Denise Caraco (later Siekierski by marriage), who as a teenager risked her life working for Bass's rescue organization, was one of those who knew André well (fig. 7). "Bass was so huge," she says, "that I was a little bit afraid of him." This from a young woman who was undaunted by the Vichy or German police. In her own memoirs, she added, "To [Poliakov's] portrait [of Bass], one must add his big sparkling blue eyes and a stentorian voice." She observed that Bass dressed well, ate prodigiously, and always traveled first class, a luxury that he paid for himself. He slept only three to four hours a night, which allowed him to read continually. Denise was impressed that he retained everything he read, which gave him a broad cultural base. She was equally impressed by his colossal temper.[15] Like most women, young and old, she adored him. Most men admired him as well.

Joseph Bass was born in 1908 in Grodno, currently in Belarus but at the time in Russian-controlled Poland. After he completed his secondary schooling in Saint Petersburg, his mother decided that he should continue his studies in Paris, where she had a sister. The young man accepted the suggestion and never saw his mother again.[16] With no money for travel, he paid for his trip by performing manual labor along the way in the Soviet Union, Poland, and Germany. The trip took months. After arriving in Paris speaking no French, he stayed with his aunt for a short time but then rented a maid's room without electricity, took a job unloading produce at Les Halles, and obtained the baccalaureate necessary for university admission. Soon his French was so good that he had almost no accent and could easily pass as an Alsatian. Next, he studied for two university degrees simultaneously while also working in a factory to support himself. After attaining credentials as both a lawyer and an engineer, he set up a legal office in Paris to advise and assist clients seeking patents for industrial property. Not surprisingly, he was soon successful.[17]

As early as 1934 Joseph Bass became involved in helping refugees, especially those who were Jewish, establish themselves in Paris. He subsequently claimed that he did not belong to any political party at this time, although at least one historian has stated that he was a militant Socialist. When the war broke out in September 1939, he tried to volunteer for military service, but, like so many immigrants at the time, he was not accepted in the French army. He continued working in Paris until October 1940 when the German and Vichy authorities enacted measures to confiscate Jewish property. At that point he transferred his patent office to his devoted non-Jewish associate, Madeleine Rocca, a war widow and also a lawyer, who kept the business going, protected its assets and documents from the Gestapo, and regularly delivered the profits to him (fig. 7). He established a second practice in Lyon, in the unoccupied zone, where he did not register as Jewish in the census ordered by the second Statut des juifs in June 1941.

After settling in the unoccupied zone, Joseph Bass traveled from time to time to Marseille, where he met dozens of prominent foreign intellectuals who were eluding the Vichy authorities and the Kundt Commission and, often, trying to emigrate. Among them, he later recalled, were the Italian Socialist Giuseppe Emanuele Modigliani, elder brother of the painter Amedeo Modigliani, and Victor Serge, a historian, novelist, and critic of both Fascism and Communism who had been born in Belgium to Russian Jewish emigrés. Also in Marseille, Bass met Boris

Vildé, an immigrant from Saint Petersburg like himself, a linguist and ethnologist at the Musée de l'Homme in Paris, and a founder in August 1940 of the Réseau du Musée de l'Homme, one of the first French resistance networks. Vildé had been sent to the unoccupied zone early in 1941 to recruit militants for the resistance in Marseille, Lyon, Toulouse, and other large cities. He told Bass about the Paris group and asked him to participate, but Bass preferred to work with refugees in the south. The two men agreed to meet again in Lyon, but when Bass went there he learned that the police had discovered the address. Vildé was arrested by the Germans in Paris on March 26, 1941, and shot on February 23, 1942, along with six others from the Musée de l'Homme group.[18]

Because Bass's association with Vildé had not escaped the attention of the Vichy police, he was under surveillance throughout the spring of 1941 not because he was Jewish but because he was considered a resister. He knew he should hide, he later related, but he lacked the material resources and what he called "the spirit." The decision was finally made for him when he was arrested as a Russian national in June or July 1941, after the German attack on the Soviet Union. He was sent to the fort of Paillet in Lyon and then interned at Argelès on July 13, 1941. There he was interrogated by the Gestapo, apparently in the context of the Kundt Commission. Looking back later, he stated that he had been recognized as a known anti-Nazi and designated for transfer to a punishment unit. At this point he escaped and, after much difficulty, reached Marseille by way of Perpignan and Nîmes. Now he had no choice but to obtain false papers and live in hiding. He later recalled, "Having become completely illegal, I thought that I could do more than before. I returned to my project of helping the persecuted, refugees and Jews." Elsewhere he added that he was now more interested in political internees than ever before, since he had shared their fate.[19]

After the expulsions of foreign Jews from unoccupied France in August 1942, Joseph Bass's "project" was to organize a group of people of different origins and backgrounds – Catholics, Protestants, and Jews – who were prepared to hide fugitives and support them systematically. When furnished with false documents and money, the fugitives could live illegally for extended periods. The project was a conscious repudiation of the many French Jewish charitable organizations such as the Oeuvre de secours aux enfants (OSE), the Éclaireurs israélites de France (EIF), and the Organisation pour la reconstruction et le travail (ORT), which were sheltering Jewish children, in particular, but had not yet moved their protégés out of legal, easily recognized Jewish institutions and into clandestine residences. Considering legal institutions to be traps, Joseph Bass refused to have anything to do with them. He strongly believed that Jews should not be clustered together either in assigned residences or in Jewish institutions, but should be dispersed anonymously in small family units throughout the countryside, especially in the remote and sparsely populated Massif Central. There they were to assume false names and documents and break all ties with their past legal existence. Better yet, they were to be escorted when possible to safety in Spain or Switzerland. Everything Bass and his group did involved encouraging clandestine life, a policy that many Jewish charitable organizations adopted later.[20]

"Little by little, I made the contacts and our group was organized," Joseph Bass remembered later. The organization came to be called the Groupe d'action contre la déportation, better known as the Service André, Bass's pseudonym. Initially consisting of about a dozen people, it rapidly grew to between thirty and thirty-five. The Jewish participants seem to have been the first to become involved. In addition to Bass, they included Adrien Benvéniste, a professor of philosophy at a lycée in Marseille who lost his position because of the anti-Jewish laws; Sammy Klein, a rabbi who was later shot by the Germans for activities with the resistance; Théo Klein, Sammy's brother-in-law and an EIF chief; and, somewhat later, the young Léon Poliakov. Also crucial to the group was Maurice Brener, the delegate in France of the American Jewish Joint Distribution Committee, or Joint. Brener introduced Bass to Raymond-Raoul Lambert, his cousin and the director in the unoccupied zone of the Union Générale des Israélites de France (UGIF), the German-imposed Jewish welfare organization. Brener and Lambert promised to support Bass's group financially.[21]

By the late autumn of 1942, Protestant pastors and Catholic priests were also involved with the Service André. The Protestants were represented by Pastor Jean-Séverin Lemaire of the Mouvement chrétien évangelique of Marseille and Pastor André Trocmé of Le Chambon sur Lignon. The major Catholic participants were Père de Parceval, the prior of the Dominican monastery at 35 rue Edmond Rostand in Marseille; Abbé Alfred Daumas, the director of the Bourse chrétienne du travail in Nice; and Père Marie-Benoît. Other close supporters among the Protestants were pastors Marcel Heuzé in Marseille, Roland Leenhardt in Tence, and Edmond Evrard in Nice. Included among the Catholics were Frère Marcolin, a Dominican friar who obtained and distributed false papers, anti-German tracts, and even arms from his monastery; and Père Brémond, an elderly Jesuit who made his monastery at 8 avenue Mirabeau in Nice available to rescuers despite the concern of some of his colleagues.

Churchmen were useful to the Service André because they could offer their buildings as much-needed assembly points. Fugitives being escorted elsewhere could pose as parishioners and come and go with a freedom that was impossible in private residences. Church buildings could also be used as factories for the manufacture of false documents. But the rescue organization was also supported by courageous young laymen and women, including Denise Caraco Siekierski, Rosette Lazare, and Jeanine Wahlsee Fraenkel among those who were Jewish, and Fernande Leboucher, Hermine Orsi, and Émilie Guth among the non-Jews. These intrepid souls did the actual escorting of fugitives from place to place and were the most exposed to danger.[22] These guides tended to be women, because the police more often stopped men, whose Jewishness was more easily discovered because of their circumcisions. Funding for these activities came from local Jewish committees sustained by the American Jewish Joint Distribution Committee and from other charitable organizations working in France.

After the war Joseph Bass recalled with amusement his first contacts with Père de Parceval and Père Marie-Benoît. Like Père Marie-Benoît, Père de Parceval had been making public statements that were favorable to the Jews and had attracted the attention of rescuers like Bass who were desperately looking for supporters. Sometime in the autumn of 1942, Bass went to Père de Parceval's Dominican monastery and asked to see him. When the puzzled prior appeared, Bass informed him: "I am Jewish and I am in an illegal situation, but that is not the problem. I am asking nothing for myself, neither money nor documents. I am simply asking you to tell me if you are going to make speeches and sermons or if, remembering your master Saint Dominic who did so much harm to the Jews, you are going to do something to make amends. What can you do?" Père de Parceval was taken aback and asked what Bass expected of him. Bass replied that it had to be "all or nothing." The priest requested some time to reflect on the matter. When Bass returned the next day, he announced, "I agree. I am at your disposition."[23]

Joseph Bass's memories of recruiting Père Marie-Benoît are similar. The two men met at the convent of the Sisters of Notre Dame de Sion. "I had the same sort of conversation with him as with Père de Parceval," Bass recalled, meaning he also challenged the Capuchin priest to "do something" more comprehensive. "He was more taciturn and reserved than the latter, but I understood immediately that he was going to 'go' with us."[24] Many who knew him confirm that Père Marie-Benoît *was* taciturn and reserved. It comes as a surprise, because in size he resembled Joseph Bass. But apparently his voice was soft, except when he used it to sing his beloved Gregorian chants.

Unlike the case in Rome after September 1943, in which Père Marie-Benoît was the director of a Jewish rescue group, the Capuchin priest never acted as a leader of the Service André. In Marseille his good friend Joseph Bass was indisputably the initiator, director, and driving force of the organization. Père Marie-Benoît was a cog in the wheel, working sometimes independently and sometimes with Bass while acquiring skills that would be indispensable later in Rome. Many Jews, along with political dissenters, Allied soldiers in flight, and even occasional German deserters came to the priest's monastery for help, and he helped them. Usually he began by escorting them to Père de Parceval's Dominican monastery in central Marseille, where Frère Marcolin was using his connections with local authorities to secure or buy "real false papers." Then he sometimes helped hide male fugitives at that same Dominican monastery and sent the women and daughters to the nearby convent of the Sisters of Notre Dame de Sion. Père Marie-Benoît also made inquiries among sympathetic parishioners to locate temporary lodgings in Marseille for fugitives with reliable false documents. The lodgings formed part of a network of some thirty rooms secured by the Service André from Catholics, Protestants, and what Bass called "freethinkers."[25]

As the weeks passed, Marseille became an increasingly dangerous place in which to hide. Police hunts intensified in September and October, but real terror struck in November 1942 when the Germans arrived. In response to the Allied landings in North Africa early that month, the Germans occupied all of the previously unoccupied zone of France except for ten departments or parts of departments east of the Rhône River that were seized by the Italians at the same time. Less than two months later, between January 22 and 27, 1943, German security forces evacuated and destroyed the Vieux Port, Marseille's old central harbor and market section. In the process they staged a sweeping roundup of Jews, Communists, and other political dissidents, along with illegal aliens, common criminals, prostitutes, and other "undesirables." Altogether they arrested 5,956 people, of whom 3,977 were eventually released. But among those not released were at least 782 French and foreign Jews. Shipped to the holding camps of Compiègne and Drancy, outside Paris, these Jews were deported on March 23 and 25, 1943, not to Auschwitz, as was usually the case, but to Sobibor and Majdanek. Five are believed to have returned.[26]

Under these conditions the Jewish protégés of the Service André had to be moved out of Marseille as quickly as possible. Toward the end of 1942, therefore, at the suggestion of Pastors Lemaire and Heuzé in Marseille, Joseph Bass traveled to Le Chambon sur Lignon (Haute-Loire), a largely Protestant village on an isolated plateau in the Massif Central. There he discovered that hundreds of Jewish and non-Jewish refugees were being hidden by Pastor André Trocmé and his wife, Magda; the pastor's distant cousin Daniel Trocmé; his friend Simone Mairesse; Pastor Édouard Theis and his wife, Mildred; the director of public schools, Roger Darcissac; and many other local people. Hundreds of additional Jews were being hidden by other courageous rescuers in various villages throughout the plateau. Bass immediately recognized the potential for his own protégés and eventually sent several hundred Jews to Le Chambon. Following the policy of the Service André, they were not placed in institutions there, but were carefully dispersed throughout the area, living in individual family units and furnished with false papers. But they formed part of the roughly twenty-five hundred Jews who ultimately passed through the village of two thousand residents. As many as six thousand to seven thousand refugees, of whom about 95 percent were Jewish, were hidden for greater or lesser periods throughout the plateau, including the village. Nearly all of them survived.[27]

The spectacular story of Le Chambon is well known, but evidence of similar efforts to hide Jewish fugitives in other parts of the Massif Central has often disappeared in the mists of time. Denise Caraco Siekierski, however, the teenager who worked for Joseph Bass and the Service André after September 1942, remembers visiting some of those other areas. Her account involves Père Marie-Benoît. Understandably, the Capuchin priest often directed refugees to the Catholic villages with which he was familiar.

In mid-December 1942, not long after the German arrival in the previously unoccupied zone, Joseph Bass asked Denise to go on a scouting mission in Catholic areas of the Massif Central to locate still more hiding places for Jewish fugitives. It was her first such mission, and she was, by her own account, a greenhorn. But just as Protestant pastors had directed Bass to Le Chambon, Père Marie-Benoît gave Denise the address of a Catholic parish priest in a small village about eight or nine kilometers from the town of Langogne (Lozère). He also wrote a general letter of recommendation "to whomever she may visit," declaring, "I know her, I have confidence in her, and she may need help and advice." Just a few days before Christmas, Denise arrived in Langogne by train at four in the afternoon, as it was beginning to get dark. She does not remember exactly why, but she had to walk the remaining distance to the village that same night. It was snowing, her shoes were flimsy, and the batteries in her flashlight were almost dead. Cold, hungry, exhausted, and terrified of getting lost, she picked her way along the route by identifying every road marker noting a kilometer completed. Although it was ten o'clock at night when she reached her destination, the parish priest took her in and gave her a meal and a place to sleep. The next day he sent her on to several other hamlets, where she met another helpful priest and secured many hiding places for future use. She says, "I never told all the details of this first mission to my friends in the resistance, because I felt guilty for my negligence in not having checked the batteries of my flashlight. I realized then that the resistance would involve unforeseeable and not always glorious tests and trials!"[28]

Sometimes with input from the Service André and sometimes independently, Père Marie-Benoît referred protégés to Catholic villages like the one where he had sent Denise Caraco Siekierski. Esther and Rachel Fallmann remember their own experience hiding in such a place. Refugees from Belgium in May 1940, they had lived in supervised residence in Villelaure (Vaucluse) until their father, Heinrich, was arrested on August 26, 1942. They would have been seized also, but their mother, Ida, was in the hospital with typhus or typhoid at the time. Heinrich was sent to Les Milles and then to Drancy, from where he was deported to Auschwitz on September 7. He did not return.[29] Vichy police returned later for Ida and her daughters but were told that Ida was still too sick to travel. That illness saved their lives. Ida Fallmann was sent back to a hospital by a French doctor trying to protect her, and her daughters were placed in a center for Jewish children in Marseille.

Knowing that their mother could not stay in a hospital in Villelaure indefinitely, Esther and Rachel brought her to Marseille. They moved with great difficulty, for in addition to Ida's inability to speak French, none of the three had the travel permits required for foreign Jews. In Marseille, Ida somehow met Père Marie-Benoît, who, as described earlier, tried without success to get them across the Swiss border early in 1943. After that narrow escape, Père Marie-Benoît sent them to Venanson (Alpes-Maritimes) in the Italian zone. There they posed as Catholic evacuees from Marseille's destroyed Vieux Port. Père Marie-Benoît provided them with false papers. Esther became Edvige, and Rachel, Renée. Their mother was now Ernestine, and their family name became Foucault. Thus they retained most of their original initials, a common practice in the event that they had some possessions with monograms. To preserve the appearance of normal life, the two girls went to a Catholic school in Venanson. All went well until the nuns at the school wanted them to participate in the sacrament of First Holy Communion. When their mother refused permission, Père Marie-Benoît sent the little group to Nice.[30]

Another witness to Père Marie-Benoît's rescue work was Fernande Leboucher, a young non-Jewish fashion designer from Paris (fig. 8). In the first year or two of the war, Leboucher married Ludwik Nadelman, a Jewish engineer born in 1906 in Warsaw who had immigrated to France in 1939 after his country was invaded by the Germans. Sometime in the autumn of 1942, but before the German occupation of the southern zone,

Nadelman was arrested and sent to Rivesaltes (Pyrénées-Orientales), an internment camp about ten kilometers from Perpignon. From this camp, among others, foreign Jews were being regularly delivered to Drancy and Auschwitz beginning in August. Not completely aware of the danger of deportation or the existence of death camps but nevertheless in despair, Leboucher went to the Capuchin monastery in the rue du Croix-de-Régnier and asked to see Père Marie-Benoît. After checking her story carefully, he consented to try to help her husband [31]

As a first step Père Marie-Benoît wrote a letter of recommendation for Fernande Leboucher to present to the commandant of the camp at Rivesaltes. With that precious document, the young woman made the harrowing trip to the camp by train, by bus, and on foot. She arrived covered with mud but was able to convince a guard at the camp to take her to the Catholic chaplain. Impressed by Père Marie-Benoît's letter, the priest brought her to the commandant, who allowed her to see her husband for half an hour. During that conversation, husband and wife concocted a rescue plan. Rivesaltes was not heavily guarded, Nadelman explained to his wife. Escape was possible but useless unless escapees could present identification documents once they were free. If caught without documents, they would simply be returned to the camp.

The plan involved the delivery of a false identification document to Nadelman that gave no indication that he was Jewish. Père Marie-Benoît provided the document, supplied by one of his contacts; Leboucher supplied the photograph. According to Leboucher, Père Marie-Benoît also supplied a false and backdated baptismal certificate. Such a document would not necessarily have been conclusive. Christians born to two Jewish parents were considered to be Jewish under the French racial laws, regardless of conversion. Baptismal certificates, false or real, could help only those individuals who could prove, with additional documents, that two of their four grandparents were not Jewish. Also, all relevant baptismal certificates had to be dated prior to June 25, 1940 (or, for those born after that date, at the time of birth). In Nadelman's case, however, in a confused situation in which the documents of his parents and grandparents were not available, the baptismal certificate that Père Marie-Benoît provided could have been helpful, especially if inspected by a French bureaucrat inclined to give prisoners the benefit of the doubt.

Armed with Père Marie-Benoît's documents carefully sewn into her skirt, Fernande Leboucher traveled back to Rivesaltes. Again the camp commander let her see her husband. This time, however, Nadelman raised another issue. He was immensely grateful for her effort, but he realized that he could not leave his four comrades in the lurch. He asked his wife to return to Père Marie-Benoît with a request for documents for them as well. He gave her their personal addresses and begged her to go to their families for photographs. Fernande was devastated, but she ultimately agreed, as did Père Marie-Benoît. As a result, Nadelman's four Jewish friends were able to escape from Rivesaltes, assemble at the monastery in the rue du Croix-de-Régnier, and, with more help from Père Marie-Benoît, cross safely into Switzerland. Indeed, the action was so successful that it became more ambitious. Père Marie-Benoît produced more documents, and Fernande Leboucher made more journeys to Rivesaltes. More prisoners were able to escape, hide, and cross the border to Switzerland.

As Leboucher gained self-confidence and the trust of her colleagues, she became involved in other activities linked with Père Marie-Benoît. She hid dozens of fugitives in her own apartment, delivered documents to Jews hiding throughout Marseille, helped escort protégés from one place to another, and even organized a fashion show to raise money for rescue. But the pressure was growing. It peaked when a Jewish fugitive was captured at the Spanish border and admitted under torture that the papers he was carrying came from Père Marie-Benoît. After that the monastery came under constant surveillance and was searched several times, fortunately when no Jewish fugitives were present. Leboucher barely escaped two other raids, one in a restaurant and one in her apartment building. She long remembered what Père Marie-Benoît said to her when she informed him that she could not continue the dangerous work: "He looked at me with a strange, intense, piercing expression. I felt that he could see into my soul. He said, in a low voice, 'You cannot leave. This is your mission, your responsibility, and you must continue to the end. You must regain your courage. If you feel yourself begin to weaken, if you are afraid, then at that moment you must communicate with me through heaven!'"[32] She continued in the rescue efforts.

With all their daring and resourcefulness, however, Père Marie-Benoît and Fernande Leboucher were ultimately not able to save Fernande's husband. After Nadelman finally agreed to escape from Rives-altes with papers from his two protectors, Père Marie-Benoît found him a hiding place in Marseille, but he was discovered by an informer. Told to wait while the informer went for the police, he refused to escape in order not to endanger those helping him. He was rearrested and sent to Gurs, from where he was expelled to Drancy. Again Père Marie-Benoît and Leboucher tried to help him. Leboucher even traveled to Drancy with a document from Père Marie-Benoît stating that Nadelman had been baptized in 1937. It is not likely that such a statement would have helped, but in any case, she arrived too late. Her husband was deported to Poland on March 6, 1943. In one of only a few exceptions to the normal destination of Auschwitz, his convoy, number 51, delivered its victims to Sobibor and Majdanek, near Lublin. Only five men from the convoy of about one thousand passengers survived. Ludwik Nadelman was not among them.[33]

After learning of the deportation, Leboucher tried to commit suicide in her apartment in the rue de l'Académie in Marseille. Waking up in a hospital, she found Père Marie-Benoît at her bedside. But instead of sympathizing, he was furious. "How dare you?" he demanded. "How dare you attempt to take that which belongs to God alone? And how dare you attempt to deprive our Jewish friends of the only hope that they have of escape? You are essential to our operation! We need you! How can you wish to desert us when Ludwik was willing to give his life for this work?"[34] And so again she continued. She helped hide fugitives and supply them with documents and money until Père Marie-Benoît was recalled to Rome in June 1943. Nothing is known about her activities in wartime France after that.

Père Marie-Benoît and Fernande Leboucher remained friends for the rest of their lives. Leboucher moved to New York after the war, but the priest's notebook indicates that she visited him often during her numerous trips to Paris. Père Marie-Benoît was recognized by Yad Vashem in Jerusalem as a Righteous among the Nations in 1966 and given the award at a ceremony at the Israeli embassy in Paris in November 1967.[35] Leboucher, similarly honored in 1973, received the award at the Israeli consulate in New York City. In 1976 Père Marie-Benoît wrote to Leboucher to ask if she would help him raise money for a trip to Israel so that he could participate in the traditional ceremony at Yad Vashem in which those designated as Righteous plant a tree with a plaque bearing their name. He also asked if she would make the trip with him. By then eighty-one years old, suffering from sciatica, and unable to walk without a cane, he was worried about traveling alone. Leboucher immediately agreed and tried to arrange the details. The two hoped to plant their trees side by side to commemorate the rescue work they had done together in Marseille. But even with Leboucher's help, the journey proved to be more than Père Marie-Benoît could undertake. In 1978 he arranged for Sister Marie-Thérèse Hoch of the Sisters of Notre Dame de Sion to travel to Israel and plant a tree in his name. The idea of two trees side by side did not materialize. Fernande Leboucher was never able to make the trip to Israel for a tree planting. After running out of planting space in 1989, Yad Vashem inaugurated a Garden of the Righteous in 1995 to honor those who did not yet have a tree. Fernande Leboucher's name is engraved on a plaque on the Wall of Honor in the garden. She died in New York in September 2002.

Rescue work in Marseille before and during the German occupation was a dangerous activity for rescuers and recipients alike. To cite only a few cases, Jeanine Wahlsee Fraenkel was arrested in Nice on November 8, 1943, and deported from Drancy to Auschwitz on December 7. She did not return. Antoine Zattara, a non-Jewish director of administrative police in Marseille, who had lost a leg in the First World War and who helped Père Marie-Benoît and other rescuers and resisters obtain blank forms for fabricating identification documents, was arrested and deported to Buchenwald, where he died on October 9, 1944.[36] Among the clergy, Pastor Lemaire was arrested for hiding Jews on March 14, 1943, tortured, and deported on April 5, 1944, to Mauthausen and Dachau, from where he returned more dead than alive after the war. Pastor Heuzé was also deported and did not survive. Frère Marcolin was forced to flee from his monastery in 1943, just ahead of the German and Vichy police. He joined the military resistance, where he fought as a partisan for many months. Père de Parceval was arrested for having helped him escape and for having delivered false documents to a Jewish fugitive who was caught. He spent several months in prison and was released after an intervention by his bishop. Joseph Bass wrote admiringly of that intrepid priest, "As soon as he was liberated, he resumed his activities."[37] Through it all, Père Marie-Benoît survived unscathed, perhaps in part because he was transferred back to Rome by the Capuchin order in June 1943, as we shall see.

Joseph Bass also survived the war. At some point in 1943 he began to organize a Jewish military resistance unit in Le Chambon. For several months he continued his work in Marseille and Nice with the Service André while also training for combat. After being arrested in Marseille and narrowly escaping in March 1944, however, he committed himself entirely to the military venture. With help from other Jewish rescue groups, particularly the Sixième, Hebrew Immigrant Aid Society (HIAS), and the Réseau Marcel, some activists from the Service André continued to bring support to their Jewish protégés in hiding until the liberation.[38]

Joseph Bass and the others in his military unit went on to distinguished careers in the broader French military resistance. They received the surrenders of German troops and Vichy French militiamen in the area of Le Puy-en-Velay in August 1944 and protected them from the crowds that wanted to lynch them.[39] They participated in the liberation of Le Puy-en-Velay on August 22, 1944, followed by that of the entire Haute-Loire. After the liberation of southern France, Bass became a captain in the Forces Françaises de l'Intérieur (FFI), the unified internal military resistance organization later incorporated into the regular army. For his wartime activities, he received the Médaille de la Résistance and the Croix de Guerre avec Palme after the war, and was named chevalier of the Legion of Honor. His son remembers that he always wore his medals proudly on his lapel.

Joseph Bass resumed his work as a patent lawyer in Paris around 1950 and was again successful. Madeleine Rocca, although a lawyer like Bass by training, served as his secretary until the end. But Bass was never interested in material success and possessions. Instead he devoted himself to refugees, workers, and the class question and militated within the Communist Party. He also became increasingly irritable and touchy with his former colleagues in rescue, apparently believing they were drawing too much attention to themselves and glorifying their wartime activities. Although he reminisced with his friend Père Marie-Benoît for many years, the Capuchin was not immune to his later invective. Bass also resented postwar accounts of Jewish rescue that simplified events and made it sound as if everyone got along well, without friction. He was, consequently, rather alone at the end of his life. Furthermore, the Service André that he created and led, and that saved the lives of thousands of Jewish refugees, has yet to receive the scholarly attention it deserves. Joseph Bass died in the French capital in 1969.[40]

SIX

With Angelo Donati in Nice

NOVEMBER 1942 TO JUNE 1943

WHILE LIFE BECAME FAR MORE DANGEROUS FOR PÈRE MARIE-Benoît, Joseph Bass, and their helpers and Jewish protégés when the Germans seized much of formerly unoccupied France toward the end of 1942, there was one important geographical exception. As the Germans moved south that November, the Italian army moved west to occupy ten French departments or parts of departments east of the Rhône, including the cities of Nice, Cannes, Valence, Grenoble, and Vienne.[1] In that new Italian zone, Jews and rescuers alike found conditions that were very different from those under both Vichy and subsequent German rule.

The nature of the Italian occupation was not immediately apparent. After all, as early as 1938 Benito Mussolini had decreed anti-Jewish laws in Italy that were as severe as the Nuremberg laws in the Third Reich. And for the most part, those laws had been thoroughly enforced. Furthermore, when Mussolini declared war on the side of the Germans in June 1940, thousands of foreign Jewish men throughout Italy were rounded up and interned in camps that initially were almost as wretched as those in France. When the Italians later occupied territories abroad, in southern Greece, along the Dalmatian coast, and finally in southeastern France, they brought their anti-Jewish laws with them. At first Jews in those areas were apprehensive.

It soon became evident, however, that, with respect to Jews, the Italians were unique. While thousands of Jews in both occupied and unoccupied France were being shipped to death camps in the east prior to November 1942 and from all of German-occupied France thereafter, those in Italy remained safe from deportation. They remained so during the entire period that Mussolini was in full control. After King Vittorio Emanuele III dismissed Mussolini in July 1943, Jews also remained free from deportation during the forty-five-day government of Marshal Pietro Badoglio, who replaced him. Only when Badoglio signed an armistice with the British and Americans on September 8, 1943, and the Germans consequently occupied most of the peninsula did Jewish deportations begin from Italy. Less than two months after the armistice, Mussolini, reinstated as a puppet ruler of the Italian Social Republic, the so-called Republic of Salò, deprived all Jews of their Italian citizenship, ordered their arrests by Italian police, and accepted their delivery to the Germans for deportation.[2]

Similarly in Italian-occupied southeastern France, after November 1942 but before Badoglio's armistice with the Allies, it became increasingly clear that Italian military and diplomatic personnel would refuse to enforce Vichy and German measures against the Jews. As early as December 1942, when the Vichy government ordered that all Jews throughout the former unoccupied zone must have their documents stamped "Juif" or "Juive," as had been the practice in the German-occupied north since the end of September 1940 and was currently being done in the newly German-occupied south, the Italians refused to allow it in their area. At the same time, when Vichy police, still operating in Italian-occupied France, attempted to arrest foreign Jews for expulsion to the German zone, the Italians ordered them released. Under no circumstances, the Italians declared, were Jews to be transferred out of their zone. Within that zone, Jews could be arrested only by Italian authorities, except in cases of violation of specific French laws.

It did not take long for Jews in German-occupied France to figure out that the Italian zone was the place to be. French Jews, not yet in the same danger even under German occupation, were a little slower to move, but foreign Jews who were anxious to escape arrest and deportation flocked to the southeast by the thousands. The area had some fifteen thousand to twenty thousand Jews before the Italians arrived, but according to the chief of the Gestapo's Jewish Office in France, it contained fifty thousand in July 1943.[3] Of these, some twenty thousand to thirty thousand were foreigners. Italian military and diplomatic administrators now had a problem, for most Jewish refugees possessed a hodgepodge of documents – legal and illegal, false and real or no documents at all. If they wandered about without valid documentation, they would be in violation of French laws and subject to arrest. The harassed, understaffed, and often demoralized Italian authorities found their own unique solution to this problem: they turned the refugees over to a Jewish committee in Nice.

Even before the Italian occupation, French and foreign Jews in Nice had organized a *centre d'accueil,* or reception center, to help Jewish refugees. The impetus seems to have come from an imposing Russian Jew named Jacob Doubinsky, who was over eighty years old and had memorable sky-blue eyes and a talent for raising money. Doubinsky's assistants included Claude Kelman, Michel Topiol, and Ignace Fink.[4] Eventually named the Comité d'Assistance aux Refugiés, the group became popularly known as the Comité Dubouchage because its offices were adjacent to the central synagogue at 24 boulevard Dubouchage. As the trickle of newcomers turned into a flood after the Italians arrived, occupation authorities encouraged volunteers from the committee to meet Jewish refugees in bus and train stations and direct them to the boulevard Dubouchage. There other volunteers urged the newcomers to destroy their false papers, if they had them, because the use of such documents was a violation of French law. Instead, Jewish refugees were to accept new documents prepared by the Jewish committee on behalf of the Italians. Copies of the resulting identification cards with photographs of the refugees were sent to the Italian police in Nice, who took the bearers under their protection.

Refugees with the new cards enjoyed many benefits. Above all, they could no longer be arrested by Vichy police as illegal aliens, a drain on the national economy, or violators of French laws against using false documents or residing or traveling without special permits. In addition, the Italians issued ration books and housing permits to the cardholders. Money for food and housing came from the Jews themselves. To support the poorest refugees, the Comité Dubouchage collected contributions from well-to-do French Jews along the Riviera, as well as from

French Jewish organizations and the American Jewish Joint Distribution Committee.

For Père Marie-Benoît in German-occupied Marseille in November 1942, the new situation in nearby Italian-occupied Nice offered a tantalizing opportunity. The Italian authorities were accepting and protecting Jewish refugees in their zone. What would be more logical than to direct some of his protégés in Marseille there? In addition, the Capuchin priest had lived in Rome for more than twenty-two years and spoke fluent Italian. He had contacts among the Catholic clergy in Nice and could easily develop new ones with Italian military and diplomatic personnel. Such contacts might reap enormous rewards.

One difficulty with the new situation was the persistent ambivalence of Joseph Bass. Even when dealing with the Italians, Bass retained his preference that his protégés should not be clustered together in obvious Jewish colonies, but should abandon their real identities, receive good false documents, and disperse throughout the countryside. Their only contact with other Jews should be with the couriers from the Service André who brought them money and supplies. The Italian zone could serve as a location for hiding places, and it might also offer a safer passage to Switzerland than had been possible under unrestricted Vichy control. But Bass preferred that his protégés not give up their false documents and become dependent on the Comité Dubouchage.

Despite his reservations, Joseph Bass was intrigued with the possibilities of Italian-occupied France. Père Marie-Benoît later testified, "Between November 1942 and May 1943 I went from Marseille to Nice and Cannes for two or three days almost every week, accompanied by M[onsieur] André [Joseph Bass] who played the role of my secretary."[5] Apparently individuals with identity papers, real or false, showing them to be French citizens had little difficulty crossing between the German- and Italian-occupied zones. In Nice, despite his different approach to rescue, Bass kept an office in the same building as the Comité Dubouchage and occasionally worked with its activists.[6]

Père Marie-Benoît and Joseph Bass were always looking for hiding places and new sources of reliable false documents. Regarding hiding, Père Marie-Benoît stated that he and Bass facilitated the passage of foreign Jews from the German-occupied to the Italian-occupied zone, especially to Nice and Grenoble. Here Père Marie-Benoît's many contacts with Catholic institutions were useful, both to his own protégés and to those whom the Comité Dubouchage wished to place. Confirming this, Ignace Fink of the committee testified after the war that many Christians helped them because of the priest's intervention. He added that Père Marie-Benoît advised him after liberation about whom they should acknowledge and thank.[7]

Regarding documents, André Chataignier, the secretary general of the mayor of Cannes, wrote after liberation, "André [Joseph] Bass often came to see me, along with his secretary Anne-Marie. I gave most of my false cards to them." He then added: "During the entire period of the occupation we delivered no fewer than 4,000 false cards for food and identity. I never wanted to know the real names of the people to whom I gave these papers. I said to myself, 'If one day you are taken: you believe now that you would not talk, but how to foresee the effect of the torture: it is better to know nothing, it is more sure for the others.'"[8] Chataignier stressed that his office never charged anyone for the cards.

And what was Père Marie-Benoît's role here? Chataignier remembered him well but was not certain about his responsibilities. "Several times Bass was accompanied by Père Marie-Benoît," he wrote. "I think it was the Capuchin father who was charged with the distribution of the cards, but I gave them to Bass who, certainly, gave them to him afterwards." Chataignier then provided an appraisal of the priest, valuable because there are so few from people who knew him: "Père Marie-Benoît gave the impression of a truly extraordinary man who, under an exterior of bonhomie, hid an intense interior life. He spoke little and moved around a great deal."

In addition to working for specific protégés during their trips to Nice, Père Marie-Benoît and Joseph Bass were also pondering future issues and cultivating relationships. In this regard, Père Marie-Benoît testified about the trips: "There [in Nice] we addressed all the current questions with the Jewish organizations and M[onsieur] Donati." The Jewish organizations were primarily the Comité Dubouchage and the Union Générale des Israélites de France (UGIF). "Monsieur Donati" was Angelo Donati, an Italian Jewish banker who was to play a significant role in Nice during the next few months. According to Père Marie-Benoît, Joseph Bass first introduced him to Donati at this time. Donati claimed he had already written to the priest, with input from Bass, as early as August 1942, explaining the situation of Jews in the unoccupied zone. But whatever the chronology of their first meeting, Père Marie-Benoît and Angelo Donati became friends for life.[9]

Angelo Donati was a good man to know, for not only did he have solid connections with the Italian authorities, but he also knew France intimately. Born in Modena in 1885, he began his career as a banker before the First World War. During the war he served for a time as an officer in the Italian air force (fig. 9). Of that period he later related an anecdote demonstrating the irony and humor that endeared him to Père Marie-Benoît. His plane, with several others, was busily engaged in dropping antiwar and pacifist literature behind the Austrian lines when the wind changed. The pamphlets so carefully prepared to demoralize the Austrians now fluttered down into Italy. Donati relished the story.[10] He later served as a liaison officer with the French army and, when the war was over, as part of the Italian delegation sent to Versailles to negotiate the peace treaty. He remained in Paris afterward, created the Banco Italo-Francese di Credito, and was elected president of the Franco-Italian Chamber of Commerce.

During the 1920s and 1930s, Angelo Donati wore many hats. In addition to banking and business, he was appointed Italian consul general in San Marino in 1925, a title later elevated to minister plenipotentiary. From their elegant apartment in the rue de Berry in Paris, he and his first wife led a sophisticated social life until her death in an automobile accident in 1929. In the words of his daughter, Donati "knew everyone," traveled to Israel, became a committed Zionist, and received Chaim Weizmann, leader of the world Zionist movement and later the first president of the State of Israel. In 1931 Donati introduced Vladimir Zwed Jabotinsky to the Italian government in the hope of opening a section of the Italian Maritime School in Civitavecchia to revisionist Zionist students. Mussolini agreed.

Donati also played a general humanitarian role before the Second World War, as demonstrated by his leadership of the Italian Red Cross in France. Like Joseph Bass, he became involved with German Jewish refugee relief work in Paris after 1933, although it is not clear whether the two men knew each other at that time. When the Germans occupied northern France in 1940, Donati moved to Nice, where he continued to work at a branch office of his bank in the boulevard Victor Hugo. There he became a well-known local character, always dapper and ebullient, something of a ladies' man, strolling along the Promenade des Anglais with a gray felt hat in winter and a straw hat in summer.[11] Many hats indeed (fig. 10).

In the terrifying August of 1942, Angelo Donati assumed yet another role – one that revealed that he was not merely a banker, community leader, philanthropist, and man about town. In August 1942 he took the first steps toward becoming a father, through adoption. It all happened without warning. In the roundup of August 26, Vichy police arrested Hilde and Carl Spier, German Jewish refugees from Erfurt by way of Brussels, with their children, twelve-year-old Marianne and ten-year-old Rolf, and threw them into prison in Marseille. Somehow made aware that unaccompanied youngsters might not be deported at this stage, Hilde and Carl made the agonizing choice of being transferred to a hospital on August 30 for assumed illnesses, without their children. Marianne remembers her mother being carried out of the prison on a stretcher, looking back at her intensely. She later realized that her mother understood that it might be for the last time. And indeed it was. Hilde and Carl Spier were seized at the hospital, expelled to Drancy, and deported on September 2.[12] They did not return.

Informed of the arrests of the Spier family by a cousin who was married to a cousin of Hilde, Angelo Donati rushed to the prison to find them gone. Learning that the children had been taken to a Jewish children's center, he went there to get them. "I saw him arrive," says Marianne. "He was so tall and big." Her mother had given her a list of the names of all those who might help her, which was folded and worn on a ribbon around her neck. Because Angelo Donati's name was on the list, Marianne trusted him. Donati amply rewarded that trust. The children spent more than a year with him in Nice, going to school and visiting his parents and six siblings in Italy for the Jewish high holidays. At this point Marianne and Rolf called him Uncle Angelo. When the Germans were about to seize the Italian zone of southeastern France in September 1943,

Donati and the children fled to Italy. The rest of their wartime story will be told in the next chapter.

A few weeks after the Italians occupied Nice, Angelo Donati visited the Comité Dubouchage to say that with his Italian connections he could do something for the Jews. The offer was immediately accepted. Ignace Fink and Michel Topiol were assigned the task of meeting with Donati at 8:00 AM every morning and giving him individual requests from those with special problems. Donati took those requests to the Italian authorities, and in most cases the issues were resolved satisfactorily. He was also able to help by raising money among wealthy local Jews whom he knew.[13]

Of greater impact than his role in individual cases, however, was Donati's intervention with the Italian occupation authorities on the subject of Jews in general. It all began, he later explained, in December 1942 when the French prefect of the department of Alpes-Maritimes, where Nice is located, issued an order expelling foreign Jews within seventy-two hours. They were to present themselves to Vichy authorities in the departments of the Drôme or the Ardèche, controlled by the Germans. Had they done so, they would have been arrested and deported. To forestall that disaster, Donati immediately went to his good friend Alberto Calisse, the Italian consul general in Nice. Calisse not only ordered the French to desist but also sent a long telegram to the Ministry of Foreign Affairs in Rome explaining that Italian acceptance of the Vichy measure would greatly compromise their prestige throughout the world. Officials at the ministry subsequently ordered the French to refrain from arresting Jews in the Italian zone, as mentioned above. Donati believed that the arrangements for issuing identification documents through the Comité Dubouchage stemmed from this basic Italian decision.[14]

With foreign Jews increasingly difficult to find in the German-occupied zone, however, and with the Vichy police still reluctant to arrest French citizens, German agents charged with providing victims for deportation looked greedily at the large Jewish population in the Italian zone. Italian authorities there and in Rome came under increasing pressure to give them up. The pressure intensified in late February 1943, when German foreign minister Joachim von Ribbentrop held a series of meetings with Mussolini in which he asked, among other things, that the

Italians do something about the "Jewish problem." German ambassador to Italy Hans Georg von Mackensen repeated the demand in another meeting with Mussolini late in the evening of March 17. During that meeting the harried and ill Mussolini agreed to give Vichy police a free hand with regard to Jews in the Italian-occupied zone. The next morning, however, the horrified deputy foreign minister, Giuseppe Bastianini, convinced him to renege, to focus instead on moving foreign Jews to the interior within the Italian zone, and to turn matters over to the Italian police.[15]

Consistent with that final decision, on March 19 Mussolini ordered Guido Lospinoso, a personal acquaintance and former police chief of Bari, to move to Nice to set up a Commissariat for Jewish Affairs. According to Lospinoso after the war, his mission was to placate the Germans by expediting the internment of all Jews in the Italian zone in a camp one hundred kilometers from the coast. The operation was to be completed within a month. The Germans were pleased. Believing that the Italian police would be tougher on Jews than Italian diplomats and military personnel had been, Heinrich Müller, chief of the Gestapo, stated optimistically from Berlin on April 2 that Lospinoso would "regulate the Jewish problems . . . in accordance with the German conception, and in the closest collaboration with the German police."[16]

But Gestapo agents were soon to be disappointed, for in the months that followed, Lospinoso was nowhere to be found. Frantic German agents reported that he had been seen in Menton and had then returned to Rome, set up headquarters in Nice, and failed to appear when a meeting had finally been arranged in Marseille. A representative he had sent to that meeting immediately declared that he had no authority to make decisions about the Jewish question. The Germans would have to speak with Lospinoso himself.[17]

What had happened? At least part of the explanation centers on Angelo Donati and Père Marie-Benoît. According to Donati, Lospinoso arrived in Nice with little understanding of the situation of Jews there and with no idea of how he was going to intern tens of thousands of people in a single camp one hundred kilometers from the coast within a month. In a quandary, he turned to the Comité Dubouchage for advice. Lospinoso confirmed Donati's explanation, declaring after the war, "Instead of executing my draconian orders . . . I made an agreement with the Jewish Committee, whose chief was . . . Angelo Donati . . . with whom I made another plan."[18]

But Père Marie-Benoît also had a role here as he explained on several occasions after the war. In one account he remembered, "Angelo Donati, an Italian Jew, . . . said to me, 'You speak Italian, you must pay a visit to the Italian police chief and the Italian generals to install a bit of conscience and tell them how to behave with the Jews.' I visited the Italian police chief, named Lospinoso. He received me very well and we were in total agreement."[19]

The Capuchin priest gave more details in an interview in which he declared:

> Angelo Donati . . . asked me to meet with Lospinoso, the inspector general of Italian police who had just arrived from Rome as a special Italian government delegate for Jewish questions. He was not a bad man, but he was totally ignorant about Jewish matters. He asked me questions that revealed this perfect ignorance. He asked me, among other things, if Christians and Jews worshiped the same God and why I, a Catholic priest, was interested in them. I answered that the Jews were our spiritual ancestors, that our religion had its roots in theirs and that our spirit of charity and justice obliged us to help them in the tragic period that they were experiencing. He answered that his intention was to act in a humane manner with regard to the Jews.[20]

On yet a third occasion, Père Marie-Benoît also remembered his meeting with Lospinoso. Referring to Donati, he wrote:

> Another of those who remain my very dear friends . . . asked me to go to see [Lospinoso], to submit some important matters to him and especially to dispose him favorably toward the Jews. I made the visit. He welcomed me willingly and since I spoke Italian, the conversation quickly took on a cordial and familiar tone. He asked me if my Superiors were aware of this step I was taking. I answered that my Superiors in Rome knew perfectly what I was doing and fully approved. Monsieur Lospinoso was a straightforward man, not especially set on an attitude toward Jewish questions. Thus he wanted to know for example if the God of the Jews is the same as that of the Christians and why I, a Catholic, occupied myself with them. I had no trouble in enlightening him and in justifying myself and he told me that he only wanted to show his good will toward the Jews.[21]

The question of Lospinoso's decision-making process is more complex than either Donati or Père Marie-Benoît reported. Historian Daniel Carpi argues that Italian military personnel in occupied France had an unwritten understanding that although Jews might be placed in supervised residences, they were not to be deported. Lospinoso spent several days with high-ranking Italian officers in Menton before arriving in Nice and would have been aware of that fact. He also would have been carefully briefed on the situation of Jews in general. Donati must have realized this, for he testified after the war, "The activities in favor of Jews in the Italian-occupied zone were possible thanks to the fact that ... within the hierarchy of the Italian administrations, both civilian and military, the great majority of the bureaucrats or officers were men without antisemitic sentiments and accessible to humane sentiments." However, Lospinoso was not a civilian or military administrator but a high-ranking police inspector in an officially antisemitic Fascist state. He may well have needed a little prodding into good behavior by Donati and Père Marie-Benoît.[22]

In addition, the new Italian commander of racial police was far less naïve about Jewish matters than he pretended. By his own admission in 1962, he had served for twelve years before the war as an intelligence officer at the Italian consulate in Nice, where he came to know the local elites. Among those he knew was Angelo Donati, who did not yet live in Nice but who visited often.[23] Nor was Lospinoso above prevarication. Ignace Fink testified after the war that Lospinoso told him he was from an old family of Marranos, Spanish Jews who were obliged to convert in the fifteenth century.[24] Lospinoso may have been trying to ingratiate Fink, to make him feel comfortable. But if his story of his descent was true, it is unlikely that he was quite as ignorant about Jews as he pretended. He was clearly less than truthful with either Père Marie-Benoît or Ignace Fink, and probably with both. And neither man ever suspected that he had been fooled.

This being the case, the question then arises as to why Donati sent Père Marie-Benoît to see Lospinoso when he, Donati, already knew the Italian police inspector and could have, or in fact may already have, informed him about the Comité Dubouchage himself. Was Donati uneasy about Lospinoso's attitudes toward Jews despite, or because of, his prior acquaintance with the man? Was he uncertain about the nature of Lospinoso's mission? In addition to being a high-ranking police officer in a Fascist state, after all, Lospinoso had been sent by Mussolini himself to establish an office of racial affairs. Was Donati worried? Perhaps, knowing that Lospinoso was a good Catholic, Donati thought Père Marie-Benoît could push him gently in the right direction and refer him politely to the Comité Dubouchage. Or were Donati and Lospinoso trying to disguise their prior acquaintance for some reason?

Whatever the explanation for Donati's use of Père Marie-Benoît, Lospinoso's less than forthright behavior seems to have been intended to give him time to formulate a policy of his own. Certainly it helped forestall the Germans, who could understand if he needed time to appraise the situation. But time was a luxury that Lospinoso could not be certain of having, since his orders from Mussolini were to move Jews inland within a month. While Père Marie-Benoît and Donati may not have been crucial in attracting his sympathies, they were decisive in showing Lospinoso how he could carry out his orders.

To ease the congestion caused by thousands of refugees in Nice and to show the Germans that the Italians were doing something about the "Jewish problem," the occupation authorities, even before Lospinoso's arrival, had begun studying the possibility of moving Jews away from the coast to supervised residences in the interior. The Comité Dubouchage had not opposed the project; on the contrary, it had even shown some interest. When Lospinoso met with Italian authorities and Jewish spokesmen in March 1943, then, the plan seemed to be the solution to his problem. Details were easily resolved. Resort villages such as Vence, Barcelonette, Saint-Martin-Vésubie, Castellane, Moustiers, Saint-Gervais, and Megève, where hotels and boardinghouses were empty because of the war, were selected as the preferred destinations. The Italian authorities agreed to requisition housing. The Comité Dubouchage would supply lists of refugees to be sent inland, provide for their transportation, and pay their rents and living expenses. Jews sent to the interior were "supervised" by Italian police and carabinieri, required to report twice a day, subjected to a curfew, and restricted in their right to travel. They were otherwise free to live as they pleased.

Donati estimated after the war that some four thousand Jews, many of them volunteers, had been assigned to supervised residence in the interior before the Italian-occupied French zone crumbled in September 1943.[25] This was far from Lospinoso's required target of some twenty-five thousand to thirty thousand Jews, and the supervised residences were much more pleasant than the internment camp that had been envisioned, but Mussolini seems not to have noticed.

True to their conviction that it was a mistake to gather many Jews together in one place, Joseph Bass and Père Marie-Benoît did not encourage their protégés to volunteer for supervised residence. They did inform them of the possibility, of course, and some refugees, fearful of the loneliness and dangers of living illegally, may have chosen to go there. It was a calculated risk. Those caught with false papers could be arrested, while those living in supervised residences with papers from the Comité Dubouchage seemed to be safe. On the other hand, by the summer of 1943, Bass, Donati, and other Jewish leaders were well aware that Jews in supervised residences were living on borrowed time. The Italians would not remain in occupied France much longer.

1. The house and mill in Le Bourg d'Iré where Pierre Péteul, the future
Père Marie-Benoît, was born in 1895.

Courtesy of Pierre Péteul, his nephew

2. Door of the Church of Saint Serge in Angers, smashed by soldiers of the French Republic during the conflict between Church and state over inventories of Church property, 1906, and preserved in semi-restored condition as evidence.

Photograph by Susan Zuccotti

3. Pierre Péteul, standing (*center*), a student at the École séraphique des Capucins in Spy, Belgium, in 1911. Standing on the left is his friend René Bériot, also born in 1895, and killed on the Marne in 1918. Seated in the center is Père Paulin de Ceton, Pierre Péteul's mentor.

Courtesy of Archives des Capucins de France, Paris

4. Pierre Péteul in his uniform as a French infantryman in the First World War. He served in the front lines throughout the entire conflict.

Courtesy of Pierre Péteul, his nephew

5. Père Marie-Benoît with his father, also named Pierre Péteul, and his brothers Louis (*left*) and Joseph (*right*), in 1938. Someone attached a photograph of the fourth brother, René Gabriel, killed on the Somme in 1916.

Courtesy of Pierre Péteul, the son of Louis and Père Marie-Benoît's nephew

6. Père Marie-Benoît with his friend Joseph Bass, who founded the Service André for Jewish rescue in Marseille in 1942. Père Marie-Benoît and other courageous rescuers worked closely with Joseph Bass.

Courtesy of Mémorial de la Shoah/CDJC, Paris

7. On the Canebière in Marseille, 1943, from left to right, Madeleine Rocca, Joseph Bass, and Denise Caraco, later Denise Siekierski. The two women were part of Joseph Bass's Jewish rescue organization, the Service André.

Courtesy of Mémorial de la Shoah/CDJC, Paris

8. Père Marie-Benoît with Fernande Leboucher, a friend and associate in Jewish rescue in Marseille, 1942–1943.

Courtesy of Archives des Capucins de France, Paris

9. Military papers of Père Marie-Benoît's friend Angelo Donati, an officer in the Italian air force and a liaison officer with the French army during the First World War.

*Courtesy of Mémorial de la Shoah/*CDJC

10. Angelo Donati, spokesman, benefactor, and protector of Jews in France
before, during, and after the Second World War.

*Courtesy of Mémorial de la Shoah/*CDJC

11. Hotel Salus, Piazza Indipendenza, Rome, where Jewish refugees from France and elsewhere, with or without legal documents, were housed during the German occupation of the city, September 1943 to June 1944.

Photograph by Susan Zuccotti

12. Père Marie-Benoît with his great friend Stefan Schwamm, with whom he worked in Rome to rescue thousands of Jews during the German occupation. The occasion here was a ceremony in which the priest received the rosette of an *officier* in the French Legion of Honor, March 14, 1984.

Photograph by Daniel Franck, Paris

13. Père Marie-Benoît with Rachel Fallmann, later Rachel Schutz, during a trip to Israel in 1958 given to him by the Jewish Community of Rome in appreciation of his wartime rescue activities. The priest saved Rachel; her mother, Ida; and her sister, Esther, later Esther Kichelmacher, in both France and Italy during the war.

Courtesy of Rachel Fallmann Schutz

14. A tree at the Memorial of Yad Vashem, the government-established Holocaust Martyrs' and Heroes' Remembrance Authority in Israel, planted in honor of Père Marie-Benoît, recognized as a Righteous among the Nations in 1966.

Photograph by Susan Zuccotti

16. (*Above*) Père Marie-Benoît with Baron Alain de Rothschild, Grand Rabbi Jacob Kaplan, and others in a procession in support of Soviet Jewry, October 17, 1976.

Photograph by Daniel Franck, Paris

15. (*Facing page*) Père Marie-Benoît, known in Italy as Padre Maria Benedetto, boarding a train for Paris, August 4, 1956, after completing a teaching assignment at a Capuchin college in Campobasso, Italy.

Courtesy of Archives des Capucins de France, Paris

Père Marie-Benoît and
the Donati Plan

JUNE TO SEPTEMBER 1943

BACK IN LATE JULY OR EARLY AUGUST 1942, AROUND THE TIME that French police in the unoccupied zone were beginning to expel foreign Jews to the Germans in the north, Père Marie-Benoît first learned that the general minister of the Capuchin order wanted to recall him to the International College in Rome, where he had been trained and had taught between the two wars. The reasons for this recall remain obscure. Père Marie-Benoît told Lospinoso that his superiors in Rome supported his work on behalf of Jews, but it is conceivable that some Capuchins in Marseille saw him as a cause of danger to them and wanted to curtail his activities. It is also possible that they believed the priest himself was in danger and they hoped to protect him. Or they may have felt that their confrere had too much freedom, wandering around Marseille without supervision, or they may have been jealous of his growing reputation. On the other hand, the decision could have been made on purely administrative grounds. The head of the Capuchin order in Rome may simply have needed a good professor of theology, or have considered that his brilliant priest in Marseille was not focusing sufficiently on intellectual pursuits. But whatever the reasons of his superior, it is crystal clear that Père Marie-Benoît did not want to go.

In a polite letter to the head of the order on August 9, 1942, Père Marie-Benoît, while stressing that he would of course obey, made up all kinds of excuses. Was his Italian good enough? Was he adequately prepared? He explained somewhat obscurely that he was more adept in "speculative disciplines than in spiritual theology." He also expressed his reluctance to interrupt what he called his "Jewish apostolate," explaining that he was preparing some fifteen people for baptism. This claim was more for the benefit of his superior than for himself; Père Marie-Benoît's ambiguity on that subject will be discussed elsewhere. But at this point he hoped that the claim would persuade his superior to let him stay. To it he added, "not to mention the support I am giving to a large number of persons or families, exposed to the worst anguish, especially since the events of these last days."[1] The delivery of foreign Jews in southern internment and work camps to the Germans in the north was in full swing, and he was working furiously to protect as many of those Jews as possible.

Père Marie-Benoît was to receive no reprieve. On December 15, 1942, he duly wrote to advise the head of his order in Rome that the French Foreign Ministry had recently informed him that he had been authorized to reside in Italy, by whom was not clear. As a result, he had applied to the Italian consul in Monaco for an entry visa. He did not know how long it would take to secure the visa or for how long it would be valid. It took a long time, but the matter was arranged by the end of May 1943. On May 23 the Capuchins of Marseille presented Père Marie-Benoît with a tribute to mark his departure. A long and beautifully handwritten poem testified to their love and respect for his knowledge, humility, patience, and goodness.[2]

Angelo Donati and Joseph Bass must have been saddened when they first learned that their associate in rescue was leaving them. However, the occasion, when it finally materialized, gave them an idea. Once he was in Rome, they realized, Père Marie-Benoît might be able to obtain an audience with Pope Pius XII. In such an audience he might be able to convince the pope to intervene with Mussolini to support Donati's plan to save Jews in Italian-occupied France. What was this "Donati plan," and why was it so important?

Almost from the moment the Italians arrived to occupy southeastern France in November 1942, Angelo Donati began to wrestle with the problem of what to do when they left. Every month brought more Jewish refugees to the area. Every month the Germans became angrier about the Italian refusal to deliver them for deportation. The winter of 1942–1943 witnessed crushing German and Italian defeats at Stalingrad and in North Africa. In March and April 1943, thousands of industrial workers went on strike in northern Italy. Some two hundred thousand German and Italian troops surrendered to the Allies in North Africa in May, clearing the path for the Allied invasion of Sicily on July 10. Meanwhile, northern Italian cities were being destroyed by American and British air raids. The Germans were losing the war, and the Italians were going down with them. But long before the conflagration ended, the Italian army was going to have to abandon its occupied territories to protect the homeland. Without protectors, Jews would be at the mercy of those who wished to exterminate them.

According to many who knew him, Angelo Donati was a good man, an optimist, even a dreamer who believed that he could solve the thorniest problems and never gave up trying.[3] Now, in the spring and summer of 1943, Donati concocted a plan that confirmed the most exaggerated descriptions of his character. Before the Germans replaced the Italians in southeastern France, he decided, at least the foreign Jews in supervised residence there must be transported to safety in northern Italy. They were the most vulnerable and endangered of all Jews in Italian-occupied France. To that end, Donati traveled to Rome several times, both before and after the king dismissed Mussolini as head of government on July 25, to try to gain the support of friends and contacts in the Italian government for the project. Deputy Foreign Minister Giuseppe Bastianini had no objections, Donati reported after the war, but Donati was told that officials at the Ministry of the Interior would raise technical difficulties. Thousands of Italian citizens fleeing from Allied bombing raids were already in desperate need of food and shelter. Furthermore, some seventeen thousand Jewish refugees from Italian-occupied Dalmatia and Croatia were allegedly being held in small and large camps throughout the Italian peninsula, where supplying them remained a problem. That number was a gross exaggeration, but the problem was real enough.[4]

As Donati puzzled over ways to bring his rescue plan to the attention of government officials in Italy during the summer of 1943, it dawned on him that Père Marie-Benoît might take the idea to the pope. Then, as the priest's departure grew nearer, Donati and Joseph Bass also realized that Père Marie-Benoît might use the opportunity of a papal audience to deliver more general information about the persecution of Jews in France. Such information would be enriched by the priest's own personal experience. For that second purpose it seemed useful that Père Marie-Benoît should consult with French Jewish leaders to collect any documents they wished to convey to Rome. During his last week or two in France, therefore, the Capuchin traveled to Lyon to meet leaders of the Consistoire central, including the president, Jacques Helbronner; the secretary, Léon Meiss; the grand rabbi of France, Isaïe Schwarz; and Rabbi René Kaplan. He also spoke with the grand rabbis of Lille, Strasbourg, and Marseille, as well as with the president of UGIF, Raymond Raoul Lambert; the highly esteemed French Jewish intellectuals Jules Isaac and Edmond Fleg; and others. All this was done, he later explained, "so that I could more truthfully present myself to the Holy Father in the name of French Judaism and also in the name of Jews of different nationalities who were refugees in France."[5]

Père Marie-Benoît finally left France on June 3, 1943.[6] After his arrival in Rome, he had some difficulty arranging a papal audience. When he told the general minister of the Capuchin order, the Belgian Père Donat de Welle, of his wish, he was told, "That is impossible; Pius XII no longer gives private audiences." Père Marie-Benoît must have looked crestfallen, or the general minister genuinely sympathized with his objectives, or both, for the latter finally said, "Write to me, put into writing what you have to say to the Supreme Pontiff, and then give me your writing." Père Marie-Benoît did so, and his superior took the document to Monsignor Clément Micara, formerly the papal nuncio in Belgium, who had been obliged to leave that country after the German invasion. Donat de Welle had known him in Belgium. Micara, who retained his title and worked in Rome on Belgian affairs, judged the matter to be important. Donat de Welle, who as head of the Capuchin order had the privilege of meeting with the pope privately on a regular basis, thus obtained permission to bring Père Marie-Benoît with him. The audience was finally scheduled for Friday, July 16. "My audience was very short," Père Marie-Benoît recalled later. Elsewhere he declared that it lasted twenty minutes.[7]

Of the reception he received, Père Marie-Benoît testified: "The pope gave me a very nice welcome and when I explained to him the horrors of the Jewish persecution in France, he answered, 'one would never have believed that possible in France.' He told me that he would personally study my entire dossier."[8] After a brief description of what he had done in

France and of the Jewish leaders with whom he had consulted in preparation for the papal audience, Père Marie-Benoît's dossier, dated the day
before the actual meeting, presented four requests. First, it informed the
pope that fifty thousand Jews had been deported from France to the east
and that only a few had been able to write back to their families. It asked
if officials of the Holy See could try to obtain news of the victims. The
second request was that the Holy See intervene with the Vichy government to improve the dismal conditions in French internment camps. The
third request asked the Holy See to urge Spanish authorities to protect
the many Spanish Jews caught in France and unable to secure rapid repatriation. The fourth concerned the Donati plan, although Père Marie-
Benoît did not use that name.[9]

There was great reason to fear for the fate of foreign Jews in Italian-
occupied France, Père Marie-Benoît informed the pope in his fourth
written request. If the Germans, "for one reason or another," decided to
seize the Italian zone, some eight thousand to ten thousand foreign Jews
in supervised residences would be in enormous danger of deportation.
"Since those groups are only a few kilometers from the Italian frontier,
would it not be possible to have them cross into Italy, where they could
be utilized in various work projects? Would a suggestion in this sense
[from the Holy See] to Italy be possible?" Père Marie-Benoît concluded
his dossier with an explanation that he had promised Jewish leaders in
France that he would convey additional messages and appeals to the
Holy Father in the future.[10]

To his dossier with the four requests, Père Marie-Benoît attached as
appendixes four documents prepared by the Jewish leaders with whom
he had met during his final days in France. Those documents listed the
names of some deportees from France, described the French camps and
the deportation process in greater detail, and provided, as Père Marie-
Benoît described it in his dossier, information about "camps in Upper
Silesia." He did not say so in the note, but Upper Silesia is the region
where Auschwitz was located. Although a team of four Jesuit scholars responsible for the publication of a selection of wartime diplomatic documents between 1965 and 1981 included Père Marie-Benoît's dossier with
its four requests in volume 9 in 1975, they did not print the appendixes.
Therefore, it is not clear whether Auschwitz was mentioned by name. The

editors explained in a footnote: "This list [of camps] gives information about thirteen concentration camps in Upper Silesia and the names of four camps in the 'General Government' (Poland occupied by the Germans) and the 'Protectorat' (Bohemia and Moravia). The authors make no reference to extermination projects, but speak of them as work camps where 'morale among deportees is generally good and they are confident about the future.'"[11]

It is difficult to imagine that French Jewish leaders in mid-July 1943 could have written that deported Jews had confidence in the future. Nevertheless, the Jesuit editors' statement raises the question of what those French Jewish leaders actually knew at that time about the fate of Jews deported to the east. One of the Vatican editors, the American Jesuit Robert A. Graham, was so interested in the question that he wrote Père Marie-Benoît, probably in the mid-1970s, to ask why the French Jewish leaders had not been more explicit on the subject of extermination. The exchange of letters between the two men seems not to have survived, but Père Marie-Benoît reported elsewhere that he explained to Father Graham that his meetings with the Jewish leaders had occurred without time for advance preparation, that the leaders had been surprised by the possibility of sending information to Rome, and that they had furnished him with preexisting documents. "What did they know at the Consistoire or elsewhere about the exterminations?" he wrote sometime after 1975, sounding rather irritated by the question. "I cannot say. Besides, I didn't need to go to the qualified authorities to inform myself personally. The Donati project itself spoke sufficiently. At what moment did we know precisely in France the type of extermination reserved for Jews by the Nazis, I do not know. In any case all my protégés were speaking about it in 1943. That is what I told Pius XII."[12]

Speaking about it, yes. But certainty was another matter, and evidence of what Jewish leaders and their people in general actually believed is contradictory. Everyone had heard rumors. Radio Moscow broadcasts in 1941, BBC broadcasts after early July 1942, and clandestine French Jewish Communist tracts and newspapers after mid-July 1942 all spoke of mass murder in Poland and the Soviet Union. Extermination also seemed a logical goal of the phenomenon of deportation of the old, the very young, the sick, and the weak. But systematic mass execution of men, women, and children, authorized by the government of a cultured and civilized nation, also seemed unbelievable, and many people were reluctant to accept rumors or logical conclusions as absolute truth.

After the war, without citing the extent or sources of his information, Grand Rabbi Jacob Kaplan claimed he had known about the systematic extermination of deported Jews as early as August 1942.[13] The Consistoire central sent a protest letter that spoke of methodical and pitiless extermination to Pétain on August 25 of that year and to other Jewish, Catholic, Protestant, and government leaders somewhat later.[14] Yet Jewish leaders rarely acted as if they actually believed what they had deduced from reports and observations. They never mentioned gas chambers or Auschwitz. The protest of the Consistoire petitioned the French government for a stop to the arrests of "young girls for whom these deportations risk having the most revolting consequences," as if sexual depravities were the worst atrocities they could imagine. Indeed, when Jacques Helbronner received a letter describing crematoriums and mass executions of Jews months later, he still found it unimaginable and sought verification from Jewish agencies in Switzerland.[15]

Illustrating the inability to believe the worst, after the war Ignace Fink of the Comité Dubouchage related the remarkable story of the return to Nice, toward the end of the Italian occupation of southeastern France, of two escapees from a forced labor camp not far from Auschwitz. Their return, therefore, was probably not long after Père Marie-Benoît's departure for Italy on June 3, 1943. Deported from Nice to Paris and from Paris to Kosel, Poland, in 1942, the two escapees returned to Nice separately. The first to arrive described what he had learned about systematic killings at Auschwitz and, Fink wrote, "no one wanted to believe that it was true. We even thought that he was mad. But alas, when we had more information after the end of the war, we realized that he had spoken the truth." Two months later the second escapee arrived and told a similar story, but, Fink declared, "again this time we did not want to believe it."[16]

The testimonies of most other Jewish leaders and activists reflect this same refusal to believe. Georges Wellers, a physician imprisoned in France for two and a half years before his deportation to Auschwitz in June 1944, spoke with many prominent Jewish leaders as they and their families passed through Drancy. He reported after the war, "None of them acted like men who knew that they were witnessing a death warrant issued against their dear ones " Wellers was at Auschwitz for three days before he learned and accepted the truth.[17] Henri Krasucki, an eighteen-year-old leader of Jeunesses communistes in Paris and aware of all the Communist-endorsed rumors, later recorded of his arrival at Auschwitz in 1943: "We knew that terrible camps existed . . . We had a certain idea of what might happen. What we did not know was the degree of the savagery and especially the existence of the gas chambers."[18] Robert Debré, a pediatrician in Paris who worked with Jewish institutions to hide children, later declared that although he had listened to the BBC regularly, he never believed rumors of gas chambers.[19] Père Marie-Benoît may well have shared these views.

With their extensive reliable contacts, Pope Pius XII and his advisors knew much more than Jewish leaders in France about the ongoing exterminations. Excluding what they regarded as biased Allied or Jewish sources, their information came from Vatican diplomats in German-occupied countries, Catholic German and Italian bureaucrats and soldiers based in the east, Italian businessmen abroad, traveling priests and chaplains, and others. Furthermore, the repetition of such reports made the unbelievable inescapable. To cite just a few examples, SS Colonel Kurt Gerstein, an observant Protestant who joined the Waffen SS to investigate rumors of Nazi atrocities, personally witnessed a gassing at Belzec in August 1942 and passed the information along to the office of Pius XII's friend Bishop Konrad von Preysing in Berlin.[20] At least two German Catholic insiders – Dr. Hans Globke, an official in the German Ministry of the Interior, and Dr. Josef Müller, an officer in the Abwehr (the German military intelligence service) – kept German bishops aware of the ongoing murders of Jews, and those bishops almost certainly passed the information on to Rome. Müller also traveled to Rome himself and met several times with the German Jesuit Father Robert Leiber, the pope's personal secretary.[21] On February 3, 1943, Italian ambassador to Germany Dino Alfieri informed Galeazzo Ciano that "even the SS talk about mass executions."[22] Ciano became Italy's ambassador to the Holy See a few days later. Then on March 6, Bishop von Preysing urged the pope to try to save Jews still in Berlin who were facing deportation that would lead, he indicated, to certain death.[23]

A day after Preysing's appeal, Vatican Chargé d'Affaires Giuseppe Bursio in Bratislava forwarded to Vatican Secretary of State Cardinal Luigi Maglione a letter from a parish priest in that city declaring that Jewish escapees from Poland were reporting that Jews were being killed with asphyxiating gas. On April 14 the Italian Jesuit Padre Pietro Tacchi Venturi, the Vatican's unofficial liaison with the Italian government, wrote to Maglione about his effort to save Jews still in Croatia from "deportation, the first step, as is known, toward a not distant, most difficult death." Then on May 5, 1943, an official at the Vatican Secretariat of State prepared a memo that said in part: "In Poland, there were, before the war, about 4,500,000 Jews; it is calculated now that there remain (including all those who came there from other countries occupied by the Germans) only 100,000 . . . Naturally many Jews have gotten away; but there is no doubt that the majority have been killed."[24] All this information reached the Vatican before Père Marie-Benoît's papal audience. Pius XII did not need the Capuchin priest or French Jewish leaders to tell him about mass exterminations of Jews. Why did the editors of the Vatican documents even raise the issue?

It is interesting that Père Marie-Benoît prefaced his requests to Pius XII with a description of his ministry in Marseille, in which he wrote that with the authorization of the bishop of Marseille and help from the Sisters of Notre Dame de Sion, he had instructed in the Catholic faith and baptized fifty-one Jews. This spiritual ministry had brought him into contact with other Jews, he explained, and consequently he had, in cooperation with other priests, nuns, and laypersons of Catholic Action, helped many converts and non-converts. He had also worked with Jewish organizations that were "demonstrating the greatest courage and the greatest devotion in defense of their co-religionists."[25]

The comments about baptism are difficult to interpret. As a conscientious and devout Catholic priest, Père Marie-Benoît may have been gratified by the fifty-one conversions. Presumably, however, he asked Jewish candidates for baptism for an indication that the conversions were genuine, as he was required to do.[26] But did he probe deeply enough to be certain that those involved were not simply acting under extreme stress and trying to avoid arrest? Did he understand that Jews who converted remained Jewish under the Vichy regime's racial laws and were thus not protected from arrest and deportation unless they were the offspring of mixed marriages who could also produce baptismal certificates dated before June 25, 1940? And if so, did he tell his prospective converts? Did he perhaps provide backdated baptismal certificates for them as well as false certificates for one or both parents? These questions will probably never be answered. In his postwar reports on his activities intended for the public, Père Marie-Benoît did not mention this aspect of his work. Clearly he was aware of the pain it caused his Jewish friends. Clearly also, in July 1943 he was aware that his report about conversions would be regarded favorably by Pope Pius XII, from whom he hoped to elicit support for the Jews of France. If he had not thought so, he would not have written it.

To put this matter into perspective, we might consider the case of another Capuchin friend of the Jews, Père Calliste Lopinot, with whom Père Marie-Benoît met in Rome in July while waiting for his papal audience to be arranged. A French- and Italian-speaking Alsatian and former missionary, sixty-five-year-old Père Lopinot was appointed by the Holy See in July 1941 expressly to minister to 85 Catholics among the 1,144 foreign Jews at the Italian internment camp of Ferramonti-Tarsia, in the southern Italian province of Cosenza.[27] According to Mirko Haler, an internee who knew him, Père Lopinot baptized about 50 Jews from October 1941 to December 1942. Père Lopinot himself claimed to have baptized 79 Jews during his entire stay at the camp, from July 1941 to September 1943. These conversions naturally made many internees uneasy, but Haler, who did not convert, nevertheless described Père Lopinot as "*molto simpatico,*" and added, "It is worth mentioning that Père Lopinot had many [unconverted] Jewish friends in the camp, and I never heard it said that he made propaganda for a change of religion."[28] Like Père Marie-Benoît, Père Lopinot proved to be a friend and defender of all Jews regardless of conversion.

In the days and weeks that followed his audience with Pope Pius XII, Père Marie-Benoît tried to follow up on his four requests, without much success. On February 20, 1945, after the liberation of central Italy and southern France made communications between the two areas possible but before the end of the war, he wrote to his friend Joseph Bass about what had been achieved. "The Vatican services have not been able to give me any news about the lists of Jewish deportees that I had submitted to them," he wrote, "because Germany systematically refuses all information even to the Vatican, when Jews are the subject." About the request that the pope petition the French to improve conditions in internment camps under their jurisdiction, he was equally discouraged. "I do not know what was done about the French internment camps," he told his friend.[29] There is no evidence of a Vatican intervention on this subject.

About the request concerning Spanish Jews caught in France, Père Marie-Benoît was more satisfied. In the same letter of February 20, he informed his friend: "On the other hand my visit prompted a measure from the Spanish government, in view of favoring the repatriation of its Jewish citizens residing in France. I have a letter from [Vatican Secretary of State] Cardinal Maglione informing me of all the details and of all the orders given to the Spanish consulates in France." Maglione had indeed written to papal nuncio Monsignor Gaetano Cicognani in Madrid on August 1, 1943, describing Père Marie-Benoît's audience with the pope and the discussion of Spanish Jews residing in France who were unable to repatriate. The problem seemed to involve their government's lengthy administrative procedures. Maglione explained that these Jews were possibly in danger of arrest in France and that was "urgent that Spain protect them effectively and immediately, for example by giving them temporary papers." He concluded by urging Cicognani to "take some step in the sense desired by the Holy Father."[30]

On August 23 Cicognani responded to Maglione, informing him that he had met with the appropriate Spanish authorities. On his request the Spanish government had agreed to grant entry visas to "all Spanish Jews, regardless of their political tendencies" and to treat evidence of citizenship "with broad generosity." On September 9 Maglione informed Père Marie-Benoît of this development.[31]

Père Marie-Benoît was again disappointed about the fourth, most critical request for a papal intervention with Italian government officials to allow entry into northern Italy to Jewish refugees in southeastern France. On Sunday, July 18, 1943, two days after the Capuchin priest's papal audience, Monsignor Domenico Tardini, secretary of the Section for Extraordinary Ecclesiastical Affairs at the Vatican Secretariat of State and number two or three in importance in that department, jotted on the dossier that Père Marie-Benoît had left with the pope, "We can say a good word to Italy."[32] Events intervened, however, and there is no evidence that this was ever done. Incredibly, however, the Donati plan, with or without papal support, *almost* happened. The story, intricately wrapped up in military and political developments in Italy, is complex and intriguing.

On Monday, July 19, Père Marie-Benoît was at the Vatican Secretariat of State "to settle my business" when the first Allied bombardment of Rome began about 11:00 A M. "It was on the other side of the city," he wrote to Joseph Bass on July 29, 1943. "I was out of any danger, and as the Vatican balconies dominate Rome, I was present at the operation as a spectator, watching and counting the planes that were arriving in successive waves and in good order." This was the attack after which Pius XII famously left the Vatican City wearing an immaculate white robe that was soon stained with blood as he visited and prayed among the victims. Five days after that, on the night of July 24–25, Mussolini received a vote of no confidence from the Fascist Grand Council. The following morning King Vittorio Emanuele III dismissed him as head of government and appointed Marshal Pietro Badoglio to replace him. Mussolini was arrested and spirited off to prison. Fascism had fallen, and the Italian people were jubilant. "Universal joy, with cries of 'Long live liberty,'" Père Marie-Benoît declared in his same letter to Joseph Bass on July 29. "But what are they going to do now? The war continues until new orders."[33] Badoglio had announced that Italy would remain at war on the side of the Germans.

Angelo Donati, who was in Rome negotiating for his project at the time, was among those who rejoiced. With a new and more favorable Italian government, he thought, he could now try a more ambitious plan. Perhaps he could convince Badoglio to accept all of the twenty thousand to thirty thousand Jews in the soon-to-be abandoned Italian-occupied zone of France. Italian diplomats in both Rome and occupied France were not opposed.[34] The problem, however, was that Italy was in no position to absorb so many refugees. In view of that reality, Donati now envisioned the transfer of thousands of Jews from Nice to American-

and British-occupied North Africa by way of Italy, in Italian ships, with money from the American Jewish Joint Distribution Committee.

Throughout the month of August 1943 Donati negotiated with Italian officials, many of whom were personal friends already sympathetic to his project. There is no evidence of a papal intervention in these negotiations. On the contrary, Vatican officials appear to have examined the matter, as presented in its initial form by Père Marie-Benoît on July 16, without acting. Among Père Marie-Benoît's papers in Paris is a copy in his handwriting of part of a note from Monsignor Jacques Martin, an official in the Section of Ordinary Ecclesiastical Affairs at the Vatican Secretariat of State. The note was originally sent to Père Didier at the Capuchin monastery in Rome. Written in French and dated August 5, 1943, it seems to have been a response to a question from Père Marie-Benoît or Père Didier about what action was being taken at the Vatican in response to Père Marie-Benoît's requests of July 16. It said, "The papers of P. Benoît Marie [sic] are being studied. We are considering his suggestions, some of which, at least, have been followed up [a reference to Maglione's letter to Cicognani on August 1 to intervene on behalf of Spanish Jews]. If oral explanations are necessary, we will 'convoke' him, as agreed. But it does not seem so."[35]

Donati did not need Vatican help to win over some Italian officials to his plan. For a move to North Africa, however, he did need the agreement of the British and American governments, with which Italy was still at war. Here, Père Marie-Benoît was truly helpful. As the Capuchin later remembered: "At that time, [Donati] had already achieved much with the Italian government. I said to him, 'I have the possibility, through a friend, a canon at Saint Peter's, to approach the representative of the United States [to the Holy See], Harold Tittmann, and the British ambassador [to the Holy See], Mr. [sic; Sir Francis Godolphin d'Arcy] Osborne, secretly.' Donati said, 'That's great, let's visit those two people!'" Elsewhere, Père Marie-Benoît declared that this conversation occurred in Rome on August 15 and that his friend at Saint Peter's was Monsignor Joseph Hérissé, who had a private apartment at the same Santa Marta complex in the Vatican City where the American and British diplomats were living. And so it happened that a French priest brought an Italian Jew, Angelo Donati, into Vatican City not once but several times for secret negotiations with Allied diplomats with the full knowledge and agreement of the Italian government.[36]

There is no evidence that Pius XII knew about those activities. On the contrary, Donati testified after the war that he had asked Monsignor Hérissé toward the end of August to introduce him to high-level prelates at the Vatican so that he could present his case, but Hérissé discouraged him. "Don't try to reach the high prelates," Hérissé declared. "They are very timid and will not do anything."[37] Nevertheless, it seems unlikely that Père Marie-Benoît would have done anything that he knew would displease Pius XII.

According to Donati after the war, negotiations with the Allies progressed well but slowly. He confirmed that Père Marie-Benoît had introduced him to the American and British representatives to the Holy See and that the Italian government was kept informed on a daily basis. He also wrote, "The American government answered that it looked on this solution with sympathy and would transmit the proposition to the Inter-Allied Committee of Refugees in London. The British government answered that it had no objections in principle to this solution which merited further study."[38] Optimistic and encouraged, Donati began other negotiations to lease four ships that had previously taken Italian citizens home from Italian East Africa. The plan seemed on the brink of success, but time was running out.

In an effort to bring the Vatican up to date about the Donati plan, Père Marie-Benoît sent another memorandum to officials at the Secretariat of State on September 6 or 7. In it he explained that while the Italian occupation forces were beginning to withdraw from France, the Italian government had agreed to a project to bring some thirty thousand Jews from southern France to Italy. Without mentioning that negotiations had occurred with diplomats accredited to the Holy See and within Vatican City, he stated that "an accord in principle" to move those same Jews on to North Africa had been reached with the British government and that the Americans were also involved. He then increased his statistic of Jews in danger to fifty thousand. He closed his note with two requests. Could the Holy See "ask its representatives in London and Washington to support and activate this enterprise? Would it be acceptable for me to introduce Mr. Angelo Donati to the [Vatican] Secretariat of State in order to present and treat the matter in a more direct and concrete manner?" The Jesuit editors of the published Vatican documents in which this memorandum is included state in a footnote that they found nothing more relating to these two requests. There is no record of a Vatican response, but Père Marie-Benoît was clearly trying to do everything he could to help.[39]

Also in early September, Père Marie-Benoît learned that a Swiss Capuchin confrere was leaving Rome by plane for missionary work in Africa and would be passing through Lisbon. When he informed Donati of that fact, Donati dictated a memorandum on September 6 to be personally delivered to the American Jewish Joint Distribution Committee in Lisbon. Père Marie-Benoît received the memorandum, which went out with the missionary on September 8. He also sent copies to the Vatican and to the Capuchin general minister.[40] The memorandum described the Donati plan in yet more detail, referring to some forty thousand to fifty thousand Jews in danger in southern France, defining the funding from the Joint as virtually assured, and mentioning the names and nature of the four leased ships. Not only had the ships already been used to repatriate Italian civilians from Italian East Africa, with British approval and protection, but also they were painted with Red Cross colors and their crews had received British security clearance. The memorandum claimed that British authorities were aware of all the details of the plan and had authorized their ambassador to the Holy See to urge the Italian government to carry out the plan. It ended with a dig at the Americans and British, "who until now have limited themselves to making speeches and threats, but have not done anything to save the lives of the unhappy persecuted Jews."

Despite all the negotiations, the Donati plan was not to be. At 6:30 PM on September 8, 1943, General Dwight David Eisenhower, the Allied commander in chief, announced prematurely that Marshal Badoglio's government had signed a document of unconditional surrender five days earlier, on September 3. Badoglio, who had expected that the announcement would not be made for at least another week, was obliged to confirm the news an hour and a half later. Italy was out of the war, he explained. The Italian army was to lay down its arms before the Allies but to "react" to attack "from any other quarter." Again the Italian people were jubilant. Harsh reality came with the dawn, as German troops already in Italy or massed on the frontier for just such an occasion proceeded with the deadly business of occupying the country. Scattered Italian resistance was easily overcome.

For Jews in southeastern France the situation was even worse. During the last week of August and the first week of September, as rumors of Donati's plan to evacuate them to Italy spread, thousands reappeared in Nice, the place of disembarkation. Overly optimistic Jewish and Italian groups had provided trucks to move them to the coast from the mountain villages where they had been living in supervised residence. On instructions from the Comité Dubouchage months earlier, many of these Jews had destroyed their false documents and accepted the papers that placed them under Italian protection. Now, as the Italian army streamed back into Italy, there was no more protection to be had. On September 10 a team of fifteen highly trained German SS police under SS Captain Aloïs Brunner of the Gestapo's Jewish Office in France arrived in Nice, and the hunt for Jews, French and foreign alike, began.

Brunner's men were operating with certain disadvantages. They were few in number, the Vichy police were increasingly unpopular and therefore reluctant to cooperate, and the former Italian authorities and Jewish agencies had destroyed their lists of the names and addresses of local Jews. In compensation the German SS police in Nice acted with a public brutality that was unusual in Western Europe during the Holocaust years but quite common in the east. The story is best described by Russian-born, French-naturalized Léon Poliakov, later a respected historian, who in the summer of 1943 was working with Joseph Bass to help Jewish refugees. Poliakov found himself in Nice that awful September and later remembered:

> Those official black Citroëns [of the police] cruised the streets of Nice, and passengers attentively scrutinized passers-by. At any moment, a pedestrian would be asked to get into a car. No useless questions or identity checks. The car went to the synagogue. There the victim was undressed and if he was circumcised, he automatically took his place in the next convoy to Drancy...
>
> The official black Citroën method was not the only one. Other teams raided hotels, boardinghouses, and furnished rooms, and took away entire Jewish families. Members of the [French] Milice, those jackals of the Gestapo, checked apartment buildings and made lists of names that sounded Jewish. Improvised physiognomists were posted in the stations.[41]

Arrested Jews were taken to the Hotel Excelsior, where many were tortured to make them reveal the hiding places of families and friends. During the next three months, some eleven hundred Jews from Nice, another three hundred from along the coast, and about four hundred from villages in the interior were shipped to Drancy on twenty-seven separate trains. From there they were sent to Auschwitz on two trains in October, one in November, and two in December 1943, and others in 1944. Few returned.[42]

Despite the horror and tragedy of the autumn roundup in Nice and the arrests and deportations that continued in newly German-occupied southern France until the end of the war, the absolute bloodbath that Angelo Donati and Père Marie-Benoît had feared did not materialize. The eighteen hundred Jews arrested initially and the several hundred who followed later represented a small proportion of the twenty thousand to thirty thousand in the former Italian zone. Even without false papers at the onset, a majority of the French and foreign Jews in the area were able to hide, usually with French families. They received little formal assistance from the Comité Dubouchage, whose members were obliged to dissolve their group and flee for their own lives in September 1943, but other individuals and groups continued to help them.[43] These included Joseph Bass, Léon Poliakov, and some from the Nice committee, as well as rescuers from the Sixième, HIAS, and the Réseau Marcel, mentioned in chapter 5. By this time French non-Jews were also more critical of the Vichy regime, more aware of atrocities against Jews, and more likely to be sympathetic to them.

While most French Jews sought refuge in France itself, at least two thousand foreign Jews took another tack. Distrustful of the Vichy regime, which had treated them badly, and impressed by Italian authorities who had protected them, some 1,100 to 1,250 who had been in supervised residence in Saint-Martin-Vésubie and the surrounding area, in the French Maritime Alps just a few kilometers from the border with Italy, chose to trek over those mountains and take their chances on the other side. They streamed out of the mountains into the little towns of Valdieri and Entracque, in valleys of the Italian Alps west of Cuneo.[44] Others in supervised residence north of Saint-Martin-Vésubie, in towns like Bourg-Saint-Maurice, crossed the Alps in small family units and entered the northwestern corner of Italy known as the Valle d'Aosta.[45] Another group fled east from Nice along the Mediterranean coast, reaching Italy by way of Ventimiglia. Still others in Nice followed the Italian soldiers on foot, struggling north along a twisting mountain road and entering Italy through the Col de Tende. A luckier few managed to find a place on the last train from Nice to Cuneo, passing through that same Col de Tende on September 10.[46]

Foreign Jews entering Italy knew that the country's leaders had signed an armistice with the Allies and ended the war. Optimistically, they expected to find a country at peace, with the Allies already present or arriving soon. Unfortunately the refugees arrived on the scene at the same time as the German army, which was now busy occupying the country, keeping the Allies at bay well south of Rome, and punishing anti-Fascists and Jews. The result was chaos and terror. Some 350 Jews from Saint-Martin-Vésubie were arrested around Valdieri and Entracque, most of them on September 18. In November they were sent back to Nice. From there they were shipped to Drancy and, for most of them, Auschwitz. No more than about 12 are known to have survived.[47] Those not arrested remained in German-occupied Italy, along with Jews from Nice, Bourg-Saint-Maurice, and elsewhere in southeastern France. They were worse off than before, without resources, friends, contacts, or even the ability to speak Italian. These foreign Jewish refugees from France, or at least those who made it to Rome, would be Père Marie-Benoît's new protégés.

Did Donati's plan, on which he and Père Marie-Benoît and others worked so hard, ever have a chance of succeeding? Italian bureaucrats at the highest levels had expressed their willingness to allow twenty thousand to thirty thousand Jews to pass through the country on their way to North Africa, but administration and management of such a project in wartime would have been daunting. The ships had been located and leased, money was apparently about to be made available by the Joint, and Donati had even printed a sample of five thousand "passports" intended to be issued to the refugees in question. The British and Americans had apparently agreed in principle, but settlement of the details required time. And time was a luxury not available by negotiation or purchase. Donati and Père

Marie-Benoît both claimed later that they had believed that the armistice was not to be announced until October, but that seems not to have been the intention of the parties directly involved. At most, Eisenhower's announcement was a week or two earlier than the Italians expected.

Angelo Donati was in Rome on September 8, 1943, meeting with Ivanoe Bonomi, whom he believed was to be made minister of the interior in Badoglio's government that same day. Bonomi agreed to give priority to the problems of Jews in Italian-occupied France and to order bureaucrats to make no difficulties at the frontier when they passed into Italy. Tittmann and Osborne were informed of that development.[48] But Donati must have been aware of incipient danger, for on this trip from Nice to Rome he brought Marianne and Rolf Spier and his Italian butler, Francesco Moraldo, with him. Marianne remembers waiting for Donati in a vast hall at the Vatican while he was meeting with Tittmann and Osborne. He emerged from that meeting very pleased and informed the children that everything was in order.[49]

Marianne also vividly recalls the radio broadcast on September 8 that informed the Italian people of the armistice. It was an unforgettable, jubilant, and terrifying moment. Angelo Donati first took the children and Moraldo to the village home, near Florence, of one of his brothers. They stayed there for about a month, but as the brutality of the occupation intensified, Donati's parents, many brothers, and sister all sought refuge in Switzerland. Apparently believing that the border crossing was too dangerous for young children, Donati entrusted Marianne and Rolf to Francesco Moraldo, who took them to his hometown, the tiny village of Creppo in the Italian Maritime Alps not far from the French border. There, without phone, electricity, or even a road other than a foot path, and known to all of the sixty villagers, the children lived with Moraldo's family until the liberation of northern Italy in May 1945.[50]

Donati himself headed for Switzerland. En route, still somewhere in Tuscany, he sought shelter in a monastery where he had some contacts, but on the instructions of the provincial minister of the unnamed order, he was refused.[51] Somehow he reached the Swiss border, where he was turned back on his first attempt to cross. He made it safely on the second try, however, and spent the rest of the war with his family in a small hotel in Montreux. He was, according to Marianne, the glue that held the family together.

After the war Angelo Donati settled in Paris with Marianne and Rolf, whom he legally adopted. The children joined his name to that of their biological parents and became known as Spier-Donati. Angelo Donati resumed his former life in all its forms, working as a business manager, diplomat, Red Cross benefactor, Jewish community leader, and Zionist activist. He was even able to return to his former apartment, which a non-Jewish prewar employee had somehow managed to save from the clutches of German and Vichy authorities. Always with Marianne and Rolf, he continued to visit his parents and siblings in Modena for the Jewish holidays as long as he was able. He died in Paris in December 1960 at the age of seventy-six.

EIGHT

Early Rescue in Rome

SEPTEMBER AND OCTOBER 1943

ON OR ABOUT SEPTEMBER 13, 1943, PÈRE MARIE-BENOÎT, OR Padre Maria Benedetto as he was now known in Italy, met his friend Lionello Alatri, an important figure in the Jewish community of Rome. Whether the meeting was by chance or by appointment is not known. Alatri informed the priest that a train carrying well over one hundred Jewish refugees, formerly in supervised residence in Saint-Gervais-les-Bains in Italian-occupied France, had just arrived in the Eternal City. The passengers were destitute, famished, and without secure documents or shelter. Padre Benedetto had arrived in Rome from Marseille only three months earlier. Did he perhaps know some of the refugees?

After the war Padre Benedetto remembered his response to Alatri's question: "I went to see [the foreign Jews] at the Jewish orphanage where they were temporarily housed and I recognized a good number of those I had previously assisted in Marseille and Nice." Among those he knew were Esther and Rachel Fallmann and their mother, Ida. Padre Benedetto was hooked. "It was impossible for me not to resume the duties of my assistance work," he recorded. "I then made the acquaintance of Delasem, with which I worked for nine months [until liberation], taking part in all its activities."[1] Delasem was a national Jewish refugee assistance committee based in Genoa but with regional offices in Rome. Its local director, Settimio Sorani, became one of Padre Benedetto's close friends and associates in Jewish rescue.

About a month later, Lionello Alatri, his wife, and his ninety-year-old father-in-law were among the 1,259 Roman Jews arrested in the German-conducted roundup of October 16, 1943. They were also among the 1,023 deported to Auschwitz two days later.[2] They did not survive. Among Lionello Alatri's many contributions to his community, however, was his recruitment of Padre Benedetto. Through the Capuchin priest he played a part in the rescue of thousands of Jews.

Who were the refugees who became Padre Benedetto's first protégés in Rome? They were in fact the remnant of a much larger group of perhaps two thousand Jews who had been in enforced residence in Megève and Saint-Gervais-les-Bains (Haute Savoie) and the surrounding area in the formerly Italian-occupied zone of southeastern France. In the days just before the Italian armistice with the Allies, most of the group of two thousand had been put on open trucks by the Comité Dubouchage to return to Nice. They planned to join the thousands of beneficiaries of the Donati plan to be sent by ship to Allied-occupied North Africa by way of Italy. The result of the ill-advised move to Nice was disaster, for the trucks reached the city at about the same time as the German army taking over from the retreating Italians. About half of the passengers in the trucks were arrested upon arrival or soon after.[3]

The remnant of some two hundred initially consisted of the elderly, the sick, and about forty young children with their parents, all of whom were considered too frail to bear the rigors of a mountain journey to Nice in autumn by open truck. That group was put on a train intended to take them by way of Grenoble to Nice, where they would join their families and friends and become part of the same Donati plan. Accompanying the group on the train were two activists from the Comité Dubouchage, a Polish Zionist known today only as Kott and a forty-two-year-old Jewish immigrant from Poland named Aron Kasztersztein, a Communist who had been active in the broader resistance around Grenoble for at least a year. Kasztersztein was accompanied by his wife, Udla (Adèle in France) Bronstein, and their young daughter, Léa.[4]

Also present on the train was Stefan Schwamm, the young lawyer from Vienna who, as mentioned earlier, moved to France after the Anschluss, was interned as an enemy alien in September 1939, served as an interpreter for the French army with the British, and was then forced to elude Vichy police in southern France because of his foreign Jewish status. He and his non-Jewish wife, Gisela, and daughter, Anita, made their way to Marseille, where he acquired false papers identifying him as a French Red Cross worker named Bernard Lioré, an actual non-Jewish friend who had died. Those papers would protect him during the years ahead.

Stefan Schwamm had odd jobs in Marseille but spent most of his time helping foreign Jewish friends secure papers and hiding places. He seems to have met Père Marie-Benoît/Padre Benedetto for the first time in that context in Marseille, for the priest's personal notebook lists a letter he wrote to "Dr. Schwamm" from Italy on July 19, 1943.[5] After innumerable adventures and narrow escapes, Schwamm moved to the Italian-occupied zone. He found himself in Saint-Gervais by chance at the time of the Italian armistice and managed to get on the train with his family and parents. Since he spoke perfect German, French, and Italian, his language skills would be useful to the travelers.[6]

Some of the other refugees on the train can be identified today. A brief look at their stories adds a human dimension to the saga of Padre Benedetto's rescue activities. Three of these refugees were twelve-year-old Hanna Rawicz; her mother, Gisela; and her father, Jakob. Hanna's family had left Germany when Hitler came to power in 1933, and eventually settled in Paris. When the war began in September 1939, Jakob volunteered for service with the French army, but that did not prevent his being interned at Les Milles a few months later. After also having nearly been caught as an enemy alien, Gisela fled to Lyon in the unoccupied zone. Hanna herself spent four years in the Jewish children's homes of Montintin and Chabannes.

On August 13, 1942, as the French police were conducting their massive roundups in the unoccupied zone, Jakob was put on a train at Les Milles for Drancy. Somehow he managed to escape, traveled to Lyon to get his wife, and moved with her to Nice. In May 1943 Hanna joined her parents in Nice, and from there the Italians sent them to Saint-Gervais. To get there the Comité Dubouchage put them on a bus in a terrible thunderstorm. They arrived in the middle of the night. Years later Hanna recalled that when she woke up the next morning, the snow on Mount Blanc was bright red with the dawn.

Jews in Saint-Gervais stayed in various chalets, several families in each one. Every family had a room, and they shared kitchens. Of this mountain village, Hanna later said: "I remember this period as the best of all the war years. We were free. We had the run of the village. The only hardship was that there was not much to eat. At first, the adults had to report to the Italian authorities twice a day, then once a day, and then they didn't even bother. We walked in the mountains every day, looking for firewood. Sometimes we begged the farmers for food. We ate mostly potatoes, cooked in all different ways."[7]

But the idyll in Saint-Gervais did not last long. In early September 1943, when Jews in the village prepared to move back to Nice, Hanna's father had a broken rib. As a result, he and his wife and daughter were included among the two hundred Jews traveling by train rather than in open trucks.

Ida Fallmann and her daughters, eleven-year-old Esther and thirteen-year-old Rachel, were also on the train from Saint-Gervais headed for Nice. As described in chapters 4 and 5, they had lost their husband/ father in the French police roundups of August 1942. Père Marie-Benoît had failed to get them across the border into Switzerland in early 1943 and had helped them in Marseille until they moved to Nice in the Italian-occupied zone. From Nice they were sent to supervised residence in Saint-Gervais, where they remained until ordered to return to the coast in early September 1943. Esther was suffering from appendicitis at the time, however, and was judged too weak for the open trucks. Again, as with her mother's typhus in France in August 1942, illness saved their lives.

For twenty-two-year-old Clara Schnabel Mandel, the condition that put her on the train from Saint-Gervais was a tragic injury. In 1941 the as-yet-unmarried Clara Schnabel had crossed the border from Belgium to France with her brother, Israel, and her younger sister, Frieda. Almost immediately she became involved with the resistance, serving as a liaison throughout southeastern France for the unit known as Combat. In 1942 Clara married a Czech Jew named Franz – or, within the family, Benjamin – Mandel, another Combat activist. Clara and Franz moved to Nîmes, where they shared living quarters with Israel and Frieda and where Clara became pregnant. In late August 1942 thirteen-year-old Frieda learned from French Jewish scouts that the police were planning a roundup. After warning Clara, Franz, and Israel, Frieda managed to hide, but the others were caught. Israel was arrested in a hospital where he was being treated; Clara and Franz declined to act on Frieda's warning and were caught at home. Franz was arrested, but Clara was spared, perhaps because she was a Belgian citizen. But the French police kicked Clara so brutally in the stomach that she lost her baby. Israel and Franz were both deported, without return.[8]

Clara and Frieda moved to Nice after the Italians occupied it in November 1942. From Nice they were sent to supervised residence first in Megève and then in Saint-Gervais. On September 8, 1943, Frieda was among those who traveled to Nice in the open trucks, only to run into German SS police there. Young and resourceful, she managed to survive after harrowing adventures and narrow escapes. Clara, on the other hand, had still not recovered from the injuries that had caused the loss of her child. She was put on the train from Saint-Gervais with the elderly, the young, and the ill. She expected to catch up with her young sister in Nice.

The family of fifteen-year-old Abraham Dresdner was on the train from Saint-Gervais for yet another reason. Abraham was the second oldest child of Jakob and Helen, born in Romania and Czechoslovakia, respectively. His parents had immigrated to Belgium in the late 1920s and fled to France just ahead of the German army in May 1940. Their train at that time left them in the unoccupied zone. After months in the Agde and Rivesaltes internment camps and still more time in a southern French village, they narrowly escaped arrest in August 1942 and moved to the Italian-occupied zone. The Italians sent them to Saint-Gervais, which they found as pleasant as did Hanna Rawicz. Abraham remembers that they did not go to school there, but the older boys held open-air classes for the younger ones. His mother sold cookies to earn a little extra money to supplement the subsidy they received from the Comité Dubouchage. They had to report to the carabinieri every morning and evening, but they were not harassed by officials or local residents.[9]

Abraham had eight brothers and sisters, the youngest of whom had been born during the Battle of France in May 1940. When Jews in Saint-Gervais were being loaded into open trucks to return to Nice, therefore, it became apparent that the trip would be too difficult for the youngest children. All eleven members of the Dresdner family were placed on the train.

The train from Saint-Gervais never reached Nice. When it arrived in Grenoble, the group's leaders heard the news of the Italian armistice.

Because the German army invading the former Italian-occupied zone now blocked the route south, the train was diverted to the Italian city of Turin. When the refugees reached that city, Hanna recalls, they were greeted by Italians holding newspapers with huge headlines, "La Guerra finita!" (The war is over!). Sadly, it was not to be. A few of the Jews from Saint-Gervais, including the entire Dresdner family, left the train in Turin, expecting to catch up with the advancing Allies. Instead they met the German army pouring into northern and central Italy with little resistance. The Dresdners moved on to Florence, where they were first sheltered at the local synagogue by Chief Rabbi Nathan Cassuto and later hidden in various convents by a group of priests and Jews working in cooperation with the local archbishop, Cardinal Elia Dalla Costa.[10] As will be seen, they ultimately made their way to Rome and caught up with the refugees they had left in Turin.

From Turin the train from Saint-Gervais turned south in an attempt to reach Nice by way of the French-Italian border town of Breil. After a journey of at least a day, the train approached Breil, only to learn that it could proceed no further, as the Germans had already occupied Nice and closed the frontier. The passengers were devastated. Many had only one or two suitcases. The rest of their possessions, including furniture, clothing, linens, family heirlooms, books, and documents, were on a second train from Saint-Gervais to Nice and now lost. Still more serious, many of the passengers, like Clara Mandel, had close family members – siblings, parents, or children – who had traveled to the coast in the open trucks and were now out of touch and in extreme danger in German-occupied Nice. At that point Kott left the train to attempt to return to Nice on his own in order to assist Jewish refugees there. Kasztersztein and Schwamm remained with the train and pondered their next step.

Clever and experienced in evading German and Vichy police, the two men concocted a plan. First they instructed all the passengers on the train to keep silent in order not to reveal their accents. Then Schwamm addressed the German police at the border. Showing his identification document in the name of Bernard Lioré, he explained that he was from the Red Cross. He was desperately trying to get the sick and elderly people on his train (with no mention that they were Jewish) to Nice. He insisted that he must get to that city. The Germans replied that it was

not possible; they had no time to bother with civilians in the newly occupied city. "Why don't you go to Rome," they suggested, "and take up
the matter with your ambassador there?" Schwamm feigned reluctance
but agreed. In fact, he was delighted. He and Kasztersztcin had already
decided they should go farther south in order to get their passengers as
close as possible to the advancing Allied lines.[11]

The entire trip from Saint-Gervais to Grenoble, Turin, Breil, and
Rome took about a week. After leaving Breil, Schwamm and Kasztersztein informed their passengers that they did not have to stay with the
group, but if they chose to remain they must follow strict discipline for
the protection of everyone. Some left, but well over half stayed. Without
documents, contacts in Italy, and the ability to speak the local language,
they had little choice. Also, most had little money, for they had lost many
possessions they might have sold. Stefan Schwamm later recalled that
the money problem was solved simply by giving everyone less to eat! The
passengers pooled what money they had and bought apples for everyone.
And according to Schwamm, Italian soldiers fleeing the Germans gave
the children as much food as they needed.[12] As for the train fare, no one
needed to pay, for in the confusion of the moment, railroad conductors
were not collecting tickets.

The train traveled through an Italy in chaos. Italian soldiers were
trying to get home, refugees were fleeing from bombed cities, former
Fascists and anti-Fascists were maneuvering for position, and the Germans were still getting the lay of the land. Initially most of the passengers
on the train were Jews from Saint-Gervais. As they progressed farther
south, however, many Italians joined them. Gradually all the passengers
realized that the present chaos was actually an advantage. There were not
many police controls during the first few days of the German occupation of Italy. The German police were too busy disarming and arresting
Italian soldiers and deserters. About 640,000 Italian soldiers became
prisoners of war at this time and were shipped to German concentration
camps, where about 30,000 of them died.[13]

Hanna Rawicz later recalled that the train stopped every night.
Sometimes the passengers slept on the hard wooden benches of the third-
class carriages, but on other occasions they left the train. In Viareggio, on
the Mediterranean coast between La Spezia and Livorno, a kind priest

met them and arranged for some to stay in his church and for others to have private rooms. It was difficult for Hanna's family to leave the train, because her injured father could not carry their two suitcases, and neither could she or her mother. They finally agreed to abandon one of the cases. One contained clothes and the other, books. They chose to keep the books.

Rachel and Esther Fallmann believe that the train reached Rome on September 13. When it finally pulled into the station, Schwamm and Kasztersztein went off to find local representatives of Delasem, still operating openly in their offices at 2 via Lungotevere Sanzio. As long as Italy had remained independent prior to the armistice with the Allies and the consequent German occupation, Delasem had been allowed to function, even in the harsh conditions created by Mussolini's racial laws. Now near the end of the second week of September, however, as the Germans were occupying most of the country, Delasem's existence was becoming more and more precarious. In Rome the organization's local section was nevertheless still trying to help the new arrivals who were fleeing from supervised residence in northern Italy and hoping to reach the Allied lines.

With the arrival of the train from Saint-Gervais, local Delasem representatives Settimio Sorani and his assistant, Giuseppe Levi, himself a refugee from Yugoslavia, were confronted by what Sorani estimated as an additional 110 Jews in need of help.[14] These newcomers were temporarily lodged in Jewish schools and especially in the Orfanotrofio Israelitico, a Jewish orphanage in via Arco de' Tolomei. Both Rachel and Esther Fallmann and Hanna Rawicz remember sleeping on the floor in a large room in the orphanage. The Fallmann sisters recall that they stayed there for a week or two.

Padre Benedetto, Schwamm, Kasztersztein, and the Roman Jewish leaders understood that given the German presence in the city, the refugees from France could not safely remain in Jewish institutions for long. Hoping to find more secure shelter, they decided to appeal to the Vatican. On September 17 an unidentified Jewish lawyer, possibly Stefan Schwamm, met with Monsignor Giuseppe Di Meglio at the Vatican Secretariat of State to ask if small groups of refugees could be dispersed in Catholic institutions throughout the city. The petitioner made it clear that the refugees were Jewish, mostly from France and Poland. The request was politely but firmly refused. The following day, Di Meglio reported, "I answered him that, in so doing [hiding in Catholic institutions], they would not escape from future searches by the German police! Since he insisted, I believed it opportune to refer him to Monsignor [Antonio] Riberi, who also stressed the absolute inappropriateness of having the Jews remain in Rome."[15] At the time, these prelates feared that their institutions, and perhaps even Vatican City itself, would be invaded by German troops. Jewish refugees, they believed, would be safer outside Rome, even though they spoke not a word of Italian and as yet had no documents and little money.

Given the impossibility of hiding their protégés in Church institutions – a condition that would change within a few weeks – Delasem representatives were obliged to look elsewhere. Now the problem was to find small hotels and boardinghouses that would accept guests without looking too closely at their identification papers or reporting their presence to the police as required by law. For this "understanding," Schwamm later wrote, the prices of rooms were higher than normal. But six or seven small hotels and boardinghouses were found and the refugees were distributed among them. Rachel and Esther Fallmann and their mother were sent to the Pensione Orania in the via Quintino Sella.

At this point Hanna Rawicz and her parents met Padre Maria Benedetto, whom they had not known in France. Hanna recalls that he instructed them and some others to go to the Pensione Haeslin at 28 via Palestro, where her small family was allotted one room. Still others in the group went to the Hotel Salus in the Piazza Indipendenza near the Stazione Termini, or to the Pensione Amalfi at 51 via Marghera. There were non-Jews as well as Jews in these places. Nearly all were refugees with faulty papers or, at first, none at all.

During the first week or ten days of the German occupation of Rome, even foreign Jews without papers were not in imminent danger of deportation. The German police and their Italian Fascist collaborators had other immediate concerns. On September 12 German glider crews led by SS Lieutenant Colonel Otto Skorzeny seized Mussolini in the mountain stronghold east of Rome where Badoglio had been holding him under house arrest. A few days later Hitler set up Mussolini as the puppet head of the new Italian Social Republic (RSI), better known as the Republic of Salò, after the town on Lago di Garda where many government offices were relocated. Meanwhile the Germans were learning their way around, dealing with Italian deserters and anti-Fascists, and considering which local officials they could work with. Those same Italian officials were deciding to what extent they would collaborate with the new occupiers of their country. Many may have agreed with the Roman police officer who headed the department's *servizio stranieri*, the section for foreigners. That man told Padre Benedetto and Sorani in the first days of the occupation that he would not bother their foreign (and illegal) protégés as long as he was able officially to claim ignorance of their presence![16]

Even under these conditions, however, Sorani's Delasem agents, of whom the most important by now was Padre Benedetto, had enormous problems. First, Jewish protégés in the various hotels and boarding-houses had to be provided with false identity cards, residence permits, ration books, and money. Sorani wrote that initially everyone in the Jewish schools and orphanage received a subsidy of twenty lire a day plus food, but that when they left for the hotels and boardinghouses, they needed forty lire per person. To meet these needs, Delasem agents drew on their own local reserves for a time, but it was obvious that they would soon require additional funding.

For the first few weeks Delasem leaders improvised. Hans Wolf de Salis, the Swiss head of the International Red Cross in Rome, provided refugees with packages of food and medicine on several occasions. Additional supplies could be bought on the black market, a dangerous and expensive operation. As further help, Hanna Rawicz recalls that local Italians, often but not always Jewish, donated clothing, blankets, and food and frequently invited refugees to their homes for dinner. She never forgot her first meal in such a home – a delicious risotto. One Roman Jewish family even invited her and others to a party for a Jewish holiday, probably Rosh Hashana. Hanna remembers that all the children received gifts. But these were temporary solutions to make life bearable, pending more stable arrangements.

Meanwhile more and more Jewish refugees were arriving. Many of those who had followed the Italian army into Italy from Nice, Saint-

Martin-Vésubie, Barcelonnette, and other French towns and villages eventually made their way to the Eternal City, usually independently but with referrals to the Roman office from Delasem agents farther north. Others came from supervised residences and internment centers in northern Italy as well as in former Italian-occupied areas in Croatia and along the Dalmatian coast, now also being seized by the German army. In time many Italian Jews also turned to Delasem for help. On May 16, 1944, Sorani recorded that his organization was supporting 2,532 people, including at least 800 Roman Jews and some 300 to 420 from other cities in Italy. After subtracting Sorani's statistics of Italian Jews from his total, the number of foreign Jews being helped comes to between 1,312 and 1,432.[17]

Like the Jews from Saint-Gervais, newcomers were referred to the Salus, Haeslin, Orania, Amalfi, and other similar small hotels and boardinghouses. Conditions in these places were far from ideal and grew worse with time. Hanna remembers the crowding. One woman gave birth in the Haeslin, she says, and hotel residents heard her screams all night long. Then a group of German soldiers was billeted at the Haeslin. "We were now extra careful," says Hanna, but one of the young women from Saint-Gervais started a relationship with one of the soldiers. The other hotel residents were horrified, afraid she would reveal their illegality or their Jewishness. They tried to stop her, but she wept and said, "What can I do? I love him." The outcome of this story is unknown.

Rachel and Esther, who were at the Orania, remember that they listened to the radio every day to learn where the Allies were – an understandable activity, but terribly dangerous in a place where it was difficult to keep secrets and where spies and informers were everywhere. Samuel Berlin recalls other illegal activities at the Salus. Seventeen-year-old Sam had seen his parents arrested and deported from Antwerp. He escaped to unoccupied France, was sent to supervised residence in Barcelonnette, crossed the Alps to Valdieri at the same time as the Jews from Saint-Martin-Vésubie, and immediately continued on alone to Rome. He does not remember how he was referred to the Salus, but he does recall what went on there. After a woman lured him upstairs to her room, her two male cousins, perhaps but not necessarily Jewish, blundered in, arguing ferociously about what they should or should not have done on the black market. As they were about to come to blows, Sam was able to skip out. He was later recruited at the Salus to join the resistance and, to his delight, was even given a handgun (fig. 11).[18]

As all these problems emerged, the possibility of a German roundup of Jews in Rome loomed ever larger. Already on September 18, German SS units had arrested some 350 Jews from Saint-Martin-Vésubie in the region around Cuneo, near Italy's northwestern frontier. The first deportation train from Italy had left two days before, carrying 35 Jews from Merano, near the Brenner Pass, to Innsbruck-Reichenau in Austria and later to Auschwitz. One of the 35 returned after the war. On September 19 in Novara, at least 3 other Jews were arrested and disappeared without a trace. The first massacre of Jews in Italy also occurred in these early weeks of the occupation, when German SS troops seized mostly foreign Jews in hotels around beautiful Lago Maggiore and murdered 54 of them, including many young children and their elderly grandparents.[19] Word of these atrocities filtered slowly down to Rome, increasing the anxiety of refugees and rescuers alike.

Gradually throughout September 1943 it became apparent that the Germans and their Fascist collaborators would not limit arrests to foreign Jews, as had initially been the case in France, but would seize Italian Jews as well. SS Lieutenant Colonel Herbert Kappler, chief of the German security police in Rome, received a message from his Berlin office on September 25 that said in part: "All Jews, regardless of nationality, age, sex, and personal conditions must be transferred to Germany and liquidated there. The success of this undertaking will have to be ensured by a surprise action and for that reason it is strictly necessary to suspend the application of any anti-Jewish measures of an individual nature, likely to stir up suspicion of an imminent action among the population."[20] While all Jews in Rome were the eventual target, then, individual Jews were not to be arrested . . . yet.

Local Jews, of course, did not know about Kappler's secret orders, but they had their fears and suspicions. The first public sign of trouble appeared in Rome on September 26 when Kappler called Dante Almansi and Ugo Foà, the presidents of the national and the Roman Jewish Communities, respectively, into his office. The SS officer informed the Jewish leaders that they must deliver fifty kilograms of gold to him within thirty-six hours. If they did, "nothing bad will happen to you," but if they failed, two hundred Roman Jews would be deported to Germany. The deadline was subsequently extended slightly, but by 4:00 PM on Tuesday, September 28, the gold had been collected from Jewish and non-Jewish donors throughout the city and delivered to Gestapo headquarters in the via Tasso.[21] All Romans now understood that the Germans were hostile toward Jews, but many believed, or wanted to believe, that the gold would ensure their physical safety.

Signs of extreme German hostility nevertheless continued. Early Friday morning, September 29, Kappler's security police invaded the Roman Jewish Community offices adjacent to the central synagogue on the banks of the Tiber and seized two million lire as well as documents, registers, minutes of meetings, and records of contributors. This made Roman Jews very nervous. Why would the Germans be interested in documents and lists unless they were preparing an anti-Jewish action? Dante Almansi quietly changed apartments during the first week of October. On October 10, the day following Yom Kippur, he closed the office of the national Union of Italian Jewish Communities at 9 via Lungotevere Sanzio and removed the archives. Settimio Sorani had taken most of his family, but apparently not his wife, to Soriano al Cimino, outside of Rome, as early as September 9. There he rented a house in the country, disguising his loved ones as non-Jewish refugees from the war. He and his wife left their Roman residence on September 12 and lived with false documents in ten different locations during the nine months of the German occupation.

Also in mid-September, Sorani removed or destroyed all compromising material at the local Delasem offices, including lists of protégés who were currently receiving assistance. He left only harmless documents to divert suspicions that some material had been removed. At the end of September, the entire Delasem operation went underground, reestablishing itself in Padre Benedetto's monastery and college at 159 via Sicilia. Filling nearly a city block and with a back door to provide an emergency exit onto the via Boncompagni, parallel to the via Sicilia, the large monastery complex provided an ideal haven. There, wrote Sorani, "Delasem found fraternal hospitality [and I had] the good fortune of being able to continue my work."[22] Before long the five local leaders of

Delasem's rescue efforts – Padre Benedetto, Settimio Sorani, Giuseppe Levi, Stefan Schwamm, and Aron Kasztersztcin – were meeting regularly in the monastery. Six large boxes of Delasem papers were stored in an attic on the premises.

Looking back years later, Padre Benedetto especially remembered the refugees. Not all of them were Jewish. Escaped Allied prisoners of war, political dissidents, and Italian draft evaders also knocked on the door. Hundreds came to the monastery every day. Some did not know whom to ask for. They told the friar who guarded the door that they were looking for "the Father of the Jews," an epithet the priest relished. Inside the monastery, daily life had totally changed. Padre Benedetto later recalled that "the exterior rooms filled with women every day. Interior rooms filled with men. Ten or twelve rooms were put at our disposition: deposits of food, clothing, reception rooms for the [Delasem] Committee."[23] With so many people coming and going, the situation soon became dangerously obvious. Rescue workers eventually set up other meeting places throughout the city and changed them regularly. Also for safety reasons, as in Marseille, they refrained from housing refugees in the monastery itself.

Events continued to hurtle toward their final tragic denouement. On Wednesday, October 13, two railroad cars rolled up on the trolley tracks and stopped in front of the central synagogue of Rome. German soldiers carefully emptied the library of the Roman Jewish Community, stealing priceless manuscripts, incunabula, books, prints, and historical documents. But worse was yet to come. At 5:30 AM on October 16, 1943, a rainy Saturday morning, 365 German military and security police finally came, not for documents and lire and books, but for human beings. Armed with carefully prepared lists of names and addresses, they pounded on doors in the old Roman ghetto and throughout the city, rousing Jewish men, women, and children from their sleep and bundling them out into the still dark streets. By the time the roundup ended early that afternoon, the police had arrested 1,259 people, including 896 women and children. After identity checks and screening at a detention center at the Italian Military College in via della Lungara, only six hundred feet from Vatican City, at least 1,023 Jews were crammed into boxcars at Rome's Tiburtina Station early in the morning of October

18. Deported to Auschwitz, 149 men and 47 women were selected on October 23 to enter the camp for hard labor. The others were gassed that same day. Of those chosen for work, sixteen survived.[24]

The victims of the Rome roundup of October 16, 1943, were all Italian Jews. The Germans had been able to secure their names and addresses but were apparently not yet aware of Delasem's refugees. This was not so clear at the time, however, and the refugees were terrified that rainy morning as word of the arrests began to circulate. Sorani later wrote that he went out early to warn his protégés to leave their rooms, go out for walks, and refrain from speaking Yiddish.[25] Rachel Fallmann remembers that it was her birthday and she had a terrible toothache. She and her mother and sister walked around in the rain all day. That night they returned to the Orania because they had no other place to go.

After that scare Padre Benedetto came to the Fallmanns' rescue. For them and for three other Jewish women, he found places in what Rachel remembers as a convent for Franciscan nuns in the via Sistina. This step was logical for him as a priest of the Capuchin order, a branch of the Franciscans. He undoubtedly asked the mother superior of the convent to accept his protégés, and she agreed. She then would have cleared the decision with the directors of the order. This was happening throughout Rome after the roundup of Jews on October 16 as hundreds, and ultimately thousands, of Roman and foreign Jews began to join the political dissidents, military deserters, and escaped Allied prisoners of war already hiding in convents, monasteries, Catholic schools and hospitals, and some Vatican properties. Fugitives, including Jews, were often introduced to the directors of individual Catholic institutions by priests like Padre Benedetto, acting on their own initiative for friends and contacts. Occasionally important prelates took the same kinds of initiatives, including bringing fugitives, sometimes with Jews among them, into their own apartments in Vatican City. Pope Pius XII and other Vatican officials were generally aware of these developments, although they did not know the extent or the details. Some officials approved, while others feared that the hiding of fugitives would provoke German attacks on Church institutions.[26]

Rachel and Esther recall that the Franciscan convent was very pleasant, although its central location made it dangerous. After a time, Padre

Benedetto tried to move them to another convent in the via Nomentana, but there the nuns refused to keep them. They stayed only a few hours, returned to the via Sistina, and were then moved into a Polish convent. There they remained until the liberation of Rome on June 4, 1944.

"Padre Benedetto was like a father to us," declare Rachel and Esther, who had lost their own father in unoccupied France in August 1942. While they were hiding in the convents, he remained constantly in contact, bringing them money and food. "He was so good, so warm, we thought he might be a descendant of a Jewish family!" they say. They also recall that he always said to them, "You are Jewish, and you must remain Jewish."

Hanna Rawicz also remembers Padre Benedetto from this period. At some point he moved her family out of the Pensione Haeslin and into the apartment of an eighty-year-old woman in the via dei Serpenti. The woman, says Hanna with amusement, was trying to live to be one hundred so that she could be in the newspapers! To make ends meet, she rented out three or four rooms to different families, who shared the kitchen. Hanna's family had a living room–dining room combination with a balcony. The owner came from the north of Italy. She claimed to have known Garibaldi, but she had photographs of Mussolini and the king and queen of Italy in the hall. She did not know that Hanna and her parents were Jewish. The other families in the apartment were not Jewish.

Of Padre Benedetto, Hanna says: "He was always ready to help with whatever was needed. He was wonderful. He was like a safety net. I did not realize that he was French [she thought he was Italian]. He was kind, friendly, he made you feel good, I never heard him say no to anything. He was a very big man, but very gentle. He always wanted to help. He was always accessible. My father loved him. He felt very strongly about him."

Life under these conditions was tolerable for Hanna's family but never normal. "We kids played hide and seek in the Colosseum," Hanna relates, "but we were always on guard." If they saw a police raid or a bus being stopped for a search, they walked quickly away. If anyone approached them, they ran. Hanna's parents sometimes met with other Jewish refugees, but they never went to each other's living quarters. Instead they met in a small park near the railroad station, talked, and caught up on the news. "We bought our own food," Hanna says, adding that she and her parents received false identity cards and ration books from Padre Benedetto. Her father Jakob Rawicz's card was in the name of Jacques Ravier to retain his initials. As he learned Italian, Jakob/Jacques tried to remember to speak the language with a French accent.

NINE

With Stefan Schwamm in Rome

SECURING DOCUMENTS FOR JEWISH RESCUE

NOT LONG AFTER THE ROME ROUNDUP OF OCTOBER 16, 1943, German police launched their first raid on the Hotel Salus. Some forty Delasem protégés were residing at the Salus at that time, most without documents, along with many non-Jews. By sheer chance, Padre Benedetto was at the hotel when the Germans arrived. "Fortunately," he recorded later, "in the back courtyard there was a wall that could be scaled by means of a ladder, and in just a few minutes everyone had cleared out. I stayed almost alone with the personnel of the hotel. After insisting with the [German] agents who searched the place several times, I was released after three hours." By "insisting" he presumably meant he was vouching for the boarders who were "out" that day.[1]

Then on October 28 Settimio Sorani paid a near-fatal visit to Cyril Kotnik, a diplomat attached to the Yugoslavian delegation to the Holy See and a loyal friend of Delasem. Unknown to Sorani, Gestapo agents had arrested Kotnik the day before and were in the process of searching Kotnik's apartment when Sorani knocked on the door. Naturally Sorani was arrested and taken to Gestapo headquarters in the via Tasso. For ten terrifying days he was interrogated, beaten, and interrogated again. He stuck to his story. He had come to the building to deliver a message for a friend and had mistaken the entry and floor. He had knocked on the wrong door. He knew no one named Kotnik. His false documents apparently stood up under intense scrutiny, and he was not recognized as Jewish. The Germans finally accepted his story and released him on November 6.[2] But while remaining director of Delasem in Rome, Sorani now had to be more careful than ever.

If Delasem's ever growing numbers of protégés were to survive, rescuers clearly had to meet three fundamental needs. As the raid on the
Salus showed, lodging was the first priority, and the use of small hotels
and boardinghouses was increasingly risky. Although those facilities
continued to be used for want of a better option, Delasem leaders came
to prefer Church institutions that were willing to accept Jews, as well
as private apartments whose owners rented rooms without asking too
many questions. Often those owners did not know that their new tenants
were Jewish. With regard to lodging, Padre Benedetto was able to help
significantly by contacting Church institutions.

But no lodging was possible without the resolution of the other two
necessities: false documents and money. Even in Church institutions,
but especially in hotels, boardinghouses, and apartments, refugees had
to have identification documents and residence permits in case of police searches. They also needed ration books if they were to buy food.
Money was required to buy food and pay rent or boarding fees. Even
most Church institutions charged modest fees if their guests had the
means, although only a few asked them to leave if they had no money.
During the entire German occupation of Rome until the liberation on
June 4, 1944, Delasem leaders in Rome and the brave men and women
who worked with them spent most of their time securing and distributing documents and money.

The problem of documents was intricate and complex. Refugees
needed cards identifying them as non-Jews, of course, but they also had
to be documented as foreigners, because they spoke Italian with heavy
accents if they spoke it at all. Identification cards were technically required to rent lodgings. Equally important, they were prerequisites for
obtaining residence permits (*permessi di soggiorno*), which were in turn
essential for receiving ration cards.

At first most false identification cards were primitive in the extreme. Stefan Schwamm remembered that homemade typed forms were
stamped with seals made by gluing characters from children's printing
toys to the inside of pocket-watch covers. Such documents would probably have fooled no one. But their creators soon grew more skilled – and
just in time, for on December 1, 1943, Mussolini's minister of the interior,
Guido Buffarini Guidi, ordered his police to arrest and intern all Jews

in Italy at any time and wherever they could be found. A local decree on December 6 then required that the names of all persons present in every building in Rome be posted daily at the entrances. Doormen, concierges, innkeepers, and other service personnel were to be held personally responsible for errors and omissions, and all unlisted individuals found in buildings were subject to arrest. A few days earlier, still another new law had announced that no refugees arriving in Rome after December 6 would be granted residence permits. False documents could be back-dated, but they were clearly indispensable. The authorities were cracking down, and vast roundups of foreigners were expected.

In these circumstances Padre Benedetto remembered that there had once been an old hand-operated printing press in his monastery in the via Sicilia, operated years earlier by a friar to produce religious publications. After a diligent search he found it, covered with dust, in a storeroom full of junk. A skilled printer among the refugees was able to use the obsolete machine to crank out convincing blank forms. The forms were filled in with the names, pertinent data, and photographs of individual refugees claiming to be from France. Among the papers of various refugees, Padre Benedetto and Schwamm were able to secure sample documents bearing seals from several different French communes. Using those samples as models, a sympathetic engraver created reliable seals.

A final challenge was posed by the fact that French identification cards usually bore French fiscal stamps, which of course were not available in the via Sicilia. To solve that problem, Delasem workers bought postage stamps in various shops catering to stamp collectors. When those did not suffice, they used old canceled French postage stamps. "It was crazy," Padre Benedetto later wrote, "but it worked." With his French-style handwriting, Padre Benedetto himself completed the documents by forging the names of the mayors of the various communes.[3] The idea of a big, bearded Capuchin priest in his flowing cassock and sandals engaging in such activities in a dingy junk room in his monastery evokes a respectful chuckle. But the final product was imminently convincing.

As further insurance, Settimio Sorani took the refugees' false identification documents to a friend named Marc Chauvet at the Swiss consulate. He later explained that the Swiss at the time represented French interests in Mussolini's Italian Social Republic. Therefore they had the power to verify documents and declare the "French citizens" who carried them to be under their protection – the protection of a neutral country that the Germans respected. The earliest documents were so poor, however, that Chauvet was embarrassed when asked for verification. He wanted to help Sorani, but he was reluctant to expose his consulate. He informed his friend that he should return with better documents. With Sorani in virtual hiding after his prison stint, Schwamm returned with the newer, far superior identification cards. Chauvet kept his word and provided letters of protection for hundreds of refugees.

Problems with documents nevertheless remained. Police headquarters in Rome lacked the personnel to issue hundreds of residence permits quickly. Needing ration books for their protégés, Padre Benedetto and Schwamm went to see Luigi Charrier, director of the Roman office of rationing for foreigners, and the vice director, Mario Cherubini. Could these officials, they asked, provide ration cards for four hundred to five hundred refugees from France before their residence permits were issued? The fact that the refugees were Jewish was almost certainly not mentioned. The officials were well disposed to the request, but some bureaucratic formalities needed to be respected.[4] It was agreed that Padre Benedetto should create a Committee for Assistance to Refugees (Comitato Assistenza Profughi, or CAP) "in formation" with himself as president. The committee would issue a certificate to each refugee, printed in the monastery and signed by Padre Benedetto. The certificate would state in two languages, Italian and German, that the bearer was under the protection of the CAP, the Swiss consulate, and the International Red Cross. Each refugee would then declare in writing on the certificate that he or she had arrived in Rome at some specified date prior to December 6.

To give the CAP certificates still greater credibility, Padre Benedetto went to visit Monsignor Umberto Dionisi, secretary general of the Vicariato, the administrative offices of the bishop of Rome, who was the pope. It was agreed that Monsignor Dionisi would sign other papers verifying that the signature on the CAP certificates was indeed that of Padre Benedetto and that the Capuchin priest was the president of CAP. These papers, bearing the seal of the Vicariato, were attached to each of the five hundred CAP certificates, giving the impression that the bearers were also under Vatican protection. By this ingenious arrangement,

Monsignor Dionisi did not involve himself or the Vatican with CAP or testify that it was legitimate. It is not even clear whether he knew the refugees in question were Jewish. He simply verified Padre Benedetto's signature. That, however, was enough for Charrier, Cherubini, and the office of rationing for foreigners. The ration cards were issued in advance of the requisite residence permits.[5]

It is interesting to note that while Monsignor Dionisi was willing to lend a hand, other Vatican officials around this time were not as enthusiastic about Padre Benedetto's activities. On November 19, for example, a priest at the Vatican Secretariat of State reported that he had learned from an informant that the Capuchin was already in trouble with the Italian authorities for forging official signatures on ration cards for Jewish refugees. This referred to an incident the month before when an unsuspecting Padre Benedetto had dealings with a shady character masquerading as a government official and selling phony ration cards. According to the priest at the Secretariat of State, the danger passed when he persuaded the informant not to issue a complaint.[6] According to Padre Benedetto, however, it passed when he discovered the fraud himself and reported it to Alberto De Dominicis, the chief Roman bureaucrat in charge of rationing, who agreed to cover him.[7] In any case, the following day an exasperated higher official in the Vatican Secretariat of State, Monsignor Angelo Dell'Acqua, noted on the original report of November 19, "I have repeatedly (and the last time very clearly) told Padre Benoît [sic; Benedetto], Capuchin, to use the maximum prudence in dealing with the Jews..: it can be seen, unfortunately, that he has not wished to listen to the humble advice given to him."[8]

About a month later, on December 29, an official at the Vatican Secretariat of State reported that he had just learned from Jewish sources about a joint organization of Jews and people "delegated by the Vatican." One purpose of the organization was to distribute among "persons of the Jewish religion" (in other words, not Jewish converts to Catholicism) false documents in both Italian and German identifying them as connected to the Vatican. A second goal was to find shelter for "those persons belonging to the Jewish religion" in various institutions. This could only have been a reference to Padre Benedetto's Committee for Assistance to Refugees, with a garbled understanding of the nature of

Monsignor Dionisi's involvement.[9] After reading the report, Monsignor Dell'Acqua recorded that he doubted the existence of such an organization and commented petulantly:

> Several times, however, I have observed that various persons employed at the Vatican or close to Vatican circles interest themselves too much (in a manner that I dare to call almost exaggerated) in the Jews, favoring them, maybe even with elegant schemes. . . . I have always believed . . . in using the maximum prudence in speaking with Jews, to whom it would be better to speak less. . . . Regarding the bilingual cards . . . in my opinion it would be opportune to make an inquiry in order to avoid possible trouble.[10]

It might be noted that Monsignor Dell'Acqua took this position despite the fact that he had few illusions in November and December 1943 about the fate of Jews in deportation. On October 27, when asked if the Vatican could make inquiries about Jews deported from Rome after the major roundup eleven days before, he wrote, "We can try . . . but I do not believe that we will succeed in getting any news of the deportees: the experience in other countries is rather eloquent in this regard." Five days later, Dell'Acqua's superior, Monsignor Giovanni Battista Montini, secretary of the Section of Ordinary Ecclesiastical Affairs of the Vatican Secretariat of State (and the future Pope Paul VI), noted that an Italian senator had told him he had been informed by a German police officer that the deported Roman Jews would never return to their homes.[11] Although he may not have known specifically about Auschwitz at the time that he was urging prudence and restraint in assisting Jews, Dell'Acqua surely knew that deported Jews were going to their deaths.

Without directly and specifically condemning the ongoing Nazi extermination of the Jews, Pope Pius XII nevertheless managed to convey his concern in several public speeches and articles. His encyclical of October 20, 1939, titled *Summi Pontificatus,* in which he wrote of "the unity of the human race" and called for compassion and charity toward all victims of the war, though without specifically mentioning Jews, has been discussed in earlier chapters. Then, in his long Christmas message of 1942, he spoke of his compassion for, among many other groups, "the hundreds of thousands who, without personal guilt, are doomed to death or to a progressive deterioration of their condition, sometimes for no other reason than their nationality or descent." On June 2, 1943, his name day, the pope spoke again of his compassion for "those who have turned an anxiously imploring eye to Us, tormented as they are, for reasons of their nationality or descent . . . and destined sometimes, even without guilt on their part, to exterminatory measures."

Pius XII was demonstrably most concerned about Jews and other fugitives in his own diocese of Rome. Ten days after the roundup of Jews there on October 16, 1943, the Vatican daily newspaper, *L'Osservatore Romano*, mentioned the pope's compassion and charity, which did not "pause before boundaries of nationality, religion, or descent." Then on October 29 it declared that "the heart of the August Pontiff is more than ever with all members of the great human family so severely affected, particularly with those closest and who suffer most, [he is] always concerned to leave nothing undone to alleviate their pain and discomfort – without distinction of nationality, descent or religion." Expressions of concern occurred again in the Vatican newspaper on December 3 and 4 when articles objected to a new Italian decree ordering that all Jews in Italy be arrested and interned within the country.[12]

These brief papal expressions of concern for "all members of the great human family" were vague and imprecise and would not have changed the minds of those who were indifferent to Jewish suffering. They also never constituted a warning about ongoing persecutions. However, Catholics who were already well-disposed toward Jews were aware of the expressions of concern and were convinced that in helping Jews and others they were following the pope's example and carrying out his will. Padre Benedetto was surely one of these. But also important in this context is what the pope may have said about Jews in private, and that is much more difficult to know. Until recently there has been almost no credible testimony by rescuers about a private papal directive to save Jews. More recent testimony focused on Rome also tends to be flawed, usually because documents appear to be backdated or because it is not clear how claimants could have known what they wrote or why they waited so long to testify.[13] It is clear that the pope knew that Jews and others were hiding in Church institutions, including some in the Vatican City itself, and he seems to have accepted the effort as long as it remained limited. However, he seems not to have known the full extent of the involvement.

Under the circumstances, Vatican officials like Monsignor Dell'Acqua felt comfortable reporting that they were trying to restrain involvement with Jews by priests like Padre Benedetto. Requests for restraint grew more insistent after the first Italian-German raids on extraterritorial Vatican properties outside Vatican City on the night of December 21, 1943. At least twenty men, including several Jews, were arrested that night at the Pontificio Seminario Lombardo, the Pontificio Istituto Orientale, and the Pontificio Collegio Russo. After that fearful event, officials at the Vatican Secretariat of State began to issue directives declaring "those who find themselves in other ecclesiastical buildings should be urged to change lodgings."[14] The concern was that overzealous rescue efforts by churchmen would provoke major German or Fascist attacks on more Catholic institutions and endanger those in hiding. They would also jeopardize Vatican efforts to maintain a dialogue with the occupiers of Rome to preserve order, minimize violence, and ensure a smooth transition when the Germans withdrew.

The attitude of Pius XII to all this seems to have been ambivalent. In an audience with the Jesuit Padre Martegani, director of *La Civiltà Cattolica*, on December 27, 1943, six days after the raid on the Seminario Lombardo, the pope declared that he no longer felt confident about the safety of refugees in ecclesiastical properties and said it was necessary to be more wary and prudent regarding them. "Exercise charity with the many pitiable cases that come up," he told Padre Martegani, "but avoid the use of false documents and any other thing that may appear fraudulent."[15] Yet as Padre Benedetto well knew, it was virtually impossible to shelter and supply anyone without false documents.

The pope's concern and desire for prudence increased still more after a Fascist raid on the extraterritorial Basilica di San Paolo fuori le Mura on the night of February 3–4, 1944. Sixty-four fugitives were arrested that night, of whom five were Jewish. Those five were subsequently deported and murdered at Auschwitz. Soon after the raid, a priest at the Seminario Lombardo recorded in his daily logbook: "Orders from the Vatican to dismiss all non-clerics. Why such a brutal blow? ... On the other hand there were grave penalties for disobeying: suspension of religious privileges for those rectors of colleges, institutions, etc., who kept young people in religious habits ... The rector who had risked his life to shelter Jews, Communists, military officers, and had done the impossible, obeyed the order . . . The young people had to leave."[16] The expulsion order was enforced at the Seminario Lombardo and several other Vatican properties. Jews and other fugitives being hidden were referred elsewhere. Some returned when the danger seemed to have passed.

About the same time, a similar expulsion order was issued to priests and prelates sheltering some fifty fugitives, including about seven who were Jewish by culture or religion (that is, not converts), within Vatican City itself. There, however, several important cardinals protested, asking Secretary of State Cardinal Luigi Maglione to speak to the pope, who had apparently approved the expulsion order in the first place. In the end, in contrast to Vatican properties outside the walls, the order was not enforced in Vatican City itself.[17]

Although Padre Benedetto occasionally received expressions of disapproval from officials at the Vatican and lukewarm support at best, the attitude of his Capuchin superior was quite different. In 1948 Padre Benedetto wrote that the general minister of the Capuchin order had always fully supported and approved of his rescue work. Padre Benedetto recalled learning after the war that someone, presumably a friar in his monastery, had gone to the general minister during the German occupation to complain that the rescue work compromised the security of everyone in the order. The general minister replied, "Don't worry about a thing; if anyone has to go to prison with Padre Benedetto, it will not be you, it will be me." Grateful for the support, Padre Benedetto reflected, "I continued my activities, but I fully realized that I was compromising for the college and that on several occasions they feared a raid and search."[18] How could it be otherwise? The Pensione Jaccarino was just down the street. In that large Tuscan-style villa at 38 via Romagna on the corner of via Sicilia, the extreme Fascist fanatics of the infamous Banda Koch operated between April and June 1944, arresting and torturing suspected partisans and political dissidents with the unofficial blessing of the occupation authorities.

After Padre Benedetto and his associates obtained French identification cards validated by the Swiss consulate and temporary ration cards from the proper Roman authorities, they still faced the problem of residence permits. Padre Benedetto and Stefan Schwamm consulted again with Monsignor Dionisi, who referred them to a friend at police headquarters. The friend put them in touch with the police chief. With no idea that the beneficiaries were Jewish, the police chief agreed to issue residence permits to the refugees from France. In order not to overload his employees, however, he asked that the applicants present themselves in groups no larger than twenty a day. This was done for two or three weeks, but then the process was suspended. In desperation, Schwamm pulled strings. In his capacity as Bernard Lioré, a French Red Cross worker, he had somehow befriended a Captain Bruto Girardi from the Italian Africa Police (PAI), a mixed Italian and African colonial police force that fought alongside the Italian army during the war. Schwamm/Lioré convinced his friend Girardi to appeal to a general in the same police force, who in turn appealed to the police chief. The issuance of residence permits was resumed.[19]

While he was more than willing to use connections, Schwamm stressed that in most of these maneuvers he and Padre Benedetto did not pay bribes. Partly, Schwamm recalled, they did not pay because they had no money to spare. But in addition they understood that payment of bribes could expose them to blackmail. Instead, Schwamm declared tactfully, "We tried to convince the relevant authorities with arguments of reason, juridical interpretations, and unexpressed but well-understood threats," all delicate references to postwar reckoning.[20]

The system of providing documents worked well, at least for the first four or five hundred refugees. But the numbers were increasing rapidly, and not all of Delasem's newest protégés were from France. Jews from Rome and other Italian cities also needed false documents to establish their new identities as non-Jews and allow them to secure ration books. In addition, Jewish refugees were arriving from points east of Italy, having nothing to do with France. At the Swiss consulate, Chauvet was able to protect only refugees from France. As a result, papers and even false ration cards for the Italians were secured from activists in the resistance or from sympathetic local bureaucrats who stole blank forms from their offices. Those for many Jews from the east were provided by the Hungarian consul general, Viktor Szasz, and the Romanian ambassador to the Holy See, Vasile Grigorcea. Both countries were allied to the Third Reich at the time and were usually able to protect their citizens abroad from the Germans if they wished. For some periods during the war, they did not choose to protect their Jewish citizens abroad, but they protected non-Jews for as long as they could. Jewish refugees from Hungary and Romania now presented themselves as non-Jews.

Just when Padre Benedetto and his assistants thought they had the problem of documents for refugees solved, however, an enormous new difficulty arose. Chauvet at the Swiss consulate informed Padre Bono detto that he could no longer provide protection for refugees with dubious connections to France – that is, for those who may have been illegal aliens in that country before moving to Italy. Chauvet's superiors were giving him trouble. The refugees would have to leave Rome for the Italian countryside or return to France. Delasem leaders seemed to be back where they had started. They certainly could not send their refugees back to France. But how could they secure new documents for five hundred people, find hiding places in the countryside for them, and arrange to supply them? There was only one solution. After consultation with Szasz, who had already been so helpful, Padre Benedetto and Stefan Schwamm obtained or fabricated blank Hungarian identification forms, transferred refugees' photographs from their old documents to their new ones, and filled in the names. Szasz even provided authentic seals from his office. The five hundred refugees from France became refugees from Hungary. Witnesses do not tell us how those new Hungarian citizens secured their residence permits and ration books.[21]

The transfer of "citizenship" was not quite as great a stretch as it may seem. Most of the refugees from France were originally from Central or Eastern Europe, often from parts of Poland or Galicia (today Ukraine) near Hungary. Many of them, therefore, had been born in the Austro-Hungarian Monarchy, which existed until 1918. Just one family member with some knowledge of Hungarian could present a claim for spouses, children, siblings, nieces, and nephews who had never been east of the Alps. Others with a birth certificate from a grandparent long deceased or a military service form from the Austro-Hungarian army could do the same. For many the claim of Hungarian citizenship was no more spurious than the French version had been.

Examples of the beneficiaries abound. Sedonie, or Sidie, Templer was born in Bratislava, Slovakia, in what had once been part of Austria-Hungary. In 1927 Sidie and her family immigrated to Belgium, where she met her future husband, Alter Shytoltz. Both families fled to southern France when the Germans invaded Belgium in May 1940, and both eventually moved into the southeastern corner of France after the Italians occupied the area in November 1942. To show the Germans that they were doing something about the "Jewish question" in their zone, the Italians sent them to supervised residence in Saint-Martin-Vésubie. Married while there, Sidie and Alter fled with their families over the Alps to Valdieri and Borgo San Dalmazzo in northwestern Italy when the Germans occupied the Italian zone on September 8, 1943. Then they barely escaped the German roundup of Jews in Valdieri and Borgo on September 18.

About two months later, Sidie took a train to Rome with her mother, sister, and brother. They had to change trains and spend one night in Florence, where, with no recommendation, they found no place to stay. They knocked on the doors of Church institutions and asked priests, friars, and nuns for assistance, but no one would help. They spent that night in the streets. Once in Rome, however, they went directly to the Hotel Salus, a short walk from Stazione Termini. Sidie believes that they had been directed there by don Raimondo Viale, the courageous parish priest of Borgo San Dalmazzo. Don Viale distributed Delasem funds to Jewish refugees hiding in and around Borgo and was in touch with Delasem agents in Rome. Sidie also recalls that she first met Padre Benedetto at the Salus.

Sidie was able to move about with some security because she already had French identification documents in the name of Suzanne Servat. The papers had been obtained not from Delasem but as a result of her earlier work with the resistance in Toulouse and Grenoble. Soon after her arrival in Rome, therefore, Sidie went to the Hungarian consulate to request identification documents for some twelve to fifteen other Jews still hiding in Valdieri and Borgo San Dalmazzo whose photographs she had carried with her on her flight south. Somehow this effort had been organized through communications between Delasem activists in Rome and don Viale in Borgo. Among the twelve to fifteen photographs were those of Sidie's father as well as her husband and his parents, who were in fact from Warsaw and had no connection to Hungary. At the Hungarian consulate a discomfited official asked Sidie how he could issue so many documents to people he had never seen. Sidie was in the early stages of pregnancy, and at that point she fainted. The official gave her the documents.

A couple of weeks later, Sidie returned alone to Borgo to deliver the precious papers. With her French documents and her blond hair, she says, she felt secure. She gave most of the documents to don Viale, who, with the help of local priests whom he recruited, then had the difficult and dangerous job of distributing them to the refugees involved. The papers of her loved ones she delivered herself. Her husband's card, which Sidie still has, identified him as Alberto Vamos, born in Budapest on December 9, 1923; occupation – student. The card bore the seal of the Hungarian consulate and an official signature confirming that the bearer's photograph and signature were legitimate. Armed with good documents, her father and her husband and his parents moved to Rome and installed themselves in the Salus in early January 1944.[22]

Another young courier who carried Delasem's Hungarian documents from Rome to Borgo San Dalmazzo was Miriam Löwenwirth Reuveni. It was no coincidence that these couriers were both women; young men were more suspect because they had to explain why they were not in military service, and young Jewish men could be detected during searches because of their circumcisions.

Miriam Löwenwirth was born in a Slovakian village near the Hungarian border in 1926. Her parents spoke Hungarian, although she did not. The Löwenwirth family immigrated to Antwerp in 1929, fled to southern France in May 1940, and moved to the Italian-occupied zone at the end of 1942. Sent by the Italians to supervised residence in Saint-Martin-Vésubie like Sidie Templer, they also crossed the Alps into northwestern Italy after September 8, 1943. On September 18, as the Germans were arresting all the Jewish refugees they could find in the area, Miriam and her parents and five siblings met don Viale, who hid them and saved their lives. A day or two later he put them in touch with a stranger from Turin, probably a Delasem worker, who escorted them first to Turin, then to Genoa, and finally to Florence. In all of those places, Delasem representatives were working with local priests and prelates to rescue

Jews.[23] In Florence, Miriam's family was hidden, mostly in local convents, although her father was placed in a private apartment.

Miriam's father was caught in Florence on January 5, 1944, and ultimately died in deportation.[24] The day after his arrest, Miriam decided that for greater security her mother, two younger sisters, and baby brother must move to Rome. She herself was determined to remain in Florence to try to help her father in prison. Miriam believes that it was Suora Crispina at the convent of the Suore Francescane Missionarie di Maria in the Piazza Carmine, where she was hiding, who gave her the name of a contact in the Eternal City – a Capuchin priest named Padre Benedetto. That priest received her mother and the children and secured a small apartment for them and another Jewish family. After that he delivered funds to them on a monthly basis. But the two older Löwenwirth boys were still in convent schools in Florence.

In mid-February the intrepid Miriam and her friend Elizabeth Dresdner, Abraham's older sister, had another challenge. Like Miriam's mother, Elizabeth's parents with their four daughters had made it to Rome, where Padre Benedetto and the Delasem group put them up at the Hotel Salus. Now they wanted their five boys, still hiding in convent schools in Florence, to join them, and Miriam's mother wanted her two older sons to be with her. Eighteen-year-old Miriam's younger sister, Zehava, and her friend, nineteen-year-old Elizabeth Dresdner, joined her in Florence, where they gathered up the seven younger children. Somehow the group of ten youngsters made it back to Rome, walking through snow and hitching rides, sometimes even with German soldiers. The trip took five full days. When they reached Rome, they stayed in the Hotel Salus for a time. But because the Salus was too dangerous, Padre Benedetto placed the Dresdner and Löwenwirth sons at the Istituto Pio XI, a boarding school for some 200 to 250 boys run by the Salesian Order. He also hid some of the daughters of the two families in a local convent.

Miriam, however, stayed in Rome for only one day. She was desperate to return to Florence on a Wednesday, she recalls, because that was the only day of the week when packages could be delivered to the prison where her father was being held. If her father did not receive a package, she knew he would conclude that his family had been arrested. But before leaving, she went to see the Capuchin priest at his monastery in the via

Sicilia to thank him for everything he had done for the Löwenwirth and Dresdner families. During that meeting Padre Benedetto asked her to carry Delasem funds back to Florence and to continue on to Borgo San Dalmazzo to deliver fifteen false Hungarian documents to Jews in hiding there. Miriam agreed, on the condition that he not tell her mother! "Padre Benedetto was a very special person," Miriam later wrote,

> and when I spoke to him I felt most comfortable. It was as though I was speaking to a rabbi and not a priest of the Catholic faith. He listened to me as I spoke to him of Zionism, my plans for going to Eretz Ylsrael after the war . . . When I left Padre Benedetto, he made a gesture that I have never forgotten. He accompanied me to the door and said that he would bless me as is customary in Judaism. He placed his two hands on my head and made a blessing. . . . When we parted he said to me: "Continue to be a good Jewess!" That was the first time I had ever had a conversation with a priest and I said to myself: "He is a good priest."[25]

Many other refugees from Saint-Martin-Vésubie who had fled on foot to the area around Valdieri and Borgo San Dalmazzo but who made their way to Rome slightly later than those from Saint-Gervais benefited from the Hungarian papers that couriers like Sidie Templer Shytoltz and Miriam Löwenwirth carried north at such great personal risk. Charles Roman, originally from Vienna, immigrated to France with his mother, Marianne, in 1938. The two were sent to Saint-Martin-Vésubie in the spring of 1943 and fled over the Alps to Italy that September. Hiding in the mountains around Valdieri, Marianne obtained from Delasem in Rome not only Hungarian identification cards for herself and her son but also an official document identifying seventeen-year-old Charles as a Hungarian national who had to report to the Hungarian consulate in Rome to be inducted into the army. After all, she could declare truthfully if asked that she had been born in 1900 in what was then Austria-Hungary. With those papers but without speaking a word of Hungarian, mother and son set off for Rome in the spring of 1944. They traveled by train through wartime Italy, escaping German searches in Florence and an Allied bombing raid in Orvieto. In Rome they sought help at the Hotel Salus, which was full. They were referred to the nearby Pensione Haeslin, where Hanna Rawicz had been.[26]

Serena Szabo Gerhard, with her two children, Régine and Jacky, and her niece Rosa Eller, had claims to Hungarian documents roughly similar to those of Miriam Löwenwirth and Charles and Marianne Roman. Serena was born in Vylok, Galicia, in 1911, at a time when that region was part of Austria-Hungary (it became part of Czechoslovakia after the First World War). Also, Serena spoke Hungarian. Following a pattern similar to that of Sidie and Miriam, she had moved from Galicia to Belgium before the war and then, during the conflict, to southeastern France, Saint-Martin-Vésubie, and Valdieri in Italy. Early in 1944, soon after a second German raid on Valdieri on January 7, she and her children and niece traveled to Rome, mostly by hitching rides in German military vehicles. Serena told everyone who asked that her husband, Leopold, was in the Hungarian army, fighting on the side of the Third Reich. In reality, after serving in a military unit associated with the French Foreign Legion fighting against the Germans in May and June 1940, Leopold had nevertheless been arrested by French police in February 1943 and deported to the east, without return.[27]

Upon their arrival in Rome, Serena and her family went straight to the Hotel Salus. "The Hotel Salus seemed huge to me," Jacky wrote in 2003. He was nine years old in 1943. "In reality it was only a little hotel of two stories, as I saw upon returning to Rome a few years ago." The hotel, fronting on a busy but tree-lined square and now painted a pretty pink, still operates. From the Hotel Salus, Serena was sent to the Hungarian consulate, where she had no trouble securing Hungarian identification documents for herself and her family.[28]

Although Hungarian documents were a great help, they were no guarantee of survival. Word leaked out. "Hungarian" refugees were not what they seemed to be. As a result, on March 1, 1944, the Fascist paramilitary Koch band raided the Hotel Salus at midnight, looking for Hungarians with false documents. Padre Benedetto was called to the scene and later recorded that he saw Sorani and Kotnik there too. Some seventeen Jews had been seized on suspicion of possessing false Hungarian documents. Faced with disaster, someone called Viktor Szasz. The Hungarian consul general arrived at the Hotel Salus in a rage. He threatened reprisals against Italian citizens living in Hungary if these refugees were not released. The Fascists left without their prey.[29] The fabrication of false documents continued, but whenever possible, refugees were housed elsewhere. But newcomers kept coming and took their places at the Salus.

Inevitably there were other close calls. Padre Benedetto recalled that Delasem was warned at one point that a hiding place at the convent of the Franciscan Sisters in the via Vicenza had been denounced to the Gestapo. All refugees lodged there had to be moved, with all of their possessions, on a moment's notice. Twice Padre Benedetto was told that individuals arrested by the Germans had given his name under torture, yet nothing came of it. On one occasion Alcide De Gasperi, then active in the resistance and later a Christian Democrat prime minister of Italy (or in other accounts De Gasperi's brother), came in person to warn Padre Benedetto that a warrant for his arrest had been issued. Another time a refugee admitted to an agent at Rome's rationing office that his card was false and that he was not really French. Fortunately the agent was Luigi Charrier, director of the office of rationing for foreigners and a friend of Delasem, who simply kicked him out and told Padre Benedetto to instruct his protégés to be more circumspect. The priest also received several anonymous letters threatening to denounce him and, in one case, demanding twenty thousand lire for silence. Padre Benedetto solved that last problem by going to a friend at police headquarters. The police agent went to the rendezvous with the money, followed by "a certain number of our people, duly instructed on what they had to do," as the priest wrote. The blackmailer, apparently a woman, sensed the trap and disappeared without the money.[30]

TEN

With Stefan Schwamm in Rome

SECURING FUNDS FOR JEWISH RESCUE

IN THE LATE AUTUMN OF 1943, PADRE MARIA BENEDETTO'S position and connections as a Catholic priest were invaluable to Delasem's efforts in yet another way. The Jewish rescue organization in Rome was desperately short of money. It had largely depleted its own local financial reserves, as well as two hundred thousand lire made available by the Union of Italian Jewish Communities at the end of September and six hundred thousand lire sent from its national headquarters in Genoa at the end of October. Another one hundred thousand lire would come from the Union of Italian Jewish Communities in early March 1944, but the total was woefully insufficient to support for eight or nine months what is generally agreed to have been about 2,532 people by May 1944. New sources of funding had to be found. Indeed, as Sorani remembered after the war, "The most difficult and tormenting problem [for Delasem's rescue activities in German-occupied Rome] was always the search for the funds necessary for helping [refugees]."[1]

One source of additional funds was the American Jewish Joint Distribution Committee, based in the United States. But how could the Joint be contacted from behind the German lines, and how could funds be transferred? Padre Benedetto provided the solution by calling again upon his good friend Monsignor Joseph Hérissé. A young American who knew the French monsignor at this time later described him as "a spry, white-haired little man with a sharp wit [who] did not hide his complete support for the Allied cause."[2] As seen in connection with the Donati plan, Monsignor Hérissé lived in Vatican City and was a neighbor of Harold Tittmann, the American chargé d'affaires at the Holy See, whom he introduced to Padre Benedetto in July 1943. Now toward the end of that same year, Padre Benedetto asked Hérissé to take him to Tittmann again. The meeting was successful.[3]

Tittmann relayed Padre Benedetto's request for funds to the Joint by coded telegram in the American diplomatic pouch from the Vatican. Communications were slow and cumbersome, however, and it was not until January 7, 1944, that an affirmative response arrived. The sum of twenty thousand dollars, initially deposited in New York and later transferred to London, was at the disposal of Delasem in Rome. Padre Benedetto was summoned by the British ambassador to the Holy See, Sir Francis Godolphin d'Arcy Osborne, to receive the news. Osborne, wrote the Capuchin priest, asked to see him alone. Much later, probably in the second half of May 1944, just a few weeks before the liberation of Rome, the Joint made another one hundred thousand dollars available. This time Sorani received the news in an undated letter from Lelio Vittorio Valobra, the national president of Delasem, who had escaped to Switzerland in November 1943.[4]

But how was the Joint money to reach Delasem in Rome in January 1944? Dollars could not be sent into wartime northern and central Italy, whose de facto government was fighting on the side of the Third Reich. It was illegal for Italian citizens to hold dollars, much less change them into the lire that Delasem leaders desperately needed to distribute to their protégés. The only hope was to convince trusted Italian non-Jews with extra lire to extend loans on the promise of repayment in dollars after the war at a favorable exchange rate. Such lenders were difficult to find, particularly because they had to be convinced that the deposits in London actually existed. Here again Tittmann and Osborne were helpful. Those two diplomats held the evidence of the Joint's letters of credit.

Now the apartment of Monsignor Hérissé became the site of frequent but highly irregular meetings. At the request of the American and British diplomats, Padre Benedetto initially brought both Sorani and Dante Almansi, president of the Union of Italian Jewish Communities, there to meet them on January 25. Cryptic entries in the priest's notebook indicate that he continued to meet with Tittmann, Osborne, Hérissé, and others every three to five days throughout February to work out the complicated details of the anticipated financial transactions. During this same period, Delasem leaders, especially Renzo Levi, the president of the Roman section, struggled to find potential lenders in Rome. Eventually Sorani and individual lenders, one at a time, visited the same apartment of Monsignor Hérissé at least once a week during the last months of the German occupation. Padre Benedetto accompanied Sorani when he could.

Even getting to those meetings was a remarkable achievement. As the major part of the sovereign and neutral country known as the Holy See, Vatican City was technically off limits for those who did not live or work there. German guards patrolled the border along the famous colonnade surrounding the enormous piazza in front of the Basilica of Saint Peter. Vatican guards, including the Swiss Guard and the Palatine Guard, prevented unauthorized outsiders from entering Vatican City through gates in the walls. Individual worshippers were permitted to attend services in Saint Peter's, but Vatican guards were supposed to prevent them from slipping into Vatican City through inner doors in the basilica itself. Access was possible only if someone with authority living and working within Vatican City vouched for visitors at the points of entry. Apparently Monsignor Hérissé was able to arrange that.

During the meetings of Padre Benedetto, Sorani, and individual lenders in Monsignor Hérissé's apartment, the amounts involved rarely exceeded the lire equivalent of $500 at a time. Individual lenders brought in the lire. They did not receive signed receipts, because they were too dangerous, but Monsignor Hérissé held written evidence of the loans in the safety of his apartment. Sorani then received the money in thousand-lire bills, which he wrapped in a newspaper. He carried these out, as he later wrote, "under the noses of the German guards . . . every time with my heart pounding, because I could always be stopped." He took the money to Padre Benedetto's monastery. But the process was so difficult that it was only possible to advance the lire equivalent of $36,000 of the available $120,000 during the German occupation.[5]

Although two Allied diplomats accredited to the Holy See and a French prelate living within Vatican City helped Padre Benedetto and Sorani borrow lire against deposits of Joint dollars, it is clear that they acted without the sanction of higher Vatican officials. In fact, a Catholic aristocrat who was well connected at the Vatican and willing to help the

Jews of Rome asked the Vatican Secretariat of State in March 1944 to provide essentially the same service – that is, to receive sixteen thousand dollars from the Joint, as would have been possible for a neutral party, and hold the money in a Vatican institution as security for him as he extended an equivalent value in lire to Delasem. Such a system would have been much safer than the one actually used, avoiding the necessity of Sorani and Padre Benedetto passing through Vatican and German security points carrying large amounts of cash. But Secretary of State Cardinal Maglione categorically refused, writing, "I do not intend to give orders or assume responsibility [for receiving and holding dollars from the Joint]. I do not even want to give suggestions."[6] Yet British Foreign Office documents indicate that at this same time a Vatican bank was extending credit in the amount of five million lire to Ambassador Osborne to assist escaped Allied prisoners of war in Rome on a British guarantee of future repayment.[7] Cardinal Maglione, second only to the pope in power and influence at the Vatican, was unwilling to extend this same service to the Jews.

Before Delasem leaders in Rome learned of the second Joint contribution in mid-May 1944, they were desperate for funds. Not only did they need to support their own protégés, but Delasem workers in Florence and elsewhere were also asking for financial aid. Consequently, Padre Benedetto and Stefan Schwamm concocted a mad scheme to travel to Genoa to request more money from the national Delasem headquarters there. The money was available in Genoa. When Lelio Vittorio Valobra had been forced to go underground a few weeks after the onset of the German occupation, he had consigned the organization's funds to Cardinal Pietro Boetto, archbishop of Genoa. Working always with Delasem personnel in hiding, Cardinal Boetto and especially his secretary, a twenty-eight-year-old priest named don Francesco Repetto, took on the dangerous job of preserving lists of Delasem protégés, finding shelter for those in the Genoa area, recruiting other priests and laypersons to help, creating widespread regional rescue networks, and distributing funds to individuals in need. But by the spring of 1944 there was no way to deliver Delasem funds from Genoa to Rome. Raffaele Cantoni, the previous courier, had been arrested, escaped, and fled to Switzerland in

December. Padre Benedetto and Schwamm, brilliant at charming local authorities and fabricating false papers but hardly experienced cloak-and-dagger conspirators, set out to take his place. While in the north they also planned to travel to Milan to inquire about possible escape routes into Switzerland for their refugees, who were growing increasingly nervous and restive.

The result was exactly what might have been expected. There was no longer any regular train service between Rome and Florence, and automobiles were rarely available. Civilians were normally not authorized to travel by automobile, and in any case automobiles could usually operate only at night because of Allied bombardments. Padre Benedetto and Schwamm set about solving these problems with their usual panache. Captain Bruto Girardi, Schwamm's old friend in the Italian African Police who had helped earlier with residence permits, had access to a German automobile. Or more correctly, as Schwamm wrote later, he "had an automobile that, let's speak frankly, he had stolen from the Germans." For authorization to use it, the two went to see Hans Wolf de Salis of the International Red Cross, who had already helped them on numerous occasions. From de Salis they obtained a letter of recommendation in Italian and German asking all authorities to help them on their mission of visiting French prisoners. Schwamm, it will be recalled, was carrying papers identifying him as French Red Cross worker Bernard Lioré. With de Salis's letter, Schwamm went to the German military command, declared that he had a private car, and received a permit to drive it.[8]

Years later Stefan Schwamm remembered that as Padre Benedetto, Captain Girardi, and he were preparing to leave Rome about 10:00 PM on April 12, the priest showed up with a large basket of bread and fruit for the journey. He solemnly explained to the others that the supplies were normally intended for the poor, but that in the present case, "The poor – it's us!"[9] The episode, so slight but so revealing, casts light on the personalities of Padre Benedetto and Stefan Schwamm and goes far to explain why the two became such fast friends. They shared a roguish sense of humor and a love for dramatic adventure. These characteristics remain apparent in Schwamm's many postwar letters to Padre Benedetto, but they are usually less clear in the priest himself. His profession demanded a restrained and dignified comportment, serious, scholarly, and contemplative. He was indeed all of those things. But he had another dimension, a cleverness, imagination, and love of action that made him a fine soldier in the First World War and a superb rescuer of refugees in the Second. He effectively straddled two worlds.

The three travelers reached Siena on the morning of April 13. Because it was not safe to travel in daylight, they spent the day in Siena and set out again when it was dark. After arriving in Florence an hour or two later, Schwamm again took de Salis's letter of recommendation to the local German military command. To their delight, the travelers were billeted in what Padre Benedetto called the best hotel in Florence, the Grand Hotel Baglioni. There they found themselves surrounded by a friendly group of German army staff officers. With German help they were even able to obtain gasoline to continue their journey. They left Florence toward the end of the next day, arriving in Bologna two and a half hours later. After spending the night there with a Protestant pastor, they finally reached Milan on April 15. In Milan they separated, going off to inquire from different sources about escape routes to Switzerland. Among other places, Padre Benedetto visited the Swiss consulate.

Two days later Padre Benedetto and Schwamm met in a restaurant to compare notes. Schwamm arrived with the name of a local contact, a woman who had agreed to help them. He telephoned her from the restaurant, and she told him to wait there; she would meet him in fifteen minutes. While they were waiting, an apparent civilian appeared at the door of the restaurant – not the woman Schwamm had called, but an unknown man, who summoned Schwamm by his false name, Lioré. Padre Benedetto watched while Schwamm went to the door, showed his papers to the man, and returned to the table for his coat. Very pale, he was able to murmur to the priest, "I am under arrest." Padre Benedetto later learned from local partisans with informants among the police that when Schwamm had telephoned his local contact, the police were in the process of searching her apartment. He had not spoken to her, but to a female police agent.

As soon as Schwamm departed, Padre Benedetto left the restaurant, picked up their luggage at the hotel where they had deposited it, told the doorman at the hotel that he was returning to Rome, and went to hide at the local Capuchin monastery. Fifteen minutes after he left the restaurant, the police, having searched Schwamm and found the letter of recommendation from Rome, went to the hotel to seize his traveling companion. The doorman relayed the information that the priest was returning to Rome. Since there were no trains that night, the police went to the station early the next morning to search the first train leaving for Florence. Of course they did not find him.

Stefan Schwamm was confined for three months in the abysmal prison of San Vittore in Milan, where his Jewishness was not discovered. As a result, he was deported in July 1944 not to Auschwitz but to a labor camp at Laband, not far away. "I organize myself as well as possible and learn a little Russian with other prisoners," he later wrote with his characteristic aplomb. Understandably, Padre Benedetto was deeply concerned about him. On June 21, 1944, he recorded in his notebook that he had received a visit in Rome from Schwamm's parents. They must have been without a place to live, for two days later he wrote that he was going to refer Schwamm's mother to a Protestant pastor who had been helping his group. Padre Benedetto's notebook entries for 1945 were much sparser than in 1944, but on September 9 he wrote with great relief, "Return of Stefan Schwamm (Bernard Lioré); I accompany him to [his family] in the via del Babuino." Schwamm had been liberated by the Russians in January 1945, but it had taken him eight months to get home by way of Cracow, Warsaw, Czestochowa, Bucharest, Vienna, and Belgrade. He had no documents under his real name.[10]

After Schwamm's arrest on April 17, Padre Benedetto remained in Milan for about a week to try to discover his friend's whereabouts, if only to be able to inform his parents and wife in Rome. After learning where he was, he sent a package of linens to the prison, taken from Schwamm's luggage back at the hotel. With that, Schwamm understood that the priest was still free. On April 24 Padre Benedetto took a train from Milan to Genoa, for Captain Girardi had already left with the car. In Genoa he went to see Cardinal Boetto and don Francesco Repetto in order to collect the Delasem funds that had been promised to him. He returned to Milan by train on May 6 and took another train for Florence the following day. From Florence he left for Rome in the evening of May 10, apparently by car, and arrived in Rome at 6:00 A M the next morning. He had secured one million lire from Delasem headquarters in Genoa.[11]

With that amount plus a contribution of twenty thousand Swiss francs from the Union of Swiss Jewish Communities, sent by Valobra from Zurich at the end of April in the form of two checks written to the Italian delegate to the International Red Cross, the Delasem organization in Rome was able to support its protégés in hiding until the city was liberated on June 4.[12]

After the war the sources of Delasem funds in Rome were the subject of much confusion. On February 25, 1961, Father Robert Leiber, a German Jesuit who was Pius XII's private secretary, advisor, and friend throughout his papacy, published an article that drastically misstated the facts. Father Leiber understood correctly that the national Delasem organization in Genoa had turned its funds over to Cardinal Boetto for distribution to its Jewish clients. But he claimed that some five million lire from those funds were delivered to Padre Benedetto by a papal nuncio in Rome to be distributed among the Jews there. Father Leiber also stated that Padre Benedetto distributed some twenty-five million lire "with the help furnished to him by Pius XII." According to Leiber, some of that money had come to the pope from what he called the Catholic Refugees Committee in the United States, as well as from American Jews.[13]

Delasem leaders Lelio Vittorio Valobra, Renzo Levi, and Settimio Sorani were quick to deny these claims. In a letter to the editor published in the Italian Jewish weekly *Israel* on June 8, they explained that Padre Benedetto not only received just one million lire from Delasem in Genoa rather than the five million claimed by Father Leiber, but he also never received twenty-five million lire from the pope, or anything remotely close to it. They pointed out that a large part of the money distributed by Delasem and by Padre Benedetto to Jewish refugees in Rome came instead from Roman non-Jews who were willing to lend lire on the promise of being repaid in dollars guaranteed by the American Jewish Joint Distribution Committee, as noted earlier.[14]

A month later, on July 6, 1961, Padre Benedetto's letter to the editor was also published in *Israel*. The priest began by explaining that he had received one, but certainly not five, million lire of the national Delasem money that had been entrusted to Cardinal Boetto in Genoa. He had not received it from a papal nuncio in Rome, however, but had collected it personally by visiting Genoa in April 1944. He added that much smaller sums had previously been delivered to Delasem representatives in Rome, again not by a papal nuncio but by a Jewish Delasem courier whose name he could not remember and who was arrested in December 1943, escaped, and fled to Switzerland. This was a reference to Raffaele Cantoni. Second, still addressing the issue of a papal nuncio, Padre Benedetto declared that he *had* received ninety-eight thousand lire from Monsignor Antonio Riberi of the Pontifical Commission for Refugee Assistance, but only *after* the liberation of Rome. Riberi was named as papal nuncio to China in July 1946, and Padre Benedetto was suggesting that this may have been the reason why Leiber evoked that title. The ninety-eight thousand lire obtained from Riberi, specifically intended for Jews who had converted to Catholicism, was not for Delasem. It was also a far smaller sum than the five million lire, not to mention the twenty-five million, claimed by Father Leiber.

In an effort to be gracious to Father Leiber, Padre Benedetto then explained that he had reported to Riberi in January 1945 that Delasem had distributed twenty-five million lire in Rome during the war and that Father Leiber must have seen the report and misunderstood the provenance of those funds. In his same letter to the editor, Padre Benedetto stated clearly that the money distributed by Delasem during the German occupation of Rome "had not been given by the Vatican." He then added unambiguously, "I and the true heads of Delasem did not receive any sum from the Vatican" during the occupation. On the contrary, he recalled, toward the end of September 1943 he and a small group of Roman Jewish leaders had gone to Monsignor Riberi (who was not yet involved with the Pontifical Commission for Refugee Assistance, which was founded in March 1944) to ask for a Vatican loan. "I still remember Monsignor Riberi's precise answer," he wrote. "'The Vatican does not make loans; if it has it, it gives it,' and we left with nothing."[15]

Padre Benedetto went on in his letter to the editor to describe the two letters of credit sent by the Joint for twenty thousand dollars and one hundred thousand dollars, and the complicated negotiations with the American and British diplomats accredited to the Holy See to help process loans in lire from Italian non-Jews. At one point, he wrote, the British Ambassador Osborne had asked him if he had permission from Vatican officials to do what he was doing. Osborne may have understood that the pope frowned on the fabrication of false documents and other illegal methods. Padre Benedetto informed the ambassador that during his private audience with Pius XII in July 1943, "I received his blessing for any future new activity in favor of the persecuted Jews."[16] The pope gave that blessing before the Germans occupied Rome and before Padre Benedetto was engaged in clandestine activities. During his meeting with Osborne in February 1944, Padre Benedetto could not evoke any more recent and precise papal encouragement. Indeed, we have seen that Vatican officials close to the secretary of state reported their disapproval of his activities and their insistence that he be more moderate and prudent.

Padre Benedetto concluded his letter to the editor of *Israel* by writing that the only supplies his group received from the Vatican consisted of a single delivery to his monastery of three hundred kilograms of flour, which was transformed into bread and distributed to Delasem's protégés. Indeed, he had recorded that delivery in his wartime notebook on February 8.[17] While the Capuchin never mentioned any other contribution from the Vatican, Sorani wrote vaguely in 1983 that Delasem leaders had *tried* to obtain a donation of clothing from Monsignor Riberi. Sorani did not mention food or money, nor did he say in that report whether the clothing was actually received. In his earlier report of May 16, 1944, however, he also referred to the request for clothing and wrote tersely, "Despite the promises, nothing has been granted as of today." On the other hand, he wrote on July 19, 1966, that Delasem *had* received some clothing from Monsignor Riberi. Presumably that donation occurred after May 16, in the last weeks of the German occupation, or, more probably, after the liberation of Rome. Sorani never mentioned receiving money.[18]

While contributions from the Vatican did not go directly to Padre Benedetto and the Delasem group in Rome, then, many of the refugees hiding in convents, monasteries, and Catholic boarding schools *did* benefit from Vatican deliveries made directly to those institutions, intended for whoever was living there. Also, on May 30 Ambassador Osborne reported to London that the Vatican was making some one hundred thousand meals a day available to the Roman poor for a price of one lira per person.[19] Some of Delasem's refugees hiding in apartments may have been able to participate in this program. Still, there is no evidence to warrant the claim of an official at the Vatican Secretariat of State on January 9, 1944, that his colleagues had been giving Padre Benedetto money and foodstuffs for Jewish refugees since the onset of the German occupation. Monsignor Riberi, the official alleged, was in charge of the matter.[20] If such a claim were true, it is inconceivable that Padre Benedetto and Sorani would have denied it. Padre Benedetto devoted his life to his church and respected the pope and his assistants. At war's end both he and Sorani were eager to advance the cause of Jewish-Catholic dialogue, a cause that would have been furthered by evidence of Vatican aid to the Jews. Yet both men recorded that they received almost no help. Years later Padre Benedetto read that Vatican official's claim of January 9, 1944, when it was published in volume 9 of the *Actes et documents du Saint Siège relatifs à la seconde guerre mondiale* (ADSS) in 1975. He commented wryly, "They [the Vatican official] also speak of [providing] foodstuffs [to his group]. To whom would they have delivered them?"[21]

Padre Benedetto corrected many other assertions and errors regarding his activities in volume 9 of the ADSS. At the end of his remarks, he summarized as follows:

> To read the totality of these observations, one would think that the editors [of ADSS] wanted to present my activities [on behalf of the Jews] as a dependency of the Vatican. Certain assertions or certain insertions that I have had to contest would lead to that interpretation. But it is not exact.
>
> I received no mission from the Vatican, because I was unknown there. The [diplomatic representative] of the United States and the ambassador of Britain had taken refuge there [in Vatican City]. We went to find them secretly . . . It was neither from a spirit of independence nor from a spirit of indiscipline. I was in no way a habitué of the Secretariat of State. My Jewish companions still less. The Vatican was for us like a mountain. We were in a hurry. As an intermediary, Monsignor Hérissé was a godsend for us.[22]

Padre Benedetto did not say that Vatican officials had refused to help. But neither had they helped, and he wanted to make that clear.

As the funds for Jews in hiding trickled in during the winter of 1943–1944, the problem of distributing them became ever more difficult. Unfortunately, little is known about this most dangerous aspect of the rescue work. Sorani later recorded that Delasem's leaders met regularly, usually in the afternoons, at Padre Benedetto's monastery in the via Sicilia. Social workers who helped with distributions did not usually come to those meetings, and all Delasem workers never came together at the same time. Social workers were assigned to groups of no more than ten refugees, for whom they were responsible but about whom only they knew the details. They met their protégés outside their hiding places, usually in the streets, in parks, or in cafés. They chose a different assembly place for every meeting. Individual Delasem leaders dealt with specific social workers, giving them the supplies they needed. Thus no single person knew too much.[23]

Again according to Sorani, financial subsidies to individual refugees that had initially been twenty and then forty lire a day had to be increased to fifteen hundred lire a month in March 1944 and then to twenty-four hundred lire in April as the cost of living soared. Apparently that monthly subsidy was less for individuals in large families, presumably on the theory that living expenses were lower per person for those sharing their room and board with others. Italian Jews and those who had arrived in Rome before September 8, 1943, also received less, because they had had time to get to know the city and find reasonable lodgings. But in nearly every case the subsidies were inadequate. Most refugees had difficulty supplementing rationed food supplies on the black market, for prices there were beyond their reach. Obtaining adequate clothing was also a problem. Refugees had arrived with no warm clothes, and it can be cold and damp in Rome in the winter. But clothing was expensive and in short supply.

To fill the gaps, Delasem tried to collect and distribute food, clothing, and medicine as needed, along with financial subsidies. They were greatly aided by packages from the International Red Cross. Sorani later recalled that during the most difficult weeks just before liberation, when it was too dangerous for Delasem workers to go to the offices of the Red Cross, the packages were dropped off for them on the corner of the Corso Trieste and the via Nomentana. He was immensely grateful. "Apart from the material aid," he noted, "what had even more value was the comfort, the cordiality, the understanding that never failed." He also noted that a refugee named Dr. Leon Silbert and a group of other doctors provided medical care, with expenses paid by Delasem.[24]

According to survivors of the period, however, subsidies were not always handed out by social workers in public places as Sorani described it. We have seen that Padre Benedetto himself visited the convent where Esther and Rachel Fallmann and their mother were hiding to check on them and deliver food and money. On the other hand, Hanna Rawicz, placed with her parents in an apartment by Padre Benedetto, recalls that from time to time she and her father went directly to the priest's monastery in the via Sicilia to get money for their room and board. They tried to go as infrequently as possible so as not to take advantage of the situation. Jakob Rawicz, a commercial designer by training, tried to earn a little money in Rome as an artist. He made drawings of the city and sold a few. He also found a job drawing decorative features for handbags. He and Hanna took long walks around the city, which, she says, "my father loved, in spite of everything. Maybe it was his artistic background."

Despite the momentous achievement of obtaining funding from Genoa, Padre Benedetto returned to Rome on May 11, 1944, to find his people in chaos. For him and for many refugees, this was the most dangerous and difficult time of the entire German occupation, and the most tragic. Several months earlier Schwamm had befriended two young non-Jewish Frenchmen who had been conscripted either into the German army or into the German labor organization Todt (reports vary). They had deserted, found their way to Rome, and come to Delasem for help in securing false documents. The two men had lived in Schwamm's house and come to know him well. Sometime while Schwamm was away in the north with Padre Benedetto, perhaps emboldened by his absence, the two men had betrayed the rescue network to the German police for money. As a result, Aron Kasztersztein, one of the five leaders of the Delasem group along with Padre Benedetto, Schwamm, Sorani, and Giuseppe Levi, was arrested at the Pensione Amalfi, where he was living with false papers under the name of Ceslav Kapciae, on or about May 1, 1944. His second child, a boy, had been born in Rome just two months before.

The loss of Kasztersztein was an enormous blow to the group, for in addition to being a dear friend, most witnesses testify that he was the brains of the operation – the man with the best ideas. He specialized in helping partisans and escaped British, Canadian, American, Russian, and Polish prisoners of war, as well as Italian and foreign Jews, to locate escape networks to Allied-held territory.[25] He also knew much about Delasem's leadership and operations. After Kaszterszteın's arrest Padre Benedetto left his monastery and went into hiding until the liberation of Rome. Sorani and, presumably, Levi were already in clandestine residences. Delasem leaders also hastened to move many of the refugees still living in the Hotel Salus to private apartments or institutions of the Church. Among those moved were Helen and Jakob Dresdner, whose son Abraham and their eight other children had already been hidden in the Istituto Pio XI, for the boys, and a convent for the girls. For the last few weeks of the German occupation of Rome, Helen and Jakob were lodged in a small room in the bell tower of a nearby Catholic church. Others went to the private residence of Protestant pastor Anselmo Ammenti, who had already been helpful on numerous occasions.

Aron Kaszterszteın was held in a prison in Rome and then sent to the Italian internment camp of Fossoli, near Modena, from where he was deported to Auschwitz on June 26, 1944. At least 347 Jews from his convoy were gassed upon arrival, but he was one of 180 prisoners to have been admitted to the camp and one of 35 to have survived. He seems to have been moved to Buchenwald when the Russians approached Auschwitz in January 1945, and he returned to Paris later that same year.[26]

Aron Kaszterszteın was not the only victim of the informers. The two Frenchmen also gave the Gestapo Schwamm's name – Schwamm, who had taken them in when they were fugitives – and German agents went to his house in Rome while he was in prison in the north. There they threatened to kill his eight-year-old daughter unless his wife, relatively safe because she was not Jewish, gave them the names and addresses of refugees in hiding. Schwamm only alluded to this terrible story in his postwar testimony, providing no details. Apparently Schwamm's wife knew no details of his work and did not talk. The little girl was spirited away to safety by an individual named De Vial at the French embassy to the Holy See, who had been a regular friend of the Delasem group.[27]

Apparently the two informers had made it their business to assemble details about other refugees in hiding. Also, once the police interrogated the first few refugees, they were sometimes able to discover more. As a result, dozens of Delasem protégés were arrested in the last weeks of the German occupation of Rome. The details are unclear. Sorani reported on May 16, 1944, that about twenty refugees had been seized because of the informers. After the war he declared that the total number of losses during the nine months of the German occupation was sixty-two, most of whom were arrested after May 1. Also after the war, Padre Benedetto wrote that "about fifty" protégés were arrested because of the informers and claimed that "without this sad incident, everyone would have been saved." This last may have been a slight exaggeration. However, May was the worst month for Delasem in Rome, and the losses were hard to bear. Sorani stressed that some arrested refugees were subsequently released because of intervention by the International Red Cross or the protecting consulates. Other refugees, he said, were deported but survived. But Sorani was occasionally inaccurate. He even seemed to have believed that Kasztersztein had not been deported but had "succeeded in fleeing" and made it to Paris.[28]

Despite efforts to move them out, an unknown number of the Jews arrested as a result of the informers were caught at the Hotel Salus and the Pensione Haeslin. Charles Roman is one of the few surviving witnesses of the Haeslin raid. He and his mother were staying in a maid's room behind the kitchen when the police arrived there. The security agents searched the main section and the kitchen but never looked in the back room.

Other victims of the informers were living in private apartments at the time. One of these was Hanna Rawicz's father. A month or two previously, Hanna had been moved, for greater safety, from the apartment where she lived with her parents to a French convent in the viale Regina Margherita. She is not sure if Padre Benedetto arranged this, but she thinks he probably did. At the convent she learned all the prayers in Latin and participated in the services. Her parents visited her regularly. On the last visit before the Allies arrived, Hanna's mother came to the convent alone. She told Hanna that her father was busy, but the girl heard her friends whispering that the father of "someone" had been arrested. She later learned that the Germans had come to the apartment for her father on May 17, 1944, two and a half weeks before liberation. It was never clear why they did not take her mother also. Jakob Rawicz, who so loved the

city of Rome, was sent to the Italian concentration camp of Fossoli on
May 22. On August 1 he was among the last group of Jews deported from
that camp as it prepared to close. Because the bridges over the Po had
been destroyed, there was no train service to Verona, where prisoners
were to be transferred to another train for Auschwitz. Therefore they
traveled to the Po in trucks and crossed it in boats on a beautiful clear
night under a full moon. In the confusion, several prisoners escaped.
Jakob Rawicz was among them.

Without help, escapees without documents and money had little
chance of eluding the authorities for long. Jakob was recaptured on August 5 at Melara, near Rovigo, and imprisoned in Rovigo until October.
Sent then to a holding camp in Bolzano-Gries, he was deported on December 14 to Flossenburg, where he died on March 31, 1945, just a few
weeks before the end of the war.[29]

Another victim of the French informers was forty-six-year-old Oser
Warszawski, a Polish writer of Yiddish who had immigrated to Paris in
1923 and become an important part of the French cultural scene. With his
wife, Marie, Warszawski fled to the south of France during the winter of
1941–1942. In the spring or summer of 1943 the couple was sent to supervised residence in Saint-Gervais by the occupying Italians, and when the
Italians withdrew from France that September, Oser and his wife made
their way to Rome. There they met Padre Benedetto, who helped them
find an apartment and provided false documents and monthly subsidies.
Oser was arrested in the apartment on May 17, the same day as Hanna's
father. Marie's real name was on the list, but somehow her false papers
protected her. Like Jakob Rawicz, Oser Warszawski was sent to Fossoli
at the end of May, from where he was deported to Auschwitz. He died in
the Nazi death camp on October 10, 1944.[30]

Padre Benedetto and the other Delasem leaders were devastated by
the losses in May 1944. On the other hand, they were justifiably proud
of certain specific achievements of the entire nine-month period of the
German occupation. At least twice, with help from friends in positions of
authority, they were able to get arrested Jews released. On another occasion Aron Kasztersztein successfully delivered a baby when women hiding in the same small hotel were too terrified to come out of their rooms
to help. But Padre Benedetto and his Delasem colleagues were aware

that many of their achievements were due in part to the broad support they enjoyed among much of the non-Jewish population. As discussed earlier, the regular, nonpolitical Roman police were often sympathetic, as were many bureaucrats in offices for foreigners throughout the city. Individuals in many embassies and consulates accredited to Italy or to the Holy See, including those of Switzerland, Belgium, France, Poland, Sweden, Portugal, Hungary, and Romania, were supportive. And men and women of the Church were willing to open their doors to refugees. Others helped in other ways. Invaluable, for example, was the help from the Salvatorian Fathers, whose monastery was contiguous to Vatican City and whose father superior, Father Pancrazio Pfeiffer, was a German priest who served as liaison between the German occupying forces and the Vatican. The Salvatorians often learned of pending Nazi raids and warned the targets.[31]

The rescue work of Delasem in Rome during the German occupation did not always run smoothly. We have seen that some lives were lost. Subsidies were often insufficient, causing hardship and complaints among the stressed, unhappy refugees. With too much time on their hands and too little security, freedom, comfort, money, food, clothing, and medicine, refugees inevitably grew demoralized and restive. Those not from France complained that Padre Benedetto's protégés received favored treatment, a condition that Delasem tried hard to avoid. Toward the end of the occupation, some refugees were angling for a reorganization of Delasem so that they could have a voice in the agency's decision-making process. But these problems cannot detract from the overwhelming accomplishment of Padre Benedetto and his Jewish partners in rescue. Together they had saved the lives of at least twenty-five hundred men, women, and children, most of them refugees without resources in a nation controlled by Nazis determined to destroy them.

ELEVEN

After the Liberation
of Rome

"I SPENT THE NIGHT AT THE FIGLIUOLI," PADRE BENEDETTO
wrote in his notebook about the night of June 3–4, 1944. He could not
stay at his monastery, because he was still in hiding. "An uproar until
midnight. The Allies enter Rome." Settimio Sorani, writing later, was
equally terse about the momentous liberation of the Eternal City. "Finally, on Sunday June 4 (13 *Sivan* 5704) the first Allied troops entered
Rome," he noted, "followed after a brief interval by the *chajalim* [the
Jewish soldiers of the Palestinian Brigade]."[1] Neither man recorded his
personal emotions on that day, but they must have been overwhelmed
with joy and relief. For them, if not yet for Italians in the north, the war
was over and their protégés were safe.

Sorani was more eloquent when describing the first public service at
the central synagogue following the liberation. "On Thursday, 8 June,"
he remembered,

> there was a ceremony at the Temple that was packed with people overjoyed to
> find each other again but dismayed by the absence of so many of our brethren.
> After the religious service, celebrated by Rabbi David Panzieri, I spoke of the
> *Tevà*. I became very emotional, I don't remember what I said; I remember
> only that many eyes were wet with tears. I was followed by Padre Benedetto,
> who began by saying that he regretted that he did not belong to the People of
> Israel for whom he had such a liking and whom he had tried to help with all his
> strength.[2]

In his notebook entry for June 8, Padre Benedetto also mentioned
the service. "Ceremony at the synagogue," he wrote in his usual com-
pact style. "Sorani invites me. 9:00 A M. Two rabbis . . . Sorani spoke . . .
The rabbis spoke, I spoke. Applause, kisses." He added that he visited

several of his protégés in the afternoon. In later references to that first postliberation synagogue service, however, the Capuchin priest was more emotional. In a letter to his "dear friend," probably Joseph Bass, in February 1945, he wrote of it: "I said a few words [and was] applauded before and after in an indescribable manner. Everyone came to shake my hand, they gave me an ovation at the exit, they called me the Father of the Jews – a name that I have kept and of which I am proud." And in another description, in 1948, he wrote of his part in the ceremony: "Thundering applause. I share the sentiments of everyone present, mixtures of joy and sorrow, because if the liberation is a fact, many are weeping for the victims, and the deportees are suffering in a distant land. More than 2,000 Roman Jews have been taken away." Writing in this case for a collection of testimonies by members of French religious orders who had saved Jews during the Holocaust, Padre Benedetto did not record that he had said he regretted not belonging to the Jewish people. Instead he wrote that he had declared, "I love the Jews with all my heart."[3]

A legend persists that after the liberation of Rome, no one could find the key to open the central synagogue. Someone thought to ask Padre Benedetto, who allegedly knew exactly where to find it. He was thus the first person to enter the temple after the German occupation. Another version of the story relates that this occurred on the morning of the first postliberation service. In their reports after the war, neither Sorani nor Padre Benedetto mentioned this incident. Some have traced it to Elio Toaff, who became the chief rabbi of Rome in 1951. On March 14, 1984, however, in his acceptance speech during the ceremony in which he received the rosette of an *officier* in the French Legion of Honor, Padre Benedetto related the story, evoking appreciative chuckles from his audience (fig. 12). He then explained, "I must say that the Italians have a vivid imagination. I never had the key in my pocket; I never had the key to the synagogue; I was not the first to enter [after liberation]. But I was there!" While it is only a legend, then, the story is indicative of the high regard many in Rome had for the Capuchin priest whom they now fondly called "the Father of the Jews." But to Padre Benedetto the story meant something more. Later in his speech in 1984, he declared about that day, "That a Capuchin priest, that a Catholic, spoke in the great synagogue of Rome was to begin that Judeo-Christian rapprochement that we are trying to realize now. And for which we are always trying to do more, in peace, in concord and in truth."[4]

In the months following the liberation of Rome, Padre Benedetto attended many other ceremonies and commemorations. Some had nothing to do with the Jews, as, for example, several receptions at the French embassy in the Palazzo Farnese to honor visiting dignitaries. These included one on June 30 for General Charles de Gaulle. Of the ceremonies concerning the Jews, a few were held in institutions of the Church. One of these was a commemorative mass at the convent of Notre Dame de Sion to mark the first anniversary of the German roundup of Roman Jews on October 16, 1943. Padre Benedetto noted that he spoke at that service. Most of the postliberation events that Padre Benedetto attended, however, were organized by Roman Jews. On June 22, for example, he was invited to a meeting at a synagogue in the via Cesare Balbo, where, he wrote in his notebook, "they applauded me." On November 1 he attended another ceremony to commemorate the anniversary of the Balfour Declaration, the pledge of British support for a Jewish national home in Palestine in 1917. He noted that he spoke at that event and was again applauded.[5]

On December 31, 1944, New Year's Eve, Padre Benedetto attended yet another Jewish-sponsored ceremony that seems to have been as moving as the one in the central synagogue on June 8. This event was intended not only to honor him but also to thank the Capuchin general minister for permitting Padre Benedetto to do what he did for the Jews and for allowing the Capuchin monastery in Rome to be used as a base of rescue activities. Gratitude was also expressed to a number of other Capuchin priests and brothers who had assisted in the rescue efforts. The general minister was unable to attend the ceremony, an absence that unfortunately remains unexplained. Representing him was Père Calliste Lopinot, whom we saw in chapter 7 as a Capuchin priest ministering to Jews in the Italian concentration camp of Ferramonti-Tarsia between 1940 and 1943. In his notebook Padre Benedetto wrote: "I go to the Jewish club with P.[Père or Padre] Callisto [sic], P. Balduino, P. Arcangelo, F.[Frère or Frate] Basilio. Speakers: 1) Paperman; 2) myself; 3) Signora Mandel; 4) Padre Callisto; 5) Outzekhowski, who presented me with a Bible; 6) singing [illegible]; 7) myself."

Again, Padre Benedetto was more eloquent in his account written in 1948. He explained that the "Jewish club" consisted of a committee of foreign Jews who met in the Albergo Raimondo and conceived of the project of honoring him on New Year's Eve. Writing in French rather than in the Italian of his notebook, he referred to Padre Balduino as Père Beaudoin, who had replaced him during what he called his "famous" trip to Milan. Père Archange, he explained, was a Yugoslavian priest who had been involved in helping his compatriots, perhaps not all of them Jewish, while Frère Basile was "the doorman [at the Capuchin monastery] known by all, whose patience had certainly been rudely tested." Padre Benedetto wrote that he received a Bible during the ceremony, signed by everyone present. He then reproduced in their entirety the speech of thanks given by Outzekhowski and a poem by Claire Schnabel Mandel, which was set to music and sung by the refugee children. He did not identify Outzekhowski, but we have seen Claire as Clara, the recently married refugee who had traveled from Saint-Gervais to Rome by train because she was suffering from injuries caused by French police who kicked her in the abdomen during her pregnancy. Now she wrote and the children sang of Padre Benedetto. Among other verses were these words: "It is he who encouraged us, it is he who protected us . . . He cared for our housing and for our food supplies, for the care of the children . . . He gave us hope for a better future, soothed us in our suffering, and saved the honor of France."[6]

Ceremonies and commemorations could not mask the fact that the first weeks, even months, of freedom found Jews in Rome in great distress. If the entire population of the city suffered from shortages of food, shelter, and medicine, the situation was worse for the Jews. Most had lost family members in addition to homes, possessions, jobs, and savings. Thousands, obliged to live on false papers for the nine months of German occupation, were now without legal identities and unable to register for ration cards and public subsidies. After going underground during the occupation, local and national Jewish community organizations needed time to reestablish themselves. Delasem's services were still in desperate demand, and Padre Benedetto remained deeply involved. As he explained in a report to Monsignor Antonio Riberi of the Pontifical Commission for Refugee Assistance on January 24, 1945, "After having had contacts with the Jews every day for nine months [of the German occupation of Rome], I could not break off all assistance from one moment to another after the arrival of the Allies."[7]

In this sad situation some incidents were amusing. Padre Benedetto noted that one day not long after the liberation of Rome, a notice in a Roman newspaper announced, "Next Tuesday, at 3:00 PM, a meeting of the Jews at the synagogue in the via Boncompagni." Since the back door of Padre Benedetto's monastery in the via Sicilia led out to the via Boncompagni, the reference was clear to all who read it. Padre Benedetto chuckled that some other Capuchin priests and friars were aghast, asking him, "Have you also set up a synagogue in our monastery?"[8] He concluded that the notice was some kind of joke, but the responses of some of his confreres suggest that not all of them were amused or pleased with the attention he had focused on their institution.

Although the interior of the monastery was not a public meeting place for the Jews after the liberation, it did serve for at least three weeks at the end of June and early July 1944 as a distribution point for matzos for all who wanted them. The matzos had been supplied to Delasem by Jewish soldiers from the Palestinian Brigade. Delasem workers had no place to store them and no means of distribution, so they asked if Padre Benedetto could do it. The priest readily agreed.[9] Again it is easy to imagine that some of his confreres might not have been happy with the public attention that resulted.

The distribution of matzos, however, was the least of what Padre Benedetto was doing for Jewish refugees during this period. His notebook indicates that he was visiting several individuals every week. On June 21 and 23 he met with the parents of his great friend Stefan Schwamm, who had had no news of their son since his arrest in Milan in April. On August 8 the priest met with the wife of Aron Kasztersztein, who, similarly, had not heard from her husband since his deportation to Auschwitz in June. On June 23 Padre Benedetto also met with Padre Beato Ambord, a Jesuit priest who had directed the German-language transmissions of the Vatican Radio during the war. Padre Benedetto wrote in his notebook that the Jesuit gave him twenty thousand lire to distribute among the Jews. He met that same day with Monsignor Antonio Riberi in what seems to have been an effort to secure a papal audience to appeal for more help for Jewish refugees in Rome. He and Monsignor Riberi discussed a possible papal audience again on July 19, but Padre Benedetto did not note the outcome.[10] The audience never occurred. Padre Benedetto later wrote that he met with Pius XII only once, in July 1943.[11]

In his notebook Padre Benedetto was unclear about the origin and precise purpose of the twenty thousand lire he received from Padre Ambord. He was equally reticent about a similar amount delivered by the same source just ten days later, on July 3. In his report to Monsignor Riberi on January 24, 1945, however, he wrote that in the weeks following the liberation of Rome, he had distributed to Italian and foreign Jews alike money donated by a Jewish man who had converted to Catholicism and who wished to remain anonymous. He explained that the money had come to him through Padre Ambord. Padre Benedetto also told Monsignor Riberi that he had received "a little more" from Padre Anton Weber, procurator general of the Pallottine religious order and director since 1942 of the Opera di San Raffaele (St. Raphaelsverein), a German Catholic organization dedicated to helping Jewish converts.[12]

As the weeks passed, the delivery of services to Jews became more organized. As Padre Benedetto explained in his report to Monsignor Riberi, special committees and the appropriate consulates eventually began to help foreign Jews. He did not record his own role in obtaining and distributing some of that help, but in his private notebook he indicated that he spent much of August 1944 trying to secure subsidies for his protégés both from the French embassy and from Jewish and non-Jewish individuals who were in a position to contribute.[13] Meanwhile, Delasem looked after Jews who were not native to Rome while the Jewish Community of Rome cared for Roman Jews. That left foreign and Italian Jews who had been baptized, whose numbers Padre Benedetto did not provide in his report to Riberi. With limited means, Jewish organizations were sometimes reluctant to help converts, while the converts themselves did not want to appeal to Jewish organizations. This issue was partly resolved with time, for Italian authorities in the liberated regions eventually subsidized all refugees, including German Jews, whether they were converts or not. At that point only Italian Jews who had converted were without some source of organized assistance.[14]

To meet the financial needs of those particular converts, Padres Benedetto and Weber sent a written appeal directly to the pope. On September 2, 1944, they explained the special needs of Jews who had converted to Catholicism. They stressed that in most cases this group had been persecuted as ruthlessly as all other Jews. Now, after the liberation of Rome, they had no organization to turn to. Some, especially among the most recent converts, were even considering returning to their former religious identities. The authors emphasized the need for a specific assistance effort for them, operated perhaps through Padre Weber's Opera di San Raffaele, which had done so much before and during the German occupation of Rome to help Jews who had converted. They calculated that about 150,000 lire a month would be required.[15]

Details about Pius XII's response are not clear, but by January 24, 1945, Monsignor Riberi's Pontifical Commission for Refugee Assistance had given Padre Benedetto ninety-eight thousand lire. By that same date the Capuchin had distributed eighty thousand lire. Padre Benedetto wrote that according to his records, he had helped about one hundred "Italian Catholic Jews." He was clearly uncomfortable with this role, however, for he explained that because he was so well known among the Jews, many who were not Catholics also came to him for assistance. He could not refuse those who were truly in need. "It seems to me that this is a way to bring Jews and Christians together," he told Monsignor Riberi, "and it is always hateful to have to say that we make religious distinctions when assisting the needy." He reported that in addition to the one hundred "Italian Catholic Jews," he had also given subsidies to about twenty "Jews," by which he meant those who remained Jewish in their culture or religion. He added that he did not issue regular monthly subsidies but gave out special grants, usually no more than five hundred lire at a time, according to need.[16] Monsignor Riberi's opinion of all this is unknown.

More than financial grants, Padre Benedetto poured his substantial energies into a series of public lectures on the Old Testament that he gave every three weeks, beginning on October 8, 1944. At first the lectures were delivered at the convent of Notre Dame de Sion in Rome, but later, to reach a wider audience, they occurred elsewhere throughout the city. "After the persecution passed, at least in Rome," he told Monsignor Riberi,

> I thought it opportune to maintain and consolidate spiritually the drawing to-
> gether of Jews and Christians that had occurred. . . . [Study of the Old Testament]
> is a common ground, I tell them, on which we can meet and meditate together
> on the great religious teachings of the word of God. . . . Despite the distances [to
> travel, within Rome, to attend the lectures], the lack of means of communication,
> the cold and bad weather, a good number of people, both Jews and Catholics, are
> always present, who demonstrate a lively interest in the lectures and in a Jewish-
> Christian drawing together.[17]

Padre Benedetto called his lecture series and the group that attended it "Amicizia ebraico-cristiana," meaning Jewish-Christian Friendship.[18]

Padre Benedetto was not alone among the wartime rescuers of Jews who continued to work for Jewish-Christian reconciliation after the conflict. We have seen that a small handful of men and women of the Church became involved in rescue precisely because they were opposed to antisemitism before 1940. It was only natural that their interest and concern would continue after 1945. Among Catholic rescuers mentioned in this study, Père Pierre Chaillet, Père Roger Braun, and Germaine Ribière in France devoted the rest of their lives to the effort. In Germany, Margarete Sommers and Gertrude Luckner did the same. Protestant rescuers and theologians in this movement were even more numerous. Padre Benedetto and others like him believed that antisemitism was an evil that must be combated and that commonalities between Christians and Jews should be emphasized through study of the Old Testament. These convictions were endorsed by the sixty-five Jewish, Roman Catholic, Orthodox, and Protestant clerics and laypersons who met at the International Emergency Conference on Anti-Semitism in Seelisberg, Switzerland, from July 30 to August 5, 1947. Pressure for change was slowly building.[19]

Unfortunately the idea of enhancing Jewish-Catholic dialogue and understanding did not meet with universal approval among the leaders of the Church in those pre–Second Vatican Council years. Deeply embedded fears persisted that prolonged personal social contact with anyone outside the Catholic faith, including Protestants, Jews, and other non-Catholics, would confuse or compromise Catholic laypersons. Such contact was favored only if it involved efforts to obtain conversions. In addition, the Holy See did not encourage Catholics to apply critical historical methods to the study of scripture, but instead promoted the reading of scripture solely according to the teaching and interpretation of the Church.[20] Some conservative churchmen were also uneasy with any undue emphasis on the religious roots shared by Jews and Christians, and feared that a focus only on the Old Testament would detract attention from the New Testament, hamper possible conversions, and promote indifferentism, the heretical belief that all religions are equally true and valid. These ecclesiastics also refused to entertain suggestions that traditional Church teachings about the Jewish people could be altered. Since Padre Benedetto challenged all of those concepts, he was often called upon to defend what he was doing.

In a report to an unidentified Vatican official on December 4, 1944, several weeks before the communication with Monsignor Riberi cited above, Padre Benedetto described his work among the Jews in a manner designed to please conservative Catholics. In Marseille between 1940 and 1943, he explained, he had instructed in the Catholic faith and baptized a number of Jews. He had also "had the opportunity to help materially both converted and non-converted Jews." He stressed that he had spoken with Pius XII in July 1943 "in the name of the Jews of France." That audience, he implied, gave his work with the Jews an enhanced legitimacy, although it is difficult to see how that could have been the case. After describing his rescue work in Rome with Delasem, Padre Benedetto also emphasized the immense "gratitude [of the Jews in Rome] to the Holy Father." He added that after the liberation of Rome, Pius XII had met with two leaders of the Roman Jewish Community, Chief Rabbi Israel Zolli and the lawyer Carlo Alberto Ottolenghi, and had agreed to grant a public audience to all the Jews of Rome later, when circumstances permitted. That public audience did not occur, but Padre Benedetto intended that all of these references to the pope should imply official approval of his own work among the Jews. He also declared that he was distributing funds put at his disposition by the Vatican, without saying that those funds were meant for converted Jews only.[21]

In explaining his lectures on the Old Testament to this Vatican official in December 1944, however, Padre Benedetto also issued a challenge to conservative Catholics generally. Using virtually the same words that he would include in his report to Monsignor Riberi on January 24, 1945, he wrote, "I thought it opportune to maintain and consolidate spiritually the drawing together that occurred between Jews and Christians during the period of the recent persecution." He added that for those who attended his lectures the results would be "a greater union with God, and then as a natural and happy consequence a greater union between Jews and Christians, to combat every form of antisemitism, to arrive at a better understanding among everyone and to promote every good work." He declared that his lectures stressed the many commonalities between Judaism and Christianity, concepts, as he put it, "of the creation of the universe, of man formed in the image of God, of monogamy, the sanctity of marriage, the unity of the species, of the human family and thus of universal brotherhood."[22] In writing thus he was deliberately ignoring the fact that "a greater union between Jews and Christians" and an emphasis on the many commonalities between Judaism and Christianity were precisely the concepts that made some conservative churchmen uneasy.

Padre Benedetto generally tried to avoid confrontation, however. His two letters of December 4, 1944, and January 24, 1945, suggest that he had been criticized by Church authorities for undue familiarity with the Jews. He understood perfectly that he was treading on delicate ground. "I am well aware of the condemnation of the Friends of Israel [Amici Israel], because I was part of it," he wrote on December 4, referring to the Vatican Holy Office's condemnation and banning on March 25, 1928, of a Catholic association of about 19 cardinals, 278 bishops, and 3,000 priests devoted to demonstrating respect for and understanding of the Jews.[23] The Vatican's published condemnation had declared only that "over time the association ... has adopted a manner of operating and speaking that is alien to the sense and spirit of the Church."[24] It did not explain that the real reason for the action was that in an effort to erase expressions of Catholic antisemitism, members of the Friends of Israel had petitioned Pope Pius XI and the Roman Curia for changes in the liturgy to attenuate references in the Good Friday mass to the *perfidis Iudaeis* – translated as "perfidious" or "treacherous" Jews. They had also asked for the introduction of kneeling and silent private prayer for the Jews during that mass, as was done for the eight other groups for whom prayers were offered on Good Friday, including the Church, pope, clergy, monarch, heretics, and pagans. The pope and the Holy Office had rejected the petition with anger and private expressions of outrage, and consequently condemned and dissolved the entire association of the Friends of Israel.[25]

Further explanation of the condemnation and banning seemed necessary, however, and so on May 19, 1928, at the request of Pius XI, Padre Enrico Rosa elaborated on the action in the Jesuit journal *La Civiltà Cattolica*. While admirable in their dedication to Jewish conversion, Padre Rosa explained, members of the Friends of Israel had erred, perhaps inadvertently, when they "covered up not only [the Jews'] defects but also their historic crimes, and attenuated the traditional [Church] language and even that used in the sacred liturgy."[26] And so the matter rested.

More than sixteen and a half years after the Vatican's banning of the Friends of Israel, and at a time when the Holocaust was still raging in parts of Europe, Padre Benedetto nonetheless felt obliged to write: "I believe that I can avoid the inconveniences of this society. I make every effort to conform my lectures to the spirit of the Church and the teachings of the Holy Fathers . . . I do not intend in any manner to propose modifications to the Sacred Liturgy, for example to the *Oremus pro perfidis Iudaeis* [prayer for the perfidious Jews] of Good Friday, or to attenuate the responsibility of the Jewish people in the trial of Jesus or other similar things."[27] The lectures were allowed to continue until the end of May 1945, but Padre Benedetto was clearly an object of suspicion in the eyes of conservative Catholics. The word *perfidis* was not removed from Good Friday prayer for the Jews until 1959, at the insistence of Pope John XXIII, Pius XII's successor.[28] Then in 1965 the Second Vatican Council "attenuated the responsibility of the Jewish people in the trial of Jesus," as Padre Benedetto put it in his letter of December 1944, by declaring that "what was committed during the passion [of Christ] cannot be imputed either indiscriminately to all Jews then living or to the Jews of our time."[29] Vatican II also emphasized the spiritual patrimony shared by Christians and Jews, as Padre Benedetto had done in 1944. Padre Benedetto lived to see the changes and was deeply gratified. But in 1944 he was a man ahead of his time.

On March 20, 1945, just a few months after his report explaining his lectures on the Old Testament, Padre Benedetto again faced inquiries about his activities. This time he was asked to describe in writing his wartime experiences regarding the conversions and baptisms of Jews.

His report was sent on July 7 to another unidentified Vatican official. The document is a shining testament to the Capuchin priest's honesty, integrity, love for his Church, and respect for the Jewish people. "I have met many baptized Jews who had received no [Catholic] religious instruction and did not observe a Christian life," he began. He went on to explain that they often admitted that they had no real Christian convictions but had converted during the war in the hope, usually futile, of avoiding Nazi persecution. "Jews converted in this way, who were not good Jews in the first place, are not now better Christians," Padre Benedetto continued. "Many times they return to Judaism once the danger has passed, or continue to go to Jewish charities where they are invited to return to the faith of their fathers." The Jews notice these things, he added, and lose respect for the Catholic clergy, whom they say took advantage of every opportunity and every means to attract converts during the years of persecution. The Jews are particularly incensed by the Church's treatment of Jewish minors hidden in Catholic institutions and indoctrinated in the absence of their parents. "If we are not careful," Padre Benedetto concluded, "we risk creating a hateful meaning to the activities of the Church in favor of the persecuted Jews."[30]

In his same report of July 7, 1945, Padre Benedetto articulated the traditional Catholic viewpoint by stating, "The Church aims at the conversion to the Catholic faith of all Jews just as with all other peoples." However, he reminded his questioner that not all means are acceptable and that according to canon law, the agreement of parents is required in cases of baptism of minors. For adults there must be an extended period of study, reflection, and prayer. But the Capuchin priest may then have raised a few eyebrows when he suggested, "Often it is better to ask [the Jews] simply to remain good Jews according to the Mosaic law and their consciences, and always to inculcate respect for individual consciences, necessary for humans to live together peacefully, whether on the part of Catholics regarding Jews or on the part of Jews regarding Catholics and baptized Jews."[31]

In 1960, still before Vatican II, Padre Benedetto published similar views on the subject of conversion. In an article in a French Capuchin provincial bulletin, he explained that he had recently had the pleasure of attending the wedding in a synagogue in Paris of the son and daughter of two of the Jews he had rescued in Rome. At a time when many priests discouraged or even prohibited their flocks from attending non-Catholic religious services, he seemed anxious to justify his presence to the Catholic leaders of the bulletin. He pointed out that the 1917 Code of Canon Law clearly distinguished between active participation in non-Catholic services, which was not permitted, and a passive presence that was tolerated when there was a sufficiently serious reason. He had never participated in a Jewish service, he declared, but he believed that a positive good stemmed from his passive presence.[32] What was that good? "Conversion is very difficult," he explained, "and one must never forget that it requires above all else the help of grace. In waiting for the hour of God, who gives it where and when he wishes, it is very useful to promote by every means in our power a climate of Jewish-Christian friendship, proceeding from supernatural charity."[33]

This statement and a few others that Padre Benedetto made elsewhere raise the question of whether he promoted Jewish-Catholic friendship after the war in order to obtain conversions. There is no doubt that the rescue work he conducted during the war was done to save lives. There is also no question that Padre Benedetto genuinely liked and admired the Jewish people. But as a good Catholic priest, that personal affinity could have made him even more committed to working for conversions, to obtain salvation for a people he cared for. His methods were always mild. Sorani wrote after the war that he had never tried to convert the Jews he was trying to protect in Rome.[34] Padre Benedetto's writings to Church officials who asked him for his views on conversions were always moderate and restrained. But was conversion nevertheless his ultimate goal?

The question is complex. After all, until Vatican II – and to some extent after it as well – many priests and practicing Catholics held that, with the possible exception of those who had no knowledge of Christ but led a moral life, salvation could be achieved only by the mediation of the Roman Catholic Church, through its teachings and the distribution of the sacraments. Put more simply, they believed there could be no salvation outside the Church.[35] Padre Benedetto, therefore, might have regarded conversion as a gift he could bring to those he cared for, making possible their salvation. But before coming to that conclusion, we must consider several factors. First, Padre Benedetto's writings on conversion before Vatican II were always directed to a Catholic audience whom he wished to ingratiate. He hoped for support from that audience for his projects of Jewish-Catholic friendship, which he believed would bring dignity and honor to both peoples. He did not want to antagonize his Catholic audience by stating unorthodox views on conversion. Second, some Catholic theologians were challenging traditional teachings on salvation well before Vatican II. Padre Benedetto was ahead of his time on many theological issues, and there is no reason to believe that he was not ahead on this one as well. He did, after all, write to one superior, as seen above, "Often [rather than insisting on conversion] it is better to ask [the Jews] simply to remain good Jews according to the Mosaic law and their consciences."

In his address to a group from Amicizia ebraico-cristiana on July 8, 1945, Padre Benedetto articulated similarly nontraditional ideas about conversion. He defined conversion for both Jews and Christians as opening one's heart to God. He added, "Thus Jews and Christians must convert themselves to God, each in the intimacy of his own conscience, to become friends of God and friends with one another, in mutual respect for conscience. Thus Jewish-Christian friendship excludes an unintelligent proselytism that wishes at any cost to impose on a Jewish brother a Christian faith that he does not feel, and prefers to trust to God the care of illuminating hearts and directing them in his ways."[36]

Also to be considered on this point is the postwar testimony of Miriam Löwenwirth, later Miriam Reuveni by marriage. As seen in chapter 9, Miriam met Padre Benedetto for the first time at his monastery in Rome in the winter of 1943–1944. When she left, he blessed her and told her always to remain a "good Jewess." Later, hiding in a convent in Florence after her father's deportation, terribly lonely, with no family or friends in the city, and with much time on her hands, Miriam found herself thinking about Jesus and his role among the Jewish people. On the eve of the liberation of Florence, August 23–24, 1944, in the basement of the church where she was hiding, with the bombs falling all around and not expecting to escape alive, she agreed to be baptized. When Padre Benedetto learned of this after the war, he was not pleased. He told her she should not have done it without consulting him first. He added that he would not have advised her to take that step. Looking back, she herself admits that if she had been able to consult with him, it would not have happened.[37]

In truth, Padre Benedetto showed himself to be deeply grieved by any allegations that conversion was a motive for his postwar activities. A good example was his response to a short notice in *L'Osservatore Romano* on October 6, 1946. The Vatican daily newspaper stated that on Saturday, October 5, a mass had been held in a convent near Padre Benedetto's monastery to initiate activities for the coming season of Padre Benedetto's group, identified as "Amicizia cristiano-ebraica." It then referred to the priest's "apostolate," in the sense of a religious mission, among the Jews, which had been so important during the war and had continued after the war in the form of his lecture series. Enraged by the article, in part because October 5 was Yom Kippur that year, local Jewish leaders wrote a letter to the Roman Jewish publication *Israel* on October 9. No mass for Amicizia cristiano-ebraica could have included Jews, they wrote, especially on that day, and no such event could possibly serve as a gesture of friendship.

On October 28 *Israel* published Padre Benedetto's response. First, he wrote, he always referred to his friendship group as "Amicizia ebraico-cristiana," and not the other way around. Second, his group never initiated its activities with a Catholic mass. He knew that the nuns in the convent mentioned held a mass once a month, on a Friday, for converts to Catholicism, including Jews, but he had never attended or ordered such a service, and it had no connection with him or his group. He added that he had never proselytized or conducted an apostolate among the Jews, as alleged by *L'Osservatore Romano,* and he charged that the description in the Vatican newspaper of his activities during the war perplexed his Jewish colleagues. Writing from his heart, he declared, "This accusation is an enormous blow for me and for my conscience, a thing that I would never have expected, and which I believe will also appear as completely untrue to all who know me."[38]

While Padre Benedetto's response is convincing, the question of why *L'Osservatore Romano* got the story so wrong remains. Was it merely a journalistic error, the result of sloppy reporting? An innocent misunderstanding? This is difficult to credit, since Padre Benedetto and the nuns in question were two entirely separate entities, not easy to confuse. Or was someone at the Vatican newspaper intentionally trying to discredit Padre Benedetto with the Jewish community, to inhibit his work for Jewish-Christian friendship? The possibility exists.

In fact, Padre Benedetto made his most conclusive statements on the complex subject of conversion of the Jews in an article for *Études franciscaines* in 1968. Writing to define the Second Vatican Council's positions regarding Jews, he was also describing his own views. Vatican II, he explained, reminded Catholics that the Jews were the people chosen by God to carry his message to humankind. That Christians carried a new message did not remove the status of chosen people from the Jews. Christians must regard Jews who remained faithful to their religion with honor and respect. If they have not become Christians, it is not because they have rejected Jesus but because God did not desire it. As he wrote, "If they do not yet have the full light of Christianity, it is not because they have rejected it; it is because they have not received that light from God. Without doubt there is a divine design that Judaism should subsist at the side of Christianity, as a witness to the first revelations and to the messianic preparations, as the original guardians of the Holy Scriptures." He then asked, "Should we go further and wish for that day, known only by God, when all peoples will invoke the Lord with a single voice and serve him with a single heart?" That may not happen for thousands of years. But "God is the master of his gifts." In the meantime, he mused, we follow God's will by living side by side with the Jews, honoring them as the people from whom Christianity emerged and as "living witnesses of the divine Scriptures and of the religious history of humanity."[39]

Padre Benedetto was not directly involved in two issues that shook the Jewish community of Rome after liberation, but he wrote about them and expressed his opinion. The issues concerned the conversion of Rome's chief rabbi, Israel Zolli, to Catholicism and the search for Jewish children hidden in Catholic institutions during the war. The first case involved the rabbi, who had hidden with Catholic families during the German occupation of Rome and played no role in rescuing his people. After the liberation of Rome in June 1944, Jewish community leaders charged Zolli with abandoning his post and relieved him as chief rabbi. The Allies reinstated him, but bitter recriminations continued. Zolli presided over religious services in the synagogue during the high holy days in the autumn of 1944, but in a sensational move in February 1945, well before the end of the war in Europe, he announced his conversion to Catholicism. He took the name Eugenio to honor Pope Pius XII, formerly Eugenio Pacelli. Zolli claimed to have had mystical visions of Jesus for a long time, though his detractors charged that his action resulted from his weak and unstable character, his wish to escape an untenable position within the Jewish community, and even his desire to embarrass and hurt those who had rejected his leadership.[40]

There is nothing in Padre Benedetto's papers to suggest an involvement in this case. He did make his views clear years later, however, in the above-mentioned article in the French Capuchin provincial bulletin for 1960. Writing in French as Père Marie-Benoît, he explained that he had known Zolli and that soon after the liberation of Rome he had discussed with him the possibility that the pope would meet with members of the Jewish community. He added, "Unfortunately for this fine project, [Zolli] abandoned Judaism for the Christian religion, and everything fell apart." He emphasized that he had played no part in the conversion, and he was anxious to present the Jewish point of view regarding the event. The news had first appeared unexpectedly in a Roman newspaper; in 1960 the Capuchin summarized, in his own words, the response of the Jewish publication *Israel* at the time: "Mr. Zolli is free to follow his conscience, but he will never make us believe that the idea of being baptized came to him in a single night; why did he continue to exercise his functions as grand rabbi until the eve of his baptism? Shouldn't he have resigned much sooner, when already he was ready spiritually to leave us?" Père Marie-Benoît said he could offer no answer to those questions, because he knew nothing "of the circumstances or the details of [Zolli's] preparation for baptism." But he was reporting the facts, "thinking that they might contain a useful lesson for similar cases."[41]

The Capuchin priest addressed the second hornet's nest of controversy in a brief postscript to his above-mentioned report on July 7, 1945. "I have just learned a delicate fact," he wrote. "The Jews of Rome are complaining that they have tried in vain to withdraw from Catholic institutions babies whose parents died in concentration camps. The Jews claim jurisdiction over these orphans and would like to raise them." But the issue was not new to Padre Benedetto. Nearly six months before, he had received a letter from Sorani, written on January 22, informing him of rumors that some Jewish children were still in Catholic institutions and asking him to speak with a particular priest who was believed to have made an investigation of the subject. Padre Benedetto had written to the priest immediately and received an answer on January 26. The priest had declared that he knew of no such cases in Rome, and Padre Benedetto had relayed that answer to Sorani on February 1.[42] The issue continued to fester, however, as evidenced by Padre Benedetto's letter in July. There is no evidence of Padre Benedetto's further involvement, and little is known about the dimensions of the problem in Rome.[43] But Padre Benedetto had made his opinions clear in that same July report – he believed that the baptism of infants without their parents' consent was contrary to canon law.

Unfortunately the issue was more complicated because, in the eyes of the Church, baptism, even if contrary to canon law, remains valid once it is performed. Some men and women of the Church after the Second World War were reluctant to return baptized children even to their surviving Jewish relatives, and many more refused, at least initially, to return them to Jewish institutions in cases where relatives did not survive. The issue emerged in every country where Jewish children were hidden in Catholic institutions.[44]

TWELVE

The Final Decades

PERHAPS NO BUREAUCRACY IN THE WORLD DISGUISES PERSONAL judgments and appraisals more effectively than that of the Catholic Church. The men – and they are nearly always men – who make decisions about promotions within Catholic institutions rarely commit their opinions to paper. There is therefore no way to be sure exactly how Padre Maria Benedetto was viewed by his superiors and peers after the Second World War. It nevertheless seems certain that in the pre–Vatican II era, his views on Jewish-Catholic relations made some of his superiors uneasy. The fact that he was often called upon to explain what he was doing and what he was trying to achieve testifies to that conclusion.

For his superiors, of course, the problem was compounded by the fact that Padre Benedetto was such a public figure. His views on Jewish-Catholic reconciliation were those of a resistance hero as well as a big burly man whom nobody could overlook. Jews and Catholics alike were aware that his superiors in the Vatican did not always share his views. Padre Benedetto admitted as much in a letter to Carlo Alberto Viterbo, a leader of the Roman Jewish Community, in 1971. Viterbo had written to ask the priest for his memories of Raffaele Cantoni, president of the Union of Italian Jewish Communities from 1946 to 1954. Cantoni had died recently, and a commemorative publication was being planned. Padre Benedetto told Viterbo that he had been invited to give a lecture at the Circolo ebraico in Rome on July 8, 1945, on relations between Jews and Catholics. Cantoni had presided at the well-attended event. Padre Benedetto recalled with some glee that after the lecture, Cantoni turned to him and said, "But you, my dear Father, you do not think like those in the Vatican."[1]

Even less certain than the attitudes of Padre Benedetto's superiors are those of his peers, his fellow priests and friars who dealt daily with a brilliant teacher who was not just popular with his young seminary students but was also a charismatic, dynamic, well-known, indeed revered public figure. Padre Benedetto was invited to elegant receptions at the French embassy. Over and over again he was lauded in the press and by hundreds, if not thousands, of Jews whom he had saved. Articles and books, though usually general and inaccurate, were written about him alone or with other rescuers.[2] He was honored not once but many times for his contribution to suffering humanity in time of war. And he was always busy, scurrying here and there, going to meetings, giving public lectures outside the monastery, never subject to the routine and repetition of normal monastery life. It seems inevitable that some of his peers would have envied and resented him.

Padre Benedetto himself inadvertently provided an example of the effect he had on his admirers in the same letter to Carlo Alberto Viterbo in 1971. He told Viterbo that after his lecture at the Circolo ebraico in July 1945, Cantoni was so enthusiastic about what the priest had said that he thanked him warmly in front of the entire audience, embraced him "with effusion," and proposed to collect, that very moment, the money necessary to print one hundred copies of the lecture.[3] It was a warm response, but one that could have made those less fond of Padre Benedetto jealous.

Still more public were the honors bestowed on the Capuchin priest in the years following the war. There were so many that it is difficult to keep track of them all. On June 18, 1946, he received a commendation for brave wartime conduct from the British government and was decorated at the British embassy in Rome. A year later, on June 6, 1947, he received a medal bearing the Cross of Lorraine of the Forces Françaises de l'Intérieur for his courageous work in both France and Italy to help "victims of Vichy and Nazism." On October 22, 1947, the French government awarded him a Croix de Guerre with a vermilion star for the same activities. Then in a ceremony in Rome on April 16, 1948, Jacques Maritain, the French ambassador to the Holy See, presented to Padre Benedetto the cross of a chevalier of the French Legion of Honor. The designation was especially for the priest's work in saving Jews, the am-

bassador declared, but it was also intended to honor his efforts to promote Jewish-Christian friendship.[4]

More honors followed. On April 17, 1955, in a ceremony marking
the tenth anniversary of the end of the war, the Union of Italian Jewish
Communities awarded Padre Benedetto and twenty-two other non-Jews
a gold medal of recognition for saving Jews in Italy during the German
occupation. Three years later, on April 27, 1958, the priest was among
several members of the French Catholic and Protestant clergy honored
by the French Comité d'Action de la Résistance for helping Jews during
the war. In 1964 American president Lyndon Johnson also paid homage
to him, and a bust of the priest was erected at the church of Saint John
the Baptist in New York City. Two years later he received the medal of
the Righteous among the Nations from Yad Vashem in Israel. Finally,
in a grand ceremony at his monastery in Paris on March 14, 1984, Padre
Benedetto, by then about two weeks shy of his eighty-ninth birthday,
was awarded the rosette of an *officier* in the Legion of Honor. The rosette
was presented by his old friend from the war years, Grand Rabbi Jacob
Kaplan, himself a *grand officier* of the Legion of Honor. Among those
present were the current grand rabbi of France, the Israeli ambassador
to France, and several prominent French Jewish leaders, as well as Stefan
Schwamm and other Jewish friends (fig. 12).[5]

Surely the most exciting honor that Padre Benedetto received was a
visit to Israel given by the Jewish Community of Rome in 1958. The offer
represented an opportunity for the trip of a lifetime to a priest committed to vows of poverty.[6] After securing permission from his superiors to
make the trip, the Capuchin priest, by then based near Tours, in France,
left Marseille on the passenger ship *Theodore Herzl* on July 20.[7] When
he arrived in Haifa four days later, he was met by representatives of the
Italian consulate, the Israeli Ministry of Religious Affairs, journalists,
photographers, and many grateful citizens and friends. For two weeks he
toured the country, visiting Jerusalem, the Galilee, and the Negev desert,
among other places. He attended receptions where he met the French
ambassador to Israel as well as prominent Italian Jews such as Umberto
Nahon, Angelo Fano, and Guido Mendes. Padre Benedetto must have
visited churches also, but he rarely wrote about it. Even more meaningful
than visits with prominent persons were those with individuals he had

protected during the war, including Rachel Fallmann, by then married and called Rachel Schutz, and her mother, Ida Fallmann. Esther Fallmann, by then Esther Kichelmacher, was out of the country at the time, but in Tel Aviv the priest was able to stay at her apartment (fig. 13).

Padre Benedetto was thrilled and touched by the entire trip, but he particularly remembered one incident in Tel Aviv. His friends there, probably the Fallmanns, maintained that he should have the privilege of saying mass in a church in Israel. Since apparently there was no church in Tel Aviv, they insisted that he go to nearby Jaffa and took him there. In Jaffa he was able to preside over mass in the large historic Franciscan church of Saint Peter. Another great pleasure was his visit to the Kibbutz Enzo Sereni, named for an Italian Zionist who founded an early kibbutz in Israel in the 1920s, joined the British army during the war, parachuted into Italy, and was captured and deported to Dachau, where he died. Padre Benedetto later wrote that he asked a man at the kibbutz if he too could live there. "Yes," replied the man, "you could teach French to the youngsters."[8]

Padre Benedetto left Israel on the steamship *Jerusalem* on August 8. His ship stopped at Cyprus and Pireas in Greece before landing in Naples. From there he traveled by train to Paris and Tours. "My trip to Israel was for me a great grace from heaven," he wrote to Rachel Fallmann when thanking her for her hospitality. In another letter to Rachel a few months later, he added, "I have only one desire, to return to Israel and, if possible, to remain there." The possibility of a return trip arose again in 1968 when Yad Vashem invited him to attend a ceremony at some future date for the planting of a tree in his honor (fig. 14). Businessmen in Israel offered to fund the journey, saying, "He has done so much for humanity. Now it is our turn to do something for him, no matter how little it is." But for some reason the trip never materialized. Padre Benedetto wrote in 1971 that he intended to make the trip, but, as seen in chapter 5, he was still trying to raise the money in 1976.[9] Two years after that, traveling was no longer physically possible for him. As he told Rachel Fallmann in a letter on June 26, 1978, "I no longer walk well, even with a cane. I tire easily."

The trip to Israel in 1958 seems to have changed Padre Benedetto's outlook on his own life. Later letters and reports of conversations suggest that his comment to the man at the Kibbutz Enzo Sereni was not fatuous but deadly serious, and that his thank-you note to Rachel Fallmann in 1958 was in earnest. He really wanted "to return to Israel and, if possible, remain there." Rachel recalls that he spoke or wrote to her of this wish on other occasions. He was particularly explicit in a letter in August 1966 when he told her, "I do not want to live in a monastery. I want to live as a Jew among the Jews, whom I like so much." The problem, he explained, was that he had no way to support himself and was too old to start again.[10]

During the 1960s Padre Benedetto also spoke seriously with his old friend Stefan Schwamm, who was then living at least part-time in Israel, about his interest in moving to the Holy Land. In October 1967 Schwamm wrote from Israel to suggest that the priest join him in teaching a course in applied linguistics at the Hebrew University to help train interpreters in religious fields. Nothing came of this suggestion, but clearly the discussion was ongoing.[11]

There is no indication that Padre Benedetto wanted to renounce his religion or his religious vows. On the contrary, he seems to have loved and cherished his faith and his Church. Rachel Fallmann believes that his faith never wavered but that he was perhaps tired of the constraints of monastic life. Those constraints must have been all the more difficult to bear after the enormous activity and excitement of his wartime work. Rachel knew nothing of Padre Benedetto's career disappointments, to be discussed below, or of the suspicions among members of the Vatican hierarchy regarding his commitment to Jewish-Christian friendship. She did understand and appreciate his great love for the Jewish people and his enthusiasm for the young state of Israel. She assumed that he wanted to share the excitement of building a new nation.[12]

While Padre Benedetto was gratified by the honors showered upon him, he also had his share of disappointments. Some of these concerned his teaching appointments. The saga began in February 1946 when the French provincial minister who headed the Capuchin province that included Paris wrote to the general minister of the Capuchin order to ask if Padre Benedetto could be transferred to his province, which was short of teachers. The provincial minister explained that he would like Padre

Benedetto to be director of studies [directeur d'études] and a teacher of the more advanced students at the Capuchin college in Paris. He pointed out respectfully that his province had given many of its best people to the international college in Rome during the last thirty years.[13]

General Minister Donat de Welle sent the provincial minister in Paris a polite refusal. "We wonder if Père Marie-Benoît would be right for the position that you intend for him and whether the international college might lose an excellent lecturer [conférencier] without [the Paris province] gaining a good director of studies," he wrote in French on March 30, ignoring the proposal that the priest would also teach upper levels of students in Paris. Donat de Welle, who had known Padre Benedetto well during the German occupation of Rome and had supported his rescue activities, was making excuses. Perhaps he truly wanted to keep his popular priest. Padre Benedetto, considered not suitable as director of studies in Paris in 1946, was given approximately that same position (préfet des études) in Rome in August 1952. On October 2, 1953, however, a new general minister in Rome informed a similarly new provincial minister in Paris that Padre Maria Benedetto "has renounced of his own free will the position of director of studies at our international college [in Rome]." But instead of Paris, he was now to be transferred to a small Capuchin monastery and college in Campobasso, in the remote mountainous region of Molise, saddled between the regions of Abruzzo and Puglia on southern Italy's Adriatic coast. He would hold the position of lecturer there. "This appointment," the general minister in Rome emphasized to the provincial minister in Paris, "in no way detracts from the esteem that we have and will keep for this priest from your province."[14]

It is difficult to believe that the transfer of Padre Benedetto from Rome to Campobasso was anything but a demotion and an exile. The international Capuchin college in Rome enjoyed the services of the finest teachers of the order and attracted the best students. With the exception of his years in Marseille from 1940 to 1943, Padre Benedetto had taught there for his entire life as a priest. Now he was being sent to an isolated provincial institution in a city of about thirty thousand people and was being demoted from director of studies to lecturer. But if the transfer was a demotion, the reasons for it are not certain. The school in

Campobasso undoubtedly needed teachers. As the number of religious vocations began to drop in the postwar years, most monastic orders suffered shortages of trained priests. There is also some reason to believe that Padre Benedetto found his administrative work in Rome a burden. But why Campobasso, a six-hour drive from Rome with all its intellectual ferment and growing ecumenism, and much farther still from dynamic, innovative Paris?

Was Padre Benedetto's new posting meant to be a punishment? If so, why? Had he provoked too many resentments and jealousies among his superiors and peers? Or were his superiors suspicious of his theology, which emphasized the religious foundations shared by Jews and Christians, dismissed the historic guilt of Jews for the death of Jesus, and even dared to suggest that Catholics should not aim, at all times and in all circumstances, to convert the Jews? Or had that same theology along with Padre Benedetto's unrelenting ecumenism and commitment to Jewish-Catholic dialogue simply irritated too many prelates within the Vatican hierarchy? Or, finally, was the transfer simply part of a broader reshuffling of personnel in the Capuchin college, which had recently received a new general minister?

An enigmatic letter from a priest who called himself an old friend of Padre Benedetto to a close associate of the Capuchin general minister in Rome hints that the reason for the transfer was delicate. A copy of the letter, unsigned and written in French, exists in the Capuchin archives in Paris, suggesting it may have been written by the same provincial general there who had requested Padre Benedetto's transfer to Paris in 1946 or by his successor. "The news of Père Marie-Benoît's resignation did not surprise me," the writer declared, "because I knew that his position [as *préfet d'études* in Rome] weighed heavily upon him . . . But I obviously could not have guessed the real reasons for his departure from Rome. What I learn from your letter pains me . . . I also sense from your letter that the Most Reverend General Minister and yourself have also been greatly pained by this matter."[15] Unfortunately the "real reasons" for the transfer remain unknown.

And so at noon on October 13, 1953, Padre Benedetto boarded a bus in Rome for the trip to Campobasso. During his three years at the Capuchin college there, he taught theology to three levels of students and Holy

Scripture to all four levels. His peers in Campobasso evidently adored him, as indicated by a commemorative scrapbook of photographs and verse that they presented to him when he left in 1956. His own thoughts are impossible to decipher. He did not complain, but his notebook is bereft of the references to interesting meetings, especially with Jewish leaders and friends, that filled the pages when he was in Rome and later in France. Instead he seems to have spent much time traveling within the region, saying mass and hearing confessions in many different towns, convents, and hospitals. Only in April 1955 did he note a short visit to Milan to receive the above-mentioned gold medal from the Union of Italian Jewish Communities. Then in August of the same year he recorded a nine-day visit with his brothers Joseph and Louis in Angers. On that same vacation he also saw Fernande Leboucher in Paris. But except for those two trips, life in Campobasso must have been lonely and more than a little dull.[16]

In 1955 the Capuchin general minister in Rome refused another request by the provincial minister in Paris for Padre Benedetto's recall to France.[17] When the provincial general in Paris asked again in June 1956, however, the request was accepted, with accolades for Padre Benedetto himself. The general minister in Rome wrote that Padre Benedetto has lived "a life of intellectual and spiritual synthesis of astonishing rigor ... [We should] add his tireless devotion outside the [Capuchin] order, especially for the Jewish cause for which the awarding of a Gold Medal can hardly acknowledge the full merits." The general minister concluded that Padre Benedetto held a prominent place among the greatest of Capuchins.[18] With that recommendation, Padre Benedetto boarded a train on August 4, 1956, for his return to France (fig. 15). With the exception of the war years 1940 to 1943, he had not lived there since 1907.

For the next seven years, Père Marie-Benoît, as he was now called again, taught theology and philosophy at a Capuchin college at 2 rue de la Pierre in Saint Symphorien (Indre-et-Loire), near Tours. From there he was able to travel frequently to Paris, where, according to his notebook, he met primarily with Jewish friends from the war years, including Aron Kasztersztein, Stefan Schwamm, Angelo Donati, and Joseph Bass, as well as with well-known French Jewish intellectuals such as Jules Isaac and Edmond Fleg. He also went often to visit his brothers in Angers. His nephew Pierre Péteul remembers that he was always present for family christenings, confirmations, birthdays, weddings, and funerals during these years and later as well.

Père Marie-Benoît's years at Saint Symphorien were not without their troubles. Most painful for him must have been an incident that began in March 1961, ten months after the capture of Adolf Eichmann in Argentina on May 11, 1960, by Israeli Mossad and Shin Bet agents, and about a month before Eichmann's trial began in Jerusalem. In a series of three articles in the Italian weekly *L'Europeo* on March 5, 12, and 19, 1961, Simon Wiesenthal, the Austrian Jewish survivor who devoted his life to hunting Nazi war criminals, described how he had searched for the former SS lieutenant colonel for years. Charged by SS leaders Heinrich Himmler and Reinhard Heydrich with organizing the deportations of Jews from most German-occupied countries, Eichmann was one of the most notorious Nazis still at large at the time. The tips and leads that Wiesenthal collected probably contributed to Eichmann's final arrest, although the agents who finally caught him tended to minimize this point.[19]

More relevant to our story is Wiesenthal's description in *L'Europeo* of the testimony of one particular informant about Eichmann. According to Wiesenthal, a man named Heinrich von Klimrod had visited him in his office in Vienna years earlier, in late 1951 or early 1952. Klimrod identified himself as a spokesman for a Viennese group of former SS veterans who were unemployed and impoverished at the time. He offered to provide Wiesenthal with information about Eichmann in exchange for what he called "Eichmann's gold" in the event of his capture. Wiesenthal declined what he later called "a proposal that disgusted me," but before doing so, he tried to get some information from Klimrod. The SS man told him that Eichmann was no longer in Europe and that he had escaped through Rome. When Wiesenthal asked where he had hidden in Rome, Klimrod produced a calling card on which was written "Padre Weber and Padre Benedetti [sic], *padri cappuccini,* via Siciliana [sic], Rome." Just below those names was another, "Hudal." When Wiesenthal asked who Hudal was, Klimrod replied that he was a bishop who headed an organization that arranged for the clandestine emigration of Nazis through

Italy. As for Weber and "Benedetti," they were "two Capuchin friars who engaged in the same activity."[20]

Père Marie-Benoît was greatly distressed by these allegations. It was little comfort that Klimrod's cryptic calling card was replete with errors. It misspelled Père Marie-Benoît's Italian name and the address of his monastery, and it misidentified the Pallottine Padre Weber as a Capuchin. Nor was Père Marie-Benoît greatly reassured a few days later by vociferous denials in an Italian Catholic weekly, *Vita,* because of the many errors and exaggerations in that article. The author of the article had interviewed the Austrian bishop Alois Hudal, who informed him that he had helped thousands of Jews and anti-Fascists during the German occupation of Rome. Hudal claimed that for several long months he had hidden many in the Collegio Teutonico, a college for German-speaking candidates for the priesthood next to the German national church of Santa Maria dell'Anima, where he was the rector. But there is no evidence of Hudal's wartime rescue claims, and Père Marie-Benoît must have known that. On the contrary, even before the conflict, Hudal was known to be sympathetic to Nazism and had publicly argued that the pope should and could reach an accommodation with Hitler in order to combat Communism more effectively.[21]

In his interview with Hudal in 1961, the author of the *Vita* article also asked about Wiesenthal's charges that he had helped German war criminals escape from Italy after the war. The author was probably only dimly aware that until 1952 Hudal had headed the Austrian subcommittee of the Pontifical Commission for Refugee Assistance or, in shorter form, the Pontifical Commission for Assistance. As seen in chapter 10, the commission was originally formed in March 1944 to help foreigners in Italy just before and after the liberation. The Austrian subcommittee was intended to focus primarily on Austrians or, at the very least, German speakers who wanted to leave the country. For several years it provided German-speaking fugitives from the Allies with the identification vouchers needed to procure documents for travel to South America from the International Committee of the Red Cross in Rome. The Austrian subcommittee and perhaps as many as nineteen other national sections of the Pontifical Commission for Assistance received financial, physical, and moral support from the Vatican. Not all those seeking assistance with emigration were war criminals, of course. Many were former German and Austrian soldiers and SS men, escaped prisoners of war, or other individuals who for countless reasons were desperate not to return to their home countries.[22]

In his answer to the *Vita* author's question about war criminals, Hudal explained his role as follows:

> On some days after 1945, more than 40 persons came to me.... They were refugees provided with Nansen passports ... or Red Cross identity cards issued in Geneva, later in Milan. All those refugees declared that they were being persecuted as anti-Communists by the Soviets and [were] in grave danger of their lives.
>
> I as a priest am not a policeman or a carabiniere, and my duty as a Christian, in those confused years, was to save those who could be saved, also to prevent people without means from remaining in Rome, where they would really be dangerous.
>
> I cannot affirm or deny that Eichmann was among those refugees, because none of them confessed his past in the Third Reich to me and because, besides, at that time no photograph of Eichmann was known.[23]

In this answer Hudal was less than forthright. First, he described the process incorrectly. Most refugees who came to him did not already have identity cards; more often they had no documents at all. They came to Hudal's subcommittee to receive identification vouchers that they could then present to the Red Cross to obtain travel documents, and they generally succeeded. Second, while Hudal could not have been expected to know the backgrounds of every person who came to him, the fact remains that neither his subcommittee nor the relevant Red Cross workers took much trouble to ask. Refugees lied about their wartime activities, and Hudal and his assistants accepted the lies at face value. Their motives varied from anti-Communism, a desire to help professed Christians and particularly Catholics, traditional Church hospitality and suspicion of secular governments, a failure to grasp the nature of Nazi crimes, and sheer sympathy with Nazism as they understood it. But as a result, many war criminals benefited. Today it is known that among those whom Hudal helped were Franz Stangl, Josef Mengele, Erich Priebke, Eduard Roschmann, Walter Rauff, and, as Klimrod suggested, Adolf Eichmann.[24]

In his memoirs published in 1976, Bishop Hudal virtually admitted all of this, writing:

> In the last stages the war of the Allies against Germany had very little to do
> with ideals. It was not a crusade, but only the rivalry of great economic com-
> plexes fighting for victory; this so-called "business" . . . used catchwords like
> democracy, race, religious liberty and Christianity as bait for the masses. All
> these experiences finally brought me to dedicate my entire charitable work after
> 1945 first and foremost to former National Socialists and Fascists, especially
> to the so-called "war criminals" who were being pursued by Communists and
> "Christian" Democrats, often with means, methods that differed very little from
> those of their opponents of yesterday.[25]

The author of the article in *Vita* who defended Hudal also praised
Padre Anton Weber's Opera di San Raffaele for wartime assistance to
some twenty-five thousand "Jews," implying that the beneficiaries were
Jewish in religion or culture. That implication was untrue. The Opera
di San Raffaele was explicitly dedicated to helping German Jews who
had converted to Catholicism emigrate from the Third Reich during the
1930s, and it continued to focus on that same group in Italy during the
German occupation. Indeed, Padre Weber specifically told interviewer
Gitta Sereny that during the war he had been "responsible for baptized
Jews only." He implied that he would have turned away any who were not
Catholics. Padre Weber has been discussed earlier in connection with
his postwar work, still with German Jews who had become Catholics.
But again by his own admission to Sereny, that work soon escalated to
include many German non-Jewish fugitives trying to escape from Eu-
rope. Some of these were war criminals, and one, disguised as "Ricardo
Klement," was indeed Adolf Eichmann. Padre Weber admitted as much,
but insisted that he had not known Klement's true identity at the time.
He added that even if he had realized that the petitioner was Eichmann,
he would not have known about his role during the war.[26]

With regard to Père Marie-Benoît, the author of the *Vita* article alleged that as Padre Benedetto he had helped Jews during the German
occupation of Rome "as a result of an official assignment from the Holy
See." This statement was also inaccurate. We have seen and will see again
below that the Vatican was not involved with Padre Benedetto's rescue efforts. The sole consolation for the priest in the article was the inclusion of
a statement from the governing office (Curia Generale) of the Capuchin
order in Rome. Addressing the claim that Eichmann had been in contact
with the Capuchins and had been hosted at their college in the via Sicilia,

it read, in part, "This governing committee . . . is able to deny in the most absolute way that [Eichmann] could have been sheltered in [our] college because the rules of the institution forbid it." That comment was true. Even during the German occupation, Jews whom Padre Benedetto was helping often came to the monastery, but they were sheltered elsewhere. The official Capuchin statement in *Vita* continued, "That [Eichmann] might have had, under a false name, contact with the same [Capuchins] is possible given the vast work of assistance that the well-known Padre Benedetto of Bourg d'Iré extended to the persecuted."[27]

The Capuchin statement was logical and honest. Padre Benedetto might have unknowingly encountered Eichmann among the many refugees whom he believed to be Jews and helped after the war. But it is extremely unlikely. First, it is not clear that Eichmann was even in Rome at all. Most scholars believe that after escaping on February 5, 1946, from an American camp in Germany called Ober-Dachstetten, where he had lived under a false name and not been recognized, Eichmann had hidden first in Prien in Bavaria and then in the little town of Eversen, near Hamburg, in the British zone. At some point he was smuggled into Alto Adige, also known as South Tyrol, south of the Brenner Pass in northern Italy, where he was hidden in a Franciscan monastery in Bolzano (Bozen in German). The exact nature of Padre Weber's help to him is uncertain, but it may have begun with a recommendation for shelter in one or more of the monasteries associated with the Opera di San Raffaele before the fugitive reached Bolzano.[28]

From the commune of Termeno (Tramin in German), near the Franciscan monastery where he was hiding, Eichmann acquired an identity card dated June 2, 1948, under the name of Ricardo Klement, born in Bolzano in 1913. With that card he eventually traveled to the Italian Red Cross office in Genoa and applied there on June 1, 1950, for a Red Cross travel document. His application was signed by a Hungarian Franciscan priest, Father Edoardo Dömöter, from his church of San Antonio in Genoa. Father Dömöter worked closely with Bishop Hudal in Rome on refugee assistance matters, receiving blank visas, instructions, and advice by mail or personal delivery. He represented the link between Hudal and Eichmann. As for Eichmann, with his Red Cross travel document in hand he went to the Argentine consulate in Genoa, where he received a permanent visa on June 14. Three days later he boarded a ship for Buenos Aires.[29]

While Eichmann's peregrinations between Germany and Argentina clearly involved both Bishop Hudal and Padre Weber, there is no incriminating evidence at all for Père Marie-Benoît/Padre Benedetto. Addressing the issue from Saint Symphorien, Père Marie-Benoît denied Klimrod's and Wiesenthal's allegations clearly and succinctly. His first written comment came in response to a request for clarification on March 15, 1961, from a Capuchin in Rome acting on behalf of the head of the order. Père Marie-Benoît answered five days later, writing: "I have never had an occasion to approach Monsignor Hudal, nor have I ever heard of this 'Clemente [sic],' who would be Eichmann. I have never provided anyone with a passport, but only with those miserable French identity cards . . . for local use in Rome. And that from 1943 to 1944." Père Marie-Benoît was quite certain that he could not have helped Eichmann without realizing it, insisting that his rescue committee consisted of and worked only with Jews.[30]

A few days after that, on April 9, 1961, Père Marie-Benoît wrote more of the same to his Italian Jewish friend Carlo Alberto Viterbo in Rome. "I have never heard about organizations for the expatriation of Nazis," he declared, "and as a French resister I would like to think that every good Italian will believe me if I say that I would have had no propensity for such activity, even forgetting about the fact that this is a question of Germans and I speak their language very badly." He repeated that he never gave a passport to anyone and pointed out that in his notebook list of interviews and meetings between the years 1947 and 1953 there was no mention of a Klement or an Eichmann. He had seen photographs of Eichmann in the newspapers recently, he went on, and he certainly did not recognize anyone he had ever known before. Furthermore, during the time that Eichmann was in Italy and was alleged to have been in Rome, he, Père Marie-Benoît, no longer met many new people, but worked almost entirely with Italian or foreign Jews whom he knew personally.[31]

But Carlo Alberto Viterbo did not need to be convinced. Even before receiving Père Marie-Benoît's letter, Viterbo's opinion was reflected in an article in the Roman Jewish newspaper *Israel.*

The assistance and rescue work for the Jews of Padre Benedetto . . . has been so prompt, merciful, and inspired, as to exclude completely the possibility that he could have given any kind of collaboration to the authors of those misdeeds that have caused him so much sincere pain and trouble. We do not know if he or his assistants might have been surprised in their good faith. If this is the case there can be no stain on their valiant operation and no lessening of our sincere and affectionate gratitude and that of all Roman Jews.[32]

And there the matter rested, but its toll on Père Marie-Benoît must have been heavy.

Another issue that troubled the last decades of Père Marie-Benoît's life involved the role of Pius XII during the Holocaust. Of particular concern to him, of course, were the claims by some representatives of the Church that Pius XII had played a role in Delasem's Jewish rescue operations in Rome. In reports to his superiors in the 1940s, Père Marie-Benoît had occasionally referred to Jewish gratitude to the pope for the rescue of Jews by men and women of the Church during the German occupation of Rome. Intended to win the support of his superiors for Jewish-Catholic dialogue, those imprecise references did not imply that the pope himself was directly involved in rescue. Rather, the pope was a symbol of an institution that had been helpful in Rome. Far more specific and unambiguous, as we have seen, was Père Marie-Benoît's letter to the editors of *Israel* in 1961 to refute the claim of the German Jesuit priest Robert Leiber, Pius XII's closest advisor throughout his papacy, that Delasem had received financial aid from the Vatican during the German occupation of Rome.[33]

The debate grew more intense in 1963 after Rolf Hochhuth's play *Der Stellvertreter (The Deputy)*, condemning Pope Pius XII's silence on the subject of the Holocaust, opened in Berlin and went on to theaters in London, New York, and other cities throughout the world. At that point the Capuchin general minister in Rome wrote to Père Marie-Benoît. Without mentioning Hochhuth, the general minister explained that the editors of the Vatican weekly *L'Osservatore della Domenica* wanted to dedicate an issue to the memory of Pius XII, who had died in 1958. They especially hoped to describe what that pope had done for the Jews, but they had little information. Could Père Marie-Benoît give them some?[34]

For the most part, Père Marie-Benoît's activities in Rome during the occupation had been limited to his work with Delasem. He was not, therefore, in a position to provide specific detailed information about other rescue activities that might or might not have been linked to Pius XII. Regarding his own activities, however, Père Marie-Benoît's response was a masterpiece of evasion. He first referred the editors of *L'Osservatore della Domenica* to his own report of his wartime activities on behalf of Jews in Marseille and Rome, published in *Livre d'Or des Congrégations françaises, 1939–1945* in 1948. That report mentions nothing about help from Pius XII, but Père Marie-Benoît did not point that out. Then he referred the editors to Renzo De Felice's *Storia degli ebrei italiani sotto il fascismo,* published in Turin in 1961. That early study described the rescue of Jews in Italy briefly but did not link rescue efforts with Pius XII. However, in addition to printing in full a report by Père Marie-Benoît on July 20, 1944, about his activities in cooperation with Delasem in Rome, De Felice furnished a list, compiled after the war by priests in Rome, of convents and monasteries in the Eternal City that hid Jews during the war. As Père Marie-Benoît described it in 1964, the statistics in the list "speak of and manifest everything that was done in Rome under Pius XII in favor of the Jews." He did not say that it was done *by* or *because of* Pius XII. Nor did he say that it was done with *no input* from Pius XII. He simply declared that it was done *during* the papacy of Pius XII.[35]

Père Marie-Benoît demonstrated his commitment to truth in the historical record again sometime after 1975 when he wrote a private letter to correct errors in volume 9, published that year, of the *Actes et Documents du Saint Siège relatifs à la seconde guerre mondiale* (ADSS), a collection of Vatican diplomatic documents from the war years. Several of the points he made have already been discussed: that Jewish leaders in France in June 1943 had not had time to prepare a statement for the pope about everything they knew about the Holocaust; that he had discovered that he had been sold fraudulent documents in Rome in October 1943 and had gone to the police himself; that the Vatican was not involved in Delasem's securing of loans in lire against deposits of the Joint in London at the end of 1943 and into 1944; and more.[36]

It is not certain to whom Père Marie-Benoît sent these corrections. The copy of the letter in the Capuchin archives in Paris is a first draft.

Probably he was writing to the editors of the A DSS. But his overall points were clear. First, he wrote, all historical details were important, and efforts should always be made to avoid or correct errors. Second, he detected an overall purpose in the errors of the A DSS – that of presenting his rescue activities as dependent upon the Vatican. That claim was false. "I received no mission from the Vatican," he wrote, just as he had written for *Israel* in 1961 that "I and the true heads of Delasem did not receive any sum from the Vatican."[37] But why was he so anxious to make this clear? He explained: "I have a tree planted in the alley of the Righteous at Yad Vashem in Jerusalem. This tree does not only represent me; it also represents the courageous Jews with whom I fought and without whom I would not have achieved a great deal. I want to name principally: Joseph André Bass, Maurice Brener, Angelo Donati, Stefan Schwamm, Settimio Sorani, Giuseppe Levi, Aron Kasterstein [*sic*]. It is in their memory and in their name that I wish to speak."[38]

Before the controversies about Eichmann and about Vatican aid to Delasem had died down, Père Marie-Benoît was called to Paris. Thus, on July 27, 1963, he left Saint Symphorien and Tours for the last time. At the age of sixty-eight he had been appointed to serve as *gardien* at the Capuchin monastery in the rue Boissonade, near the boulevard du Montparnasse in Paris's 14th arrondissement. This was an administrative management position, made usually for three years. As gardien he supervised finances, supplies, construction, maintenance, health care for the residents, and other similar issues. Although he was delighted to be in Paris, he probably did not relish the specific responsibilities of this position, for he was an intellectual and speculative man rather than a manager. But perhaps he felt that at last he had come home, for his notebook entries of trips ended with his arrival in the rue Boissonade.

A year after his appointment to Paris, Père Marie-Benoît came close to being transferred back to Italy. In 1964 the Capuchin general minister in Rome asked the provincial minister in Paris if the now elderly priest could be sent to Foggia, in the southern Italian region of Puglia, to be director of studies at a Capuchin school there.[39] In his response the provincial minister explained that Père Marie-Benoît was now nearly seventy years old and suffered from arthritis, which made walking difficult and painful. The rest of his letter, however, defined the important role of

Père Marie-Benoît in Paris and was in effect a powerful tribute to him. He was "an extremely valuable advisor, carefully listened to by a large number of priests and friars as well as by [Capuchin] provincial directors and *gardiens*. Is it necessary, in this moment of delicate *aggiornamento,* to deprive the French provinces of such an advisor?" *Aggiornamento* was a term evoked by the current Pope John XXIII to describe the updating of Church doctrine currently being addressed at the Second Vatican Council (October 1962–December 1965). Père Marie-Benoît shared the views of those favoring aggiornamento, especially as it concerned receptivity to dialogue with the Jews. At last his voice was being heard and respected. He was, apparently, much more than a gardien.

In his response to the general minister, the provincial general in Paris went on to explain that Capuchins and Franciscans in France were founding a center of study and research and were planning a new version of their *Études franciscaines*. Père Marie-Benoît's contribution to this project was invaluable. And finally, he wrote, Père Marie-Benoît, "because of his past activities and the ties of friendship that he has created, enjoys an exceptional role at the heart of *Amitiés Judéo-Chrétiennes* and, in general, in the Jewish world . . . Can we, at the moment when the [Second Vatican] Council is opening new perspectives on dialogue with the Jewish world, sacrifice to the interests of one province the unique situation of P. Marie-Benoît, so well placed to pursue this dialogue?"[40] The request for transfer was withdrawn, and Père Marie-Benoît remained in Paris.

After his three-year stint as gardien, Père Marie-Benoît was retired in 1966 and allowed to remain at the monastery in Paris without any particular assignment. At last he was free to do what he liked best: to study, write, and engage in the cause of Jewish-Christian friendship. But he may have wanted to be more active. The years 1966 and 1967 were a period when, as seen above, he inquired most about the idea of moving to Israel. Perhaps he was disheartened by his personal disappointments of the 1950s and 1960s. Or perhaps he felt that his years of service to his order were complete, and he was now free to go elsewhere. But instead of moving, he continued to live at the Parisian monastery for another twenty-three years, writing, meeting friends, participating in ceremonies and demonstrations commemorating the Holocaust, and working for dialogue with the Jews. On October 17, 1976, for example, accompanied by Alain de Rothschild, Grand Rabbi Jacob Kaplan, and other important French Jewish figures, he headed a procession in support of Russian Jews whose government refused them the right to immigrate to Israel (fig. 16).

According to those who knew him during the last two decades of his life, Père Marie-Benoît remained an impressive presence. He said the 8:00 AM mass at his monastery every morning and then walked to the nearby Luxembourg Gardens, where he sat on the same bench each day and engaged in conversation with anyone who was interested. He remained modest, quiet, and undemonstrative. One Capuchin at the monastery in the rue Boissonade during this period recalls that he never drew attention to himself or said much about the causes that were dear to him.[41] He remained an intensely private man. Yet his life still seemed to revolve around Jewish friends and Jewish issues. His files of correspondence from the 1970s and 1980s consist almost exclusively of letters from Jewish friends and former protégés from all over the world. Women who were no longer young wrote from Paris, New York, Israel, Italy, Ireland, Germany, Australia, and elsewhere to tell him of the deaths of parents or the births of children and grandchildren. Settimio Sorani wrote to him in 1980 and probably many times before that. Miriam Löwenwirth Reuveni, whom he had sent to northern Italy from Rome in the winter of 1943–1944 to deliver false documents to Jewish refugees hiding there, wrote to him on January 23, 1990, to reminisce about her visit with him in Paris in 1968 when he had accompanied her to the train station as she set off to try to find the German camp where her father had died. A Japanese university student sent the elderly priest photographs of their meeting in Paris.

Naturally most of the letters in Père Marie-Benoît's archives are those sent to him rather than those he sent, but one letter that he wrote apparently was returned. In it, Père Marie-Benoît, writing to a former protégé in Paris, described briefly how he passed his days. He was seventy-six years old when he wrote, "These days I am cultivating philosophy and theology, starting with the grand Platonic currents through the Augustinians and the Franciscans, where I try in some small way to place myself. Don't be afraid of these great names: above all else, one studies with them the love for existence and goodness and the meaning of death."[42]

Undoubtedly the friendship that meant most to Père Marie-Benoît during these final years was the one he enjoyed with Stefan Schwamm. In part this was because his other friends – Jules Isaac, Edmond Fleg, Joseph Bass, Aron Kasztersztein, Settimio Sorani, Angelo Donati, all of them Jewish – had died. But there was a special chemistry between Père Marie-Benoît and Stefan Schwamm, who was fifteen years younger. The many letters from Schwamm that Père Marie-Benoît carefully preserved are full of the intelligent, lively, often caustic humor that must have appealed to the priest in the first place. Schwamm wrote of his second marriage, after his first wife died, to Simone Sarras, a non-Jewish French woman, on April 18, 1975. He sent Père Marie-Benoît the formal wedding announcement and then, the following year, an announcement of the birth of a son, Xavier, on June 7, 1976. Père Marie-Benoît baptized the child, who lived with his parents near Frankfurt am Main, in Germany. As the years passed, Schwamm sent the priest photographs of the boy and descriptions of his antics and education. He wrote also of his own career – first, for a short time after the war, as a lawyer in Vienna, and then as a translator, interpreter, business consultant, and teacher in Israel, Canada, and Germany. The two men also exchanged critiques of new articles and books about the Holocaust and the involvement of men and women of the Church. Schwamm informed his friend that he had been asked to write a book about his wartime experiences. He would do it, he said, "in my case with accuracy, unlike what James Rorty and, less inaccurate, Sam Waagenaar have written." The Capuchin in turn told Schwamm that a new French book about Pius XII and the Holocaust contained, at least in the parts about him, "as many errors as words."[43] Schwamm often visited Père Marie-Benoît at his monastery, which must have greatly pleased the older man.

In the end, however, even these quiet activities became impossible. On May 14, 1987, Père Marie-Benoît wrote a short note to Schwamm to explain that he could no longer type.[44] In 1989, ill and frail, severely deaf, and with shaky handwriting, he left Paris for the last time. He settled in the Capuchin monastery in Angers, which operated a facility for elderly and ailing priests and friars. He died there on February 5, 1990, just a few miles from the little village of Le Bourg d'Iré, where he had been born nearly a century before. His great friend Stefan Schwamm, severely incapacitated for nine long months by a stroke, died in Frankfurt four years later, on February 9, 1994.

Epilogue

DURING THE LONG LIFETIME OF PÈRE MARIE-BENOÎT, EVERYDAY life in France changed more dramatically than in any other historical period of comparable length. The boy who grew up where villagers brought their wheat to be ground at a water mill lived to hear from Stefan Schwamm about the vexing new "electronic communications" known as computers. The earnest lad who was raised in the shadow of the French Revolution, witnessed French police smashing church doors, and left his family in order to be trained as a Capuchin priest in a foreign country, lived to see widespread popular indifference to religion, as manifested by huge declines both in attendance at Catholic mass and in the number of men and women choosing religious vocations. Far from constituting a threat to secular society, as many in France believed it to be at the end of the nineteenth century, the Church that Père Marie-Benoît loved became politically irrelevant during his lifetime. And the young priest who experienced the Vatican's abolition in 1928 of an organization devoted to treating Jews with greater respect lived to welcome the Second Vatican Council's *Nostra Aetate* in 1965, which declared that not all Jews at the time of the death of Jesus and no Jews since then could be considered guilty of the death of Jesus.

Throughout all this, Père Marie-Benoît did not change outwardly. While many men and women of the Church replaced their habits with secular clothing, he wore the traditional long brown cassock and sandals of his order until the end. Inwardly, however, he changed greatly. From the earnest and obedient young man who scrupulously reported to his Capuchin superior every penny of expense, even while facing annihilation in the trenches during the First World War, he grew into a thoughtful priest capable of questioning the traditional teachings of the Church, especially regarding Jews. During the late 1940s and 1950s he became an enthusiastic advocate of friendship between Jews and Christians, insisting that each group could learn from the other. He quietly challenged the Catholic obsession with converting the Jews, explaining that the determining factor in conversion was God's grace and will, not the efforts of men. He was always in the forefront of Catholic theologians who argued for the reforms of Vatican II.

One wonders whether this Capuchin priest ever regretted the choice he made as a young and inexperienced boy to join a religious order and become a priest. Such decisions taken today are made by young men rather than by children, and thus with much more information and understanding. Certainly Père Marie-Benoît thrived on his decision. As a boy from a conservative Catholic family with a modest income and from a traditional Catholic village, education in a university of the French Republic would have been, if not technically impossible, at least personally inconceivable. In its stead the Capuchins recognized his talents and gave him a superior education in theology and philosophy. Had he remained a layman, Père Marie-Benoît might have gone into business, but he probably would not have had a career as an intellectual, which is what he wanted to be and what he became.

Père Marie-Benoît's Capuchin education broadened his horizons in other ways, at least after he moved to Rome for advanced studies in 1921. Paradoxically, his introduction to the world beyond the Church, begun with military service in the First World War, was completed from a monastery in the Eternal City. Rome in the 1920s and early 1930s, with Mussolini in charge and Fascist thugs threatening dissenters, including priests, was certainly no paradise. But for a young man from a small village and for a war-scarred veteran of years of horror, it must have seemed close to heaven. Père Marie-Benoît thrived on the sun and the light, so different from the somber damp of northern France, Belgium, and the Netherlands. He enjoyed visits and concerts in Rome's many churches, retreats and vacations at Tivoli, and, above all, the proximity to the Vatican and the sense of being in the center of the Catholic world.

There is no evidence that Père Marie-Benoît ever regretted the absence of a wife and family. He visited the lively families of his brothers in Angers and enjoyed them, but he never expressed regrets. He certainly enjoyed the presence of women, and women liked him, as witnessed by the plentiful exchange of letters between him and many women friends and protégés. But he was equally warm with men and equally anxious to preserve their friendships. Above all, however, he liked the Jewish people. Perhaps he found them less constrained, more expansive, and more interesting than the serious and quiet men he knew in his monastery. Certainly he was drawn to Joseph Bass, Angelo Donati, and Stefan Schwamm, all of whom shared his wry and ironic sense of humor, his immense energy, and his creative imagination. Père Marie-Benoît did not give reasons for his affection for the Jews, nor, probably, did it ever occur to him to do so. But in 1945 he wrote from Rome to Joseph Bass, "The Jewish newspaper *Israel* has reappeared, some Jews have kindly given me a subscription and I am thus informed about everything that interests the Jewish world. I remain on the watch for anyone who may ask for my help in the sense that we liked to discuss together in France, and I dream and wish to do a great deal still for those who have unjustly suffered so much and have taken such a large place in my heart."[1] This he did until he died.

Père Marie-Benoît's life as a Capuchin priest was not without its sacrifices and drawbacks. He may not have missed having a family of his own. Neither was he interested in material things – in clothes, gourmet food and wine, automobiles, art, beautiful objects, or comfortable homes. But he would have cherished the freedom to choose his own career path without the obligation to go wherever the Capuchins sent him. He would have enjoyed the freedom to travel and live wherever he wished without the constraints that his vows of poverty and obedience imposed upon him. His fascination with Morocco after the First World War and with Israel in 1958 reveal his intellectual curiosity and zest for the travel and adventure that he could not afford. He never wrote that he was bored or restless in his monastery during the last decades of his life, but it is clear that he would have liked to retire in Israel. Such a step was impossible, if only for financial reasons.

Despite these sacrifices Père Marie-Benoît was fortunate in finding his religious vocation. He enjoyed teaching philosophy and theology to the young, and he was good at it. During the war he flourished while working among the Jews whom he so liked and admired, but he then returned to teaching and writing. These activities gave meaning and continuity to his life. This Capuchin priest was also fortunate in other respects. Above all, he was lucky to have survived the carnage of the First World War, in which he served from beginning to end. He was also lucky to have survived the Second World War. If he had been arrested along with Stefan Schwamm that night in Milan in 1944, or at any other time during the German occupations of France and Italy, he might well have died in deportation. Military service from 1914 to 1918 and Jewish rescue activities from 1940 to 1944, however difficult and dangerous, enriched the life of this intellectual, who was also a man of action, and provided him with a postwar role in the world outside the monastery and a store-house of memories and friendships for his old age.

If Père Marie-Benoît was personally fortunate, however, those around him were lucky to have known him. Most fortunate, of course, were those whose lives he saved, and their descendants. Fortunate too were his many students, who evidently adored him and thrived on his brilliance and fierce warmth. His Capuchin confreres in Marseille, Campobasso, and Paris were similarly appreciative, although less is known of those in Rome and Saint Symphorien. Many who knew him remember his earnestness, his devotion to his vocation, and his obvious goodness. Even those who disagreed with him benefited, although they may not have realized it. They benefited because he made them think about the value of tolerance, of listening, of respecting the rights and beliefs of others.

The study of Père Marie-Benoît's life, moving in its own right, also sheds valuable light on aspects of the Second World War and postwar history. Above all, his wartime experience reveals much about the phenomenon of Jewish rescue during the Holocaust. Of course it indicates, if more indication is needed, how much difference a single individual could make. But more than that, his example shows how much a collaborative group of rescuers could accomplish. For our Capuchin priest rarely acted alone. In both Marseille and Rome he worked closely with like-minded people, mostly Jewish but also non-Jewish. The rescue organizations he helped create saved many more people than any single individual could have done.

Rescue organizations existed in all German-occupied countries, certainly, but they tended to be much smaller and more restricted in Central and Eastern Europe than in the west. Several conditions had to be met if such groups were to operate successfully. Most effective was the participation of both Jews and non-Jews, for many reasons. The Jews were usually the first to perceive the needs of their communities, and they brought that information to the attention of non-Jews of goodwill who, busy with their own problems, might otherwise not have noticed. Non-Jews then became involved and contacted others who could help. Also, Jewish rescuers were best placed to contact individuals in need and win their trust, while non-Jews could locate safe houses and guide their protégés to them. Jewish rescuers could often raise funds from within local and international Jewish communities, while non-Jews could obtain contributions of food, clothing, and medicine from social welfare agencies and church charities. But such cooperation required that Jewish rescuers, or at least their leaders, be familiar with the language and customs of the country and have contacts among non-Jews – conditions that were not always frequent in the east. And non-Jews needed to be comfortable with Jews and free from antisemitism – conditions that also could not be taken for granted, but which were more usual in Western Europe than in points farther east.

Equally crucial for successful rescue was the broader context in which it occurred. It is true that Vichy bureaucrats and police instigated, organized, and executed the terrible deportations from unoccupied France in August 1942 and continued to cooperate with the Germans until the bitter end. Of the 330,000 Jews in the country in 1940, about 80,000 were deported to the east or were killed in France.[2] Through drawing up lists, making arrests, tolerating dreadful internment camps, guarding the trains, informing, actual murder, or other means, French citizens were involved with the deaths of most of these victims. But the environment in France was not invariably hostile to Jews. In Marseille in 1942 and early 1943, for example, Père Marie-Benoît's confreres at his monastery knew he was helping Jews, but no one turned him in to the police. Some of the Capuchin's French Catholic communicants who worked in government offices in Marseille provided blank forms for the creation of false identification cards. A French doctor kept Ida Fallmann in the hospital in August 1942 to help her avoid deportation. French nuns running a hospital near the Swiss frontier accepted the three Fallmann women when they were rejected at the border, without turning them in. A French internment camp commander allowed Fernande Leboucher to visit her husband not once but many times. These may have been small things, but they helped save lives.

The danger period for Jews in Italy during the German occupation from September 1943 to the spring of 1945 in the north was shorter but equally intense. Of approximately 32,300 Jews present in the country during the entire period of occupation, excluding those able to flee to Switzerland or to the Allied-controlled south, some 8,128 were either deported, killed within the country, or lost and unaccounted for.[3] German agents made many arrests, organized the trains, and took over the larger camps, but Italian police or Fascist fanatics assisted them, Italian bureaucrats helped prepare lists, and informers existed. But the goodwill of many bystanders was often evident. Padre Benedetto and his Catholic and Jewish friends could never have accomplished what they did without the passive cooperation of many among the Roman police and municipal bureaucrats. They also benefited from the men and women of the Church who opened convents, monasteries, Catholic boarding schools, and hospitals throughout Rome to refugees in need of shelter, including Jews. The assistance of Rome's diplomatic communities was also remarkable. Diplomats at the Swiss and Hungarian consulates, as well as many French, Belgian, Romanian, Yugoslavian, and other officials, granted protective documents to refugees unknown to them without asking too many questions. Informers were an ever present danger, but in an environment generally hostile to the German occupiers and often at least mildly sympathetic to Jews in hiding, they had to operate with caution and restraint, and their reports were sometimes ignored.

Père Marie-Benoît's wartime activities also demonstrate the different problems and situations faced by foreign and native Jews. In both Marseille and Rome the priest's protégés were notably needy foreigners. In Marseille this was in part because the arrests and deportations of native Jews remained the exception rather than the rule during the years when Père Marie-Benoît was in France. But in Rome also, the Capuchin priest dealt mainly with foreign Jews. This occurred partly because of his interest in refugees from France, but there were other factors as well. In most cases native Jews in both France and Italy were less dependent on consistent outside help from the beginning to the end of the German occupation of their countries than were the foreign Jews. Native Jews usually had friends and contacts from whom they could obtain false documents and good advice. Often they had some financial resources, however depleted. They spoke the local language and could disguise themselves as non-Jews with some ease. Foreign Jews enjoyed none of these advantages. They were totally alone in a profoundly threatening world. Père Marie-Benoît and the Jews and non-Jews who worked with him were keenly aware of their needs.

The study of Père Marie-Benoît's life also sheds light on postwar relationships between Christians and Jews. Antisemitism clearly did not end with the revelation of Auschwitz. People competing for scarce resources in the immediate postwar period continued to regard each other with suspicion. Under the circumstances, Jewish distrust of Christians in 1945 was understandable, but hostility on the part of Christians toward the Jews was unpardonable. Still worse was the failure of leadership from spokesmen of the Catholic and Protestant churches. Père Marie-Benoît understood all this and did what he could to help. He was not alone. Other thoughtful men and women did the same. Change came slowly during the second half of the twentieth century. But the need for increased tolerance and understanding among all national, religious, racial, and cultural groups remains a challenge for the present and for the future.

Notes

INTRODUCTION

1. Settimio Sorani to Harold Tittmann, "1943–1945; 1961–1962: Reports on the Situation of Jews in Italy," in English translation, January 22, 1962, file 716, collection 33/44, Archives of the American Jewish Joint Distribution Committee, New York.

2. Sorani to Eloisa Ravenna, July 19, 1966, 5 pp., 3, b. 13-B, f. Roma, Centro di documentazione ebraica contemporanea, henceforth cited as CDEC, Milan. Unless otherwise indicated, all translations from a source cited in French, Italian, and German throughout this book were made by me.

3. Toaff quoted in Elio Venier, *Il clero romano durante la Resistenza: Colloqui con i protagonisti di venticinque anni fa* (Rome: Colombo, 1972), 87. The book was also published in *Rivista Diocesana di Roma*, no. 11–13, 1969, and no. 1–2, 1970.

4. Père Marie-Benoît to Simone Sarras Schwamm (Stefan's second wife, whom he married after the death of his first wife, Gisela), February 2, 1984, in Stefan Schwamm private archives, Frankfurt am Main.

5. Père Marie-Benoît to Stefan Schwamm, May 2, 1987, in Schwamm private archives.

1. PIERRE PÉTEUL: FAMILY HERITAGE AND EDUCATION

1. Although much of it has deteriorated, part of the mill still exists, as does the stone house nearby where Pierre Péteul was born.

2. The population statistic is from Paul Joanne, *Le Maine-et-Loire d'autrefois* (1896; La Mothe-Achard, France: Les Chemins de la Mémoire, 2003), 80. In 2007 Angers had a population of 156,327; Segré, 7,155; and Le Bourg d'Iré, about 720.

3. For this information I am grateful to Jean-Pierre Legourgeois, a local historian of Le Bourg d'Iré, interview, October 15, 2007. On windmills, see Philippe and Catherine Nédélec, *L'Anjou entre Loire et Tuffeau* (Luçon: Éditions Ouest-France, 2001), 25.

4. Nédélec, *L'Anjou entre Loire et Tuffeau*, for information about parental preferences and the closing of the local school. Statistics of population and public schools in the Maine-et-Loire are from Joanne, *Le Maine-et-Loire*, 39.

5. For Pierre Péteul's failure to gain admission to the seminary in Angers, see Marie-Hélène de Bengy, former archivist at the Archives des Capucins de France, Paris, lecture in Le Bourg d'Iré, April 8, 2006. Roman Catholic priests can serve in parishes under the supervision of the local diocesan bishop or be members of religious orders. The former are called diocesan or secular priests, while the latter are called regular priests, because they

live according to the strict rules (from *regula* in Latin) of their orders. Members of most religious orders can be ordained as regular priests or be non-ordained brothers. Brothers in mendicant, preaching, or teaching orders such as the Franciscans, Capuchins, Carmelites, and Dominicans tend to be called friars, while those in monastic orders dedicated to contemplation and study such as the Benedictines and Cistercians are usually called monks. A few religious orders consist only of brothers, and still fewer, including the Oratorians and the Paulists, are comprised only of priests. I am grateful to Kevin Spicer, C.S.C., for his help on this point.

6. Pierre's genealogy and the information about his aunts and uncle are from Jean-Pierre Legourgeois. For a biography of Pierre's uncle, see n.a., *Un moine cistercien: Le P. Marie-Benoît (René Péteul), 1854–1886* (Montreal: Librairie Granger, 1909).

7. Jean-Pierre Legourgeois, interview. For the background of seminary students elsewhere in France, see Christian Dumoulin, *Un séminaire français au 19ème siècle: Le recrutement, la formation, la vie des clercs à Bourges* (Paris: Téqui, 1977), 348–49. Dumoulin presents evidence that the seminary in Bourges in 1902 also had more students than it could easily handle (423).

8. Jean-Pierre Legourgeois, *Aux Armes! Histoire de la Chouannerie au Bourg d'Iré, village du Haut-Anjou, 1789–1799* (Le Bourg d'Iré: Assoc. "Passé-Présent du Bourg d'Iré," 2007), 14.

9. These measures were a culmination of French Gallicanism, the conviction that the organization of the Church in France should be determined by the temporal authorities independently of Rome. They repudiated ultramontanist theories that the Church must be controlled entirely by the pope. For details, see especially François Furet, "Civil Constitution of the Clergy,"

in *A Critical Dictionary of the French Revolution*, ed. François Furet and Mona Ozouf and trans. Arthur Goldhammer (Cambridge, MA: Harvard University Press, 1989), 449–57.

10. For statistics for the Vendée and Maine-et-Loire, see Legourgeois, *Aux Armes!*, 25. For statistics only for Angers, see Célestin Port, *Pays de Loire: Le Maine-et-Loire* (Doue-la-Fontaine, France: Éditions C.M.D., 2001), 108. For details and statistics for the entire country, see Timothy Tackett, *Religion, Revolution, and Regional Culture in Eighteenth-Century France* (Princeton, NJ: Princeton University Press, 1986).

11. François Furet, "Vendée," in Furet and Ozouf, *Critical Dictionary*, 168.

12. Legourgeois, *Aux Armes!*, 105. For the descriptions of atrocities, see 66–81.

13. Ibid., 35, 69–71, 109, and 112.

14. In addition, by the terms of the concordat, the pope recognized the French Republic and agreed to accept the confiscation of Church lands in France. The state acknowledged Catholicism as the religion of the great majority of the French people and agreed to pay clerical salaries. All existing bishops resigned and new bishops were appointed, with representation from both the refractory and the oath-taking clergy. For details, see William Roberts, "Napoleon, the Concordat of 1801, and Its Consequences," in *Controversial Concordats*, ed. Frank Coppa (Washington, DC: Catholic University Press, 1999), 34–80.

15. The Ferry laws also made education free and compulsory for boys and girls between the ages of six to thirteen.

16. Jean-Michel Duhart, *La France dans la tourmente des Inventaires: La séparation des Églises et de l'État* (Joué-lès-Tours, France: Alan Sutton, 2001), 10. See also Pierre Pierrard, *Un siècle de l'Église de France, 1900–2000* (Paris: Desclée de Brouwer, 2000), who estimated that there

were 3,216 religious orders in France in 1900, with 35,000 men and 125,000 women involved in teaching, hospital work, and other services (39).

17. I am grateful to Frère Bruno Marie at the Cistercian Trappist Abbey in Oka, Quebec, for this information.

18. Duhart, *La France dans la Tourmente*, 10–13.

19. Because all faiths were involved, historians usually do not refer to the separation of Church and state but use the more awkward term, separation of "the churches and the state." For details, see Jean-Marie Mayeur, *La Séparation des Églises et de l'État* (Paris: Les Éditions ouvrières, 1991); and Jean Tulard and André Damien, *Histoire de la laïcité à la française: Loi de 1905: le livre du centenaire official* (Paris: Académie des science morales et politiques, 2005).

20. For details, see Émile Poulat, ed., *La Séparation et les Églises de l'Ouest; Actes du colloque tenu à l'Université Catholique de l'Ouest à Angers, les 1er et 2 décembre 2005* (Paris: L'Harmattan, 2006).

21. Marie-Hélène de Bengy, letter to this author, January 15, 2008. For more on Père Paulin, see "Le R. Père Paulin," in *Annales franciscaines* (January 1934): 46–51; and P. Théobald, *Le Réverend Père Paulin de Ceton: Frère Mineur-Capucin* (Paris: Société et Librairie Saint-François, 1934).

22. It will be noted that Capuchin priests and friars often follow their signatures with the letters O.F.M. Cap., meaning Order of Friars Minor Capuchin.

23. R. P. Paulin, *René Bériot: Frère Eleuthère de Montreuil-sur-Marne de l'Ordre des Frères Mineurs Capucins* (Paris: Pierre Tequi, 1926), 184. I am grateful to Cécile de Cacqueray at the Bibliothèque franciscaine des capucins and Frère Dominique Mouly at the Archives des Capucins de France in Paris for identifying Père Paulin and René Bériot in this photograph and for the information about the overcoat.

24. A provincial minister is the head of the order within a specific administrative region called a province, not to be confused with a secular province.

25. For more on the Vichy regime and conservative Catholics, see chapter 4.

2. PIERRE PÉTEUL AND THE FIRST WORLD WAR

1. Père Robert Levet, "Le Père Marie-Benoît, le 'Père des Juifs,'" *L'Église aujourd'hui à Marseille* 13 (July 1, 2008): 180. I am grateful to Père Levet for making his work available to me. According to Pierre Pierrard, *Histoire des curés de campagne de 1789 à nos jours* (Paris: Plon, 1986), 23,418 secular clergymen and 9,231 regular clergymen served in the French military during the First World War. Of these, 3,101 secular and 1,517 regular clergymen were killed; 7,759 and 2,655 received citations or decorations (292).

2. This information is from a document in the possession of Pierre Péteul, the son of our Pierre's brother Louis, kindly shown to me during my interview with him and his sister Françoise Péteul Huet and their cousin Marie-Joseph Péteul Zenit, daughter of our Pierre's brother Joseph, Angers, June 10, 2008.

3. All information about Pierre Péteul's regimental assignments, citations, and awards is from his nephew Pierre Péteul, who has preserved his military documents. The priest Pierre Péteul, writing as Père Marie-Benoît, also mentioned his military awards in his testimony in *Livre d'Or des Congrégations françaises: 1939–1945* (Paris: D.R.A.C., 1948), 305. They obviously meant a great deal to him. For more on *Livre d'Or*, see chapter 4.

4. Pierre Péteul, "Souvenirs de la guerre, 1914–1918," *Les Amis de St. François* (July–October 1970): 163–66. Pierre Péteul did not mention assisting a second officer on February 25, as his citation stated. Although by 1970 he was known

in France as Père Marie-Benoît, the priest signed this article with his secular name. I am grateful to his nephew Pierre Péteul for showing me this publication. The "Lévesque" referred to in this article was probably Jean Lévesque de Burigny (1692–1785), a Catholic historian and philosopher who combined Enlightenment ideas with a keen interest in the history and theology of the Church.

5. Ibid.

6. P. Marie-Benoît, "Lettres de la guerre, 1914–1919," Archives des Capucins de France, Paris, 13 LM 77, henceforth cited as ACF, Paris.

7. On the other hand, in his "Souvenirs de la guerre," Pierre Péteul wrote sympathetically of some German soldiers he had encountered in the opposite trenches in Alsace at an unstated date. They too wanted peace and a return to their families, he reflected. He recalled that the trenches had been quiet for a time, with the Germans hurling grenades at the French only when their officers were in the area. As the officers approached, the German soldiers threw stones to warn the French that a grenade attack was about to begin.

8. Although the day and month of each of Pierre Péteul's letters are usually clear, he often did not state the year, and it sometimes cannot be determined from the context. The mutinies in the French army on the Western Front began in May 1917 as a result of the horrendous casualties during General Robert Nivelle's offensive at Chemin des Dames in April. They eventually spread to sixteen army corps. By July, when Pierre Péteul was writing, the worst was over. Some twenty-eight hundred men had received sentences, of whom about fifty had been condemned to death. In addition to the punishments, however, the new commander in chief, General Henri Philippe Pétain, improved conditions in the French army.

9. Péteul, "Souvenirs de la guerre."

10. ACF, Paris, 13 LM 76. For a description of the notebook, cited by its French name as Carnet, see chapter 3, note 1. Sadly, Pierre Péteul, by then a priest and professor at the Capuchin college in Rome, was also unable to be present when his father died in 1950.

3. THE YEARS BETWEEN THE WARS, 1919 TO 1939

1. Pierre Péteul kept a brief listing of meetings, trips, and other events in his daily life in cramped handwriting in a little black pocket notebook, about three by six inches in size. The account began when he left Breust on August 11, 1921, and ended in June 1961. Unfortunately there are large gaps in the notations between 1926 and 1935, 1937 and the first half of 1938, 1941–1943, and 1945–1957. After 1957 the entries are more regular but remain few in number. See the notebook, cited as Carnet, ACF, Paris, 13 LM 76.

2. ACF, Paris, 13 LM 82.

3. Unidentified priest at the college to a Capuchin provincial minister, ACF, Paris, 2 C.

4. This personal description, drawn on her archival research, is from Marie-Hélène de Bengy, lecture in Le Bourg d'Iré, April 8, 2006.

5. Examples of his communications can be found in ACF, Paris, 7 LG 10 and 10 LJ 11.

6. In the Lateran Accords the Italian government also agreed to define Roman Catholicism as the official religion of the nation, recognize and register all marriages performed in accordance with canon law, grant freedom to Catholic Action as long as it refrained from political involvement, make religious education compulsory for Catholic pupils in the public primary and secondary schools, and pay compensation for Vatican properties not restored to the Church. In turn the

Holy See recognized the Italian state with Rome as its capital, agreed that groups identified with Catholic Action would not engage in politics, and promised to remain neutral in any international conflicts.

7. See an application from an unclear source to a director of the Société nationale des chemins de fer in Paris for a reduced train fare for Père Marie-Benoît and another priest obliged to travel from Rome to France to be mobilized, in ACF, Paris, 5 E 13 1.

8. For the full text of the Manifesto of Racial Scientists, see Renzo De Felice, *The Jews in Fascist Italy: A History,* trans. Robert L. Miller (1961; New York: Enigma, 2001), 679–80.

9. For more on the anti-Jewish laws, their content, enforcement, and impact, see Michele Sarfatti, *Mussolini contro gli ebrei: Cronaca dell'elaborazione delle leggi del 1938* (Milan: Silvio Zamorani, 1994) and *The Jews in Mussolini's Italy: From Equality to Persecution,* trans. John and Anne C. Tedeschi (Madison: University of Wisconsin Press, 2006); and De Felice, *Jews in Fascist Italy.*

10. In addition to the text in *L'Osservatore Romano* for the dates mentioned, see analysis of the speeches in Susan Zuccotti, *Under His Very Windows: The Vatican and the Holocaust in Italy* (New Haven, CT: Yale University Press, 2000), 33–36.

11. Emphasis mine. Ciano passed the ambassador's report along to Mussolini. It is cited in full in De Felice, *Jews in Fascist Italy,* 684–85.

12. Description of the papal speech is in Alberto Cavaglion and Gian Paolo Romagnani, *Le interdizioni del Duce: A cinquant'anni dalle leggi razziali in Italia (1938–1988)* (Turin: Albert Meynier, 1988), 130–31. For *L'Osservatore Romano* article, see "Il paterno elogio di Sua Santità ai pellegrini della Gioventù Cattolica del Belgio," September 9, 1938, 1.

13. "Un'omelia del Vescovo di Cremona: La chiesa e gli ebrei," *L'Osservatore Romano,* January 15, 1939, 2.

14. For details, see Georges Passelecq and Bernard Suchecky, *The Hidden Encyclical of Pius XI,* trans. Steven Rendall (New York: Harcourt Brace, 1997). While the draft of the encyclical condemned antisemitism based on concepts of race, it perpetuated several traditional Catholic anti-Jewish attitudes, explaining that Jews can only be redeemed for their rejection of the Messiah by repentance and acceptance of Jesus and declaring that the Church is not blind "to the spiritual dangers to which contact with Jews can expose souls, or . . . unaware of the need to safeguard her children against spiritual contagion."

15. For the text of *Summi Pontificatus,* see *The Papal Encyclicals,* ed. Claudia Carlen Ihm, vol. 4: *1939–1958* (Raleigh, NC: McGrath, 1981), 5–22. The encyclical is also available in English translation online.

16. Père Marie-Benoît, *Carnet,* August 25, 1939, ACF, Paris.

17. Ibid., September 2 and 3, 1939.

18. Père Marie-Benoît to "Très Révérend Père," Lettres aux supérieurs, October 11, 1939, ACF, Paris, 6 E 1 24.

19. Ibid., December 24, 1939.

4. FIRST STEPS TOWARD JEWISH RESCUE: MARSEILLE, MAY 1940 TO AUGUST 1942

1. Père Marie-Benoît, *Carnet,* ACF, Paris, 13 LM 76.

2. Testimony of Père Marie-Benoît in *Livre d'Or des Congrégations françaises: 1939–1945,* no ed. (Paris: D.R.A.C., 1948), 306. *Livre d'Or* is a collection of testimonies by French men and women in Catholic religious orders who participated in the resistance during the German occupation. Père Marie-Benoît wrote in *Livre d'Or* that his date of departure from Rome was June 19, but he meant May 19 as he clearly indicated in his notebook at the time. The

Capuchin monastery in Marseille, some twelve to fifteen blocks northeast of the Saint Charles train station and southeast of the public garden, was located in the countryside when it was built in 1826. It does not exist today, having been torn down between 1967 and 1970 to make way for the apartment buildings now numbered 32 to 34. Even the name of the street has been somewhat altered, for it is now called Impasse Croix-de-Régnier. I am grateful to Dominique Paquier-Galliard, archivist at the Archevêché de Marseille, for this information.

3. "L'extraordinaire histoire du Père Marie-Benoît," *Le Soir*, September 11, 1946.

4. Also lost were the French departments of Moselle, Bas-Rhin, and Haut-Rhin in Alsace and Lorraine that had been German between 1871 and 1918 and were now annexed to the Third Reich; the departments of the Nord and the Pas-de-Calais in northeastern France, placed under the administration of a German military governor based in Belgium; and the city of Menton and part of the Vallée de la Tarentaise east of Bourg-Saint-Maurice, in southeastern France near the Italian frontier, awarded to the Italians.

5. For the first wave of refugees, see Vicki Caron, *Uneasy Asylum: France and the Jewish Refugee Crisis, 1933–1942* (Stanford, CA: Stanford University Press, 1999), 259; François Delpech, *Sur les juifs: Études d'histoire contemporaine* (Lyon: Presses Universitaires de Lyon, 1983), 298; Julian Jackson, *France: The Dark Years, 1940–1944* (Oxford, UK: Oxford University Press, 2001), 363; and Renée Poznanski, *Jews in France during World War II*, trans. Nathan Bracher (1997; Hanover, NH: University Press of New England, 2001), 24. For the later wave, see Michael R. Marrus and Robert O. Paxton, *Vichy France and the Jews* (New York: Basic Books, 1981), 15.

6. Serge Klarsfeld, *Le calendrier de la persécution des juifs en France, 1940–1944*

(Paris: Les Fils et Filles des Déportés Juifs de France, 1993), 16.

7. For more on these internments, see Susan Zuccotti, *The Holocaust, the French, and the Jews* (New York: Basic Books, 1993), 31–37.

8. Marrus and Paxton, *Vichy France and the Jews*, 68.

9. Within the next three years, a special commission established by the Ministry of Justice reviewed, among others, the cases of 13,839 Jews, revoking the citizenship of 7,055. See report of Maurice Gabolde, keeper of the seals, to Fernand de Brinon, Vichy representative to the German occupying forces in Paris, recorded by de Brinon, September 8, 1943, Mémorial de la Shoah, Centre de documentation juive contemporaine (henceforth cited as CDJC), Paris, XXVII-47.

10. See the report prepared by the Comité de Nîmes, a coordinating committee of Jewish and non-Jewish assistance organizations, for Vichy officials in October 1941, reprinted in Joseph Weill, *Contribution à l'histoire des camps d'internement dans l'Anti-France* (Paris: Éditions du Centre, 1946),167–71; and Gérard Gobitz, "Les déportations de l'été 1942," in *Les camps du sud-ouest de la France, 1939–1944: exclusion, internement et déportation*, ed. Monique-Lise Cohen and Eric Malo (Toulouse: Privat, 1994), 173–80.

11. For the text of the two Statuts des juifs, see *Journal Officiel* (henceforth cited as JO), October 18, 1940, and June 14, 1941. According to the first statute, anyone with three grandparents "of the Jewish race" was to be considered Jewish regardless of possible conversion, as well as anyone with two grandparents "of the same race" who had a Jewish spouse. The second statute made the same provisions for any person with three grandparents "of the Jewish race," but stipulated that anyone with two grandparents of the "Jewish race" would be considered Jewish if he or

she was married to someone similarly half Jewish. It then added that a person with two Jewish grandparents was, despite his or her spouse, also to be considered Jewish unless he or she could provide a baptismal certificate dated before June 25, 1940. For evidence that the Vichy statutes were not imposed by the Germans, see Zuccotti, *Holocaust, the French, and the Jews*, 56.

12. The number 140,000 is from Commissariat générale aux questions juives (henceforth cited as CGQJ) to the Controleur général d'armée, December 2, 1941, CDJC, CXCIII-86. It apparently does not include the several thousand foreign Jews in internment camps in the unoccupied zone. According to Serge Klarsfeld, *Vichy-Auschwitz: Le rôle de Vichy dans la solution finale de la question juive en France: 1942* (Paris: Fayard, 1983), of the 109,983 Jews over age fifteen included in the census, 59,344 were French and 50,639 were foreigners (22).

13. See Prefect of Police to Militärbefehlshaber in Frankreich, CDJC, LXX-IXa-10. Of the 149,734 Jews in and around Paris, 85,664 were citizens and 64,070 were foreigners.

14. For the text of the law, see JO, October 18, 1940. Internment statistics can be found in Anne Grynberg, *Les camps de la honte: les internés juifs des camps français (1939–1944)* (Paris: La Découverte, 1991), 12; and Georges Wellers, *L'étoile jaune à l'heure de Vichy: de Drancy à Auschwitz* (Paris: Fayard, 1973), 99. About three thousand Jews died of exposure, disease, and malnutrition in French internment camps, many of them in the terrible first winter of the war. The names of two thousand are recorded in Serge Klarsfeld, *Memorial to the Jews Deported from France, 1942–1944* (New York: Beate Klarsfeld Foundation, 1983), 612–40.

15. For a copy of the order, see "Internement des Israelites," CDJC, CCXIII-125. It is also printed in Klarsfeld, *Calendrier de la persécution*, 94.

16. For discussion of these measures, see Poznanski, *Jews in France*, 177.

17. Testimony of Père Marie-Benoît in *Livre d'Or*, 306.

18. "Père Marie-Benoît d'après l'interview accordé à M. Ansky," n.d., but not long after the war, 1, CDJC, CCCLXXIII-25.

19. Information about the first request for help is from Père Marie-Benoît, interview with this author, Paris, April 25, 1988. About referrals, see testimony of Père Marie-Benoît in *Livre d'Or*, 307. In her testimony about the help her convent gave to Jews, Sister Yeritza confirmed that the first Jewish refugees, from Germany, arrived in September 1940. See Sister Yeritza, "Marseille: ma ville, mon quartier, mon lycée," n.d., 5 pp., in Archives of the Sisters of Notre Dame de Sion, Paris, 4 M 6. For more on the Sisters of Notre Dame de Sion, see Madeleine Comte, *Sauvetages et baptêmes: Les religieuses de Notre-Dame de Sion face à la persécution des Juifs en France (1940–1944)* (Paris: L'Harmattan, 2001), 13–26.

20. Père Marie-Benoît, interview with this author, Paris, April 25, 1988.

21. For more on the Opus sacerdotale Amici Israel, founded in Rome in 1926, see chapter 11.

22. For details, see Pierre Pierrard, *Juifs et catholiques français: D'Édouard Drumont à Jacob Kaplan (1886–1994)* (Paris: Cerf, 1997), 245–85.

23. For more on these rescuers, see Gay Block and Malka Drucker, *Rescuers: Portraits of Moral Courage in the Holocaust* (New York: Holmes and Meier, 1992); Patrick Henry, *We Only Know Men: The Rescue of Jews in France during the Holocaust* (Washington, DC: Catholic University of America Press, 2007); *Les Justes de France*, no ed. (Paris: Fondation pour la Mémoire de la Shoah, 2007); Mordecai Paldiel, *The Path of the Righteous: Gentile Rescuers of Jews during the Holocaust* (Hoboken, NJ: KTAV, 1993); Michael Phayer and Eva

Fleischner, *Cries in the Night: Women Who Challenged the Holocaust* (Lanham, MD: Rowman and Littlefield, 1997); and Tela Zasloff, *A Rescuer's Story: Pastor Pierre-Charles Toureille in Vichy France* (Madison: University of Wisconsin Press, 2002). For more on Protestants, see *Les protestants français pendant la seconde guerre mondiale: Actes du colloque de Paris, Palais du Luxembourg, 19–21 novembre 1992*, ed. André Encrevé and Jacques Poujol (Paris: SHPF, 1994).

24. On Père Marie-Benoît's friendships with Jews in Rome, see Fernande Leboucher, *Incredible Mission*, trans. J. F. Bernard (Garden City, NY: Doubleday, 1969), 14; information on his fluency in Hebrew is from Rachel Fallmann Schutz and Esther Fallmann Kichelmacher, interviews with this author, Tel Aviv, February 26, 2008, and March 10, 2009. Unless otherwise noted, all subsequent information about the Fallmann sisters is from these interviews.

25. In fact, although they stressed the importance of family values and moral order, Vichy officials granted few concrete pro-Church measures. They did provide some financial assistance to Catholic schools, arranged for public schools to grant free time for voluntary religious instruction off their premises, and restored some Church property. Of greater direct relevance to Père Marie-Benoît, they also permitted the public wearing of monastic habits, abolished the system of authorization for religious orders, and allowed those orders officially to return to France. The orders had been trickling back unofficially since the more relaxed atmosphere of the early 1920s.

26. Nechama Tec, *When Light Pierced the Darkness: Christian Rescue of Jews in Nazi-Occupied Poland* (New York: Oxford University Press, 1986). Other works that examine rescuers' motivations include Eva Fogelman, *Conscience and Courage:*

Rescuers of Jews during the Holocaust (New York: Doubleday, 1994); David P. Gushee, *The Righteous Gentiles of the Holocaust: A Christian Interpretation* (Minneapolis: Fortress Press, 1994); and Samuel P. Oliner and Pearl M. Oliner, *The Altruistic Personality: Rescuers of Jews in Nazi Europe* (New York: Free Press, 1988).

27. Testimony of Père Marie-Benoît in *Livre d'Or*, 307.

28. Testimony of Sister Gabriella Maria, cited in "Initiatives catholiques de secours et de sauvetage à Marseille," extract from Laetitia de Traversay, *Résistance spirituelle au nazisme (1940–1944): Le rôle de catholiques marseillais*, mémoire de maîtrise (equivalent of a master's essay) under the direction of Philippe Joutard, Aix-en-Provence, 1989, available at the Archives of the Sisters of Notre Dame de Sion, Paris, 4 M 6.

29. Both quotations are from testimony of Père Marie-Benoît in *Livre d'Or*, 307.

30. Ibid.

31. This story is told by the Fallmann sisters, but Père Marie-Benoît also recorded it in a formal testimony, probably written in support of some sort of restitution being considered for the Fallmanns at the time. See his report, June 11, 1957, f. 2: Activités de guerre, ACF, Paris, 13 LM 84.

32. Formal declaration by Père Marie-Benoît, October 2, 1949, f. 2, ACF, Paris, 13 LM 85.

33. These two stories are told in testimony of Père Marie-Benoît in *Livre d'Or*, 307; and *Le Soir*, September 11, 1946.

5. WITH JOSEPH BASS IN MARSEILLE, AUGUST 1942 TO JUNE 1943

1. For discussion of negotiations and preparations for this action, see Serge Klarsfeld, *Vichy-Auschwitz: Le rôle de Vichy dans la solution finale de la question juive en France: 1942* (Paris: Fayard, 1983), 63–162; and Serge Klarsfeld, "La livraison

par Vichy des juifs de zone libre dans les plans SS de déportation des juifs de France," in *Les camps du sud-ouest de la France, 1939–1944: exclusion, internement et déportation*, ed. Monique-Lise Cohen and Eric Malo (Toulouse: Privat, 1994), 133–54. For a copy of the order of August 5, see Klarsfeld, *Vichy-Auschwitz: 1942*, 318–19.

2. Klarsfeld, *Vichy-Auschwitz: 1942*, 158. Most of those already interned in unoccupied France were deported from Drancy on convoys 17 to 21 between August 10 and 19, 1942. Most forced laborers were deported on convoys 24, 25, and 26 between August 26 and 31. There were, of course, individual exceptions.

3. Ibid., 339–40 and 348–53, for copies of orders about non-separation of families, issued on August 18 and 22, 1942; and 159 for statistics. Most recent immigrant and refugee Jews arrested in the unoccupied zone between August 26 and mid-September 1942 were deported on convoys 27 to 33, 37, 40, and 42 between September 2 and November 6, 1942. See Serge Klarsfeld, *Memorial to the Jews Deported from France, 1942–1944* (New York: Beate Klarsfeld Foundation, 1983), 236–343, for descriptions and lists of names.

4. "Initiatives catholiques de secours et de sauvetage à Marseille," extract from Laetitia de Traversay, *Résistance spirituelle au nazisme (1940–1944): Le rôle de catholiques marseillais*, mémoire de maîtrise under the direction of Philippe Joutard, Aix-en-Provence, 1989, p. 3, at the Archives of the Sisters of Notre Dame de Sion, Paris, 4 M 6. Sister Marie Rose, a nun at the convent of the Sisters of Notre Dame de Sion in Marseille, remembered reading *Témoignage Chrétien* secretly, because the bishop disapproved of it. See her "Quelques souvenirs de temps de guerre 1940–45 à Marseille," 7 pp., 1, written after the war, in same archives, also 4 M 6.

5. For a full text of the letter, see CDJC, CIX-115. For discussion of this and other

letters of protest, see Susan Zuccotti, *The Holocaust, the French, and the Jews* (New York: Basic Books, 1993), 146–48.

6. CDJC, CIX-113.

7. For Gerlier, see CDJC, CCXIV 6; for Delay, see "Lettre de S. Exc. Mgr. Delay," extract from *La Documentation Catholique*, January 21, 1945, CDJC, CCXVIII-72. Bishop Delay's letter was not printed in *L'Echo de Notre Dame de la Garde: Semaine Religieuse de Marseille*, the weekly diocesan bulletin, which often carried messages from him and from the pope, but it was distributed throughout the diocese by Catholic Boy Scouts.

8. Authorization document signed by the vicar general of Marseille and a local police chief, September 11, 1942, ACF, Paris, 13 LM 84.

9. *Actes et Documents du Saint Siège relatifs à la seconde guerre mondiale* (ADSS), ed. Pierre Blet, Robert A. Graham, Angelo Martini, and Burkhart Schneider, 11 vols. (Vatican City: Libreria Editrice Vaticana, 1965–1981), vol. 2, doc. 105, Pius XII to Preysing, April 30, 1943, 324. The ADSS is a collection of Vatican wartime diplomatic documents culled from Vatican archives by a team of Jesuit scholars. For calls from German ecclesiastics, especially in Berlin, for charity and compassion, see Kevin Spicer, *Resisting the Third Reich: The Catholic Clergy in Hitler's Berlin* (DeKalb: Northern Illinois University Press, 2004), esp. 126–38.

10. For an example dating before the French prelates' protests, see especially the encyclical *Summi Pontificatus*, October 20, 1939, discussed in chapter 3. For later papal appeals for compassion, see chapter 9.

11. Père Marie-Benoît, *Carnet*, entry for August 5, 1942, ACF, Paris, 13 LM 76.

12. For events on August 10, see "Les conditions de la déportation dans la région Marseillaise," n.d., CDJC, CCXIII-114. Most of the children were

turned over to Jewish organizations, especially OSE and ORT. Regarding Pastor Manen, see his journal entry published in *Les Camps en Provence: Exil, internement, Deportation, 1933–1942* (Aix-en-Provence: Alinéa et LLCG, 1984), 209. For expulsions on August 11 and 13, see Klarsfeld, *Vichy-Auschwitz: 1942*, 146; and André Fontaine, *Le camp d'étrangers des Milles, 1939–1943: Aix-en-Provence* (Aix-en-Provence: Édisud, 1989), 147–49.

13. "Père Marie-Benoît d'après l'interview accordé à M. Ansky," n.d., but not long after the war, 5, CDJC, CCCLXXIII-25.

14. Léon Poliakov, *L'auberge des musiciens: Mémoires* (Paris: Mazarine, 1981), 93.

15. Denise Siekierski, *MiDor LeDor (De géneration en géneration)* (Paris: L'Harmattan, 2004), 110 and 125; and interview with this author, Jerusalem, March 2, 2008.

16. Henri-Pierre Bass, son of Joseph Bass, interview with this author, Paris, February 28, 2011. Joseph Bass did not visit his mother, because he feared that since he was a Soviet national the Soviet government might not let him leave. His mother somehow survived the Holocaust and died in 1967. Henri-Pierre Bass does not know what happened to his grandfather, Joseph's father.

17. Siekierski, *MiDor LeDor,* 110–11, and "Joseph Bass," *Revue d'Histoire de la Shoah* 168 (January–April 2000): 140–74; Poliakov, *L'auberge*, 93–94; and Siekierski and Henri-Pierre Bass interviews.

18. Interviews with Joseph Bass, Fonds Annie Latour, CDJC, DLXI-4; and Joseph Bass, Mouvement de résistance juive, connu sous le nom de Groupe d'action contre la déportation (Service André), CCCLXXXIV-41. Neither document has a date, but both testimonies were taken soon after the war. Annie Latour claimed that Bass was a militant Socialist, but he

denied it. All testimonies from the Fonds Annie Latour were made before 1970; Latour used them to write *La résistance juive en France, 1940–1944* (Paris: Stock, 1970), which later appeared in English as *The Jewish Resistance in France (1940–1944),* trans. Irene R. Ilton (New York: Holocaust Library, 1981). Latour donated transcripts of her interviews to CDJC.

19. Bass, CDJC, CCCLXXXIV-41 and DLXI-4. Siekierski and Poliakov wrote that Bass was imprisoned at Le Vernet, but he himself claimed that he was at Argelès.

20. Bass, CDJC, DLXI-4.

21. Ibid.

22. Bass, CDJC, CCCLXXXIV-41; and Bass, n.d., but not long after the war, CDJC, CCXVIII-84. Of those mentioned here, Pastors Lemaire, Trocmé, and Leenhardt, Père Marie-Benoît, Émilie Guth, Fernande Leboucher, and Hermine Orsi were designated as Righteous among the Nations by Yad Vashem after the war. For more on the Righteous, see note 35 below.

23. Bass, CDJC, DLXI-4. Although Saint Dominic may not personally have harmed Jews, the Dominican order that he founded in 1216 was subsequently charged by the Vatican with rooting out heresy and conducting the Inquisition. Groups investigated and persecuted included, among others, Cathars, Moors, and Jews.

24. Ibid.

25. Although Père Marie-Benoît often met those seeking help at his own monastery, he seems not to have lodged them there. The reason is not clear. Perhaps he thought they would not be safe there, especially in light of his own exposure, or perhaps his superior requested that he hide them elsewhere.

26. See Renée Dray-Bensousan, *Les Juifs à Marseille (1940–1944)* (Paris: Les Belles Lettres, 2004), 307–13; Serge Klarsfeld, *Le calendrier de la persécution des juifs en France: 1940–1944* (Paris: Les Fils et Filles des Déportés Juifs de France,

1993), 721, and *Memorial to the Jews,* 410; Christian Oppetit, *Marseille, Vichy et les Nazis: Le temps des rafles, la déportation des juifs* (Marseille: Amicale des Déportés d'Auschwitz et des camps de Haute-Silesie, 2005); and Donna Ryan, *The Holocaust and the Jews of Marseille: The Enforcement of Anti-Semitic Policies in Vichy France* (Urbana: University of Illinois Press, 1996).

27. The tragic exceptions included eighteen young men, mostly students, at La Maison des Roches, two kilometers from Le Chambon, arrested on June 23, 1943, along with their director, Daniel Trocmé. All but seven died in deportation. Daniel Trocmé died at Majdanek on April 2, 1944. Daniel Trocmé was designated as Righteous among the Nations at Yad Vashem, along with Pastor Trocmé and his wife, Magda; Pastor Theis and his wife, Mildred, and daughter, Louise; Simone Mairesse; and Roger Darcissac. On Le Chambon generally, see Pierre Fayol, *Le Chambon-sur-Lignon sous l'occupation: Les résistances locales, l'aide interalliée, l'action de Virginia Hall (OSS)* (Paris: L'Harmattan, 1990); Philip P. Hallie, *Lest Innocent Blood Be Shed: The Story of the Village of Le Chambon and How Goodness Happened There* (New York: Harper Colophon, 1980); Patrick Henry, *We Only Know Men: The Rescue of Jews in France during the Holocaust* (Washington, DC: Catholic University of America Press, 2007), 45–63; and *Weapons of the Spirit,* a film directed by Pierre Sauvage, released in 1989, and distributed by the Chambon Foundation, Los Angeles, California. For Bass's account, see CDJC, DLXI-4 and CCXVIII-84. See also interviews with André and Magda Trocmé, Fonds Annie Latour, CDJC, DLXI.

28. Siekierski, *MiDor LeDor,* 118; and interview.

29. Heinrich Fallmann is listed as a deportee on convoy 29, September 7, 1942, in Klarsfeld, *Memorial to the Jews,* 254. His convoy was one among several from Drancy in 1942 that stopped at Kosel, near Auschwitz, where many men able to work were disembarked for labor in nearby camps.

30. Rachel Fallmann Schutz and Esther Fallmann Kichelmacher, interviews with this author, Tel Aviv, February 26, 2008, and March 10, 2009; and Père Marie-Benoît, testimony, June 11, 1957, in f. 2: Activités de guerre, ACF, Paris, 13 LM 84. For the Fallmann women's attempt to flee to Switzerland, see chapter 4.

31. Fernande Leboucher tells this story in her memoir, *Incredible Mission,* trans. J. F. Bernard (Garden City, NY: Doubleday, 1969), 12–36 and 57–90. Leboucher made many errors regarding the chronology and broader background of her story, which she researched from secondary sources. The errors are particularly serious when she discusses Père Marie-Benoît's experiences in Rome. She worked with him only in Marseille and did not go to Rome. While the book cannot be relied upon as a general history, then, there is little reason to doubt her account of her personal experiences in Marseille. Père Marie-Benoît vouched for that account in a letter to Yad Vashem on September 29, 1971, when Leboucher was being considered for the medal of the Righteous. See Leboucher file 791, Yad Vashem Department of the Righteous, Jerusalem. Ludwik Nadelman was the nephew of Elie Nadelman (1882–1946), a Polish sculptor who moved to Paris in 1904 and to New York in 1914.

32. Leboucher, *Incredible Mission,* 71.

33. Ludwik Nadelman is listed as a deportee on convoy 51 in Klarsfeld, *Memorial to the Jews,* 407.

34. Leboucher, *Incredible Mission,* 82.

35. The Memorial of Yad Vashem, the Israeli government–established Holocaust Martyrs' and Heroes' Remembrance Authority, honors non-Jews who risked their lives during the Holocaust to save Jews. Nominations as Righteous among

the Nations are made by Jewish survivors who hid in Père de Parceval's Dominican
who have been saved by the non-Jewish in-
dividual concerned. Those survivors then
deliver sworn testimony on behalf of their
rescuers. The final determination is made
by a special commission, created in 1964,
presided over by a judge of the Israeli Supreme Court, after careful scrutiny of the
accuracy and objectivity of the accounts.

36. Zattara was arrested in November 1943 but released. He immediately
returned to his resistance work and was
arrested again in June 1944. He left behind
a wife and five children. Père Marie-
Benoît's link to this courageous resister
is confirmed by the priest's reference to a
letter he wrote from Rome to Zattara in
Marseille in July 1943. See list of recipients
of letters written by Père Marie-Benoît,
ACF, Paris, LM 76.

37. Bass testimony, CDJC, CCXVIII-84.

38. The Sixième was a clandestine Jewish rescue group that developed from
the Éclaireurs israélites de France. See
especially Alain Michel, *Les Éclaireurs Israélites de France pendant la seconde guerre
mondiale, Septembre 1939-Septembre 1944:
action et évolution* (Paris: Éditions des
EIF, 1984). The Hebrew Immigrant Aid
Society's rescue work in France and links
with Joseph Bass are described in Valery
Bazarov, "Jews Rescuing Jews: Operation
Rescue, the Hebrew Immigrant Aid Society in France (1940–44)," in *Holocaust
Persecution: Responses and Consequences,*
ed. Nancy Rupprecht and Wendy Koenig
(Newcastle upon Tyne: Cambridge Scholars Publishing, 2010), 98–119. The Réseau
Marcel, organized in Nice by Odette
Rosenstock and Moussa Abadi, hid and
supported 527 Jewish children during the
war, with protective cover from the local
bishop, Monsignor Paul Rémond. The
bishop was named a Righteous among the
Nations in 1991.

39. I am grateful for this information
to Claude S., a German Jewish refugee

who hid in Père de Parceval's Dominican
monastery for a time, was escorted to
Le Chambon with his mother by agents
working for Joseph Bass, and eventually
joined Bass in the resistance. Claude S.
asks that his full name not be cited. Interview with this author, June 8, 2010.

40. I am grateful to Joseph Bass's son
Henri-Pierre Bass for sharing personal information about his father with me.

6. WITH ANGELO DONATI
IN NICE, NOVEMBER
1942 TO JUNE 1943

1. Elsewhere on or east of the Rhône,
however, the Germans seized Marseille,
Avignon, Lyon, and Toulon, although
the latter was completely surrounded by
Italian-occupied territory.

2. On November 14, 1943, Fascist
Party delegates who had convened at
Verona approved a manifesto declaring,
among other things, that all Jews in Italy
were foreigners and members of an "enemy nationality." Then on November 30
the minister of the interior announced
that all Jews residing in Italy were to be
arrested and interned in concentration
camps within the country. There was
no specific measure ordering that Jews
should be handed over to the Germans,
but Mussolini knew that once they were
in camps, he could not protect them from
deportation.

3. SS First Lieutenant Heinz Röthke,
"Present State of the Jewish Question in
France," July 21, 1943, reprinted in full
in English translation as document 25
in Léon Poliakov, "The Jews under the
Italian Occupation in France," in Léon
Poliakov and Jacques Sabille, *Jews under
the Italian Occupation* (Paris: Éditions du
Centre, 1955), 104–106. This estimate may
have been somewhat high.

4. Interview with Ignace Fink, Fonds
Annie Latour, n.d., but before 1970, 24 pp.,
1 and 21, CDJC, DLXI.

5. "Père Marie-Benoît d'après l'interview accordé à M. Ansky," n.d., but not long after the war, CDJC, CCCLXXIII 25. On another occasion, Père Marie-Benoît wrote that the two men left Marseille for Nice and Cannes every Sunday night and stayed until Wednesday or Thursday. He added that Joseph Bass "remains my very good friend." See testimony of Père Marie-Benoît in *Livre d'Or des Congrégations françaises: 1939–1945* (Paris: D.R.A.C., 1948), 308.

6. Fink interview, 19, CDJC, DLXI.

7. Ibid., 21.

8. Chataignier report, April 19, 1945, CDJC, CCXVIII-93a. For the intense debate about the role of Anne-Marie, see Léon Poliakov, *L'auberge des musiciens: Mémoires* (Paris: Mazarine, 1981), 125–41.

9. Père Marie-Benoît interview with Ansky, CDJC, CCCLXXIII-25; and récit de Monsieur Donati, CDJC, CCXVIII-78. In her memoir, *Incredible Mission*, trans. J. F. Bernard (Garden City, NY: Doubleday, 1969), Fernande Leboucher wrote that Père Brémond introduced Donati and Père Marie-Benoît, but Père Marie-Benoît's memory was probably more accurate.

10. Incident related by Marianne Spier-Donati, Angelo Donati's daughter, interview with this author, Paris, June 9, 2010.

11. Paolo Veziano, ed., *Angelo Donati: Un ebreo modenese tra Italia e Francia,* catalog for a show in Modena, January 27, 2004, 15; and Madeleine Kahn, *De l'oasis italienne au lieu du crime des allemands* (Nice: Bénévent, 2003), 31–32.

12. Marianne Spier-Donati interview. See also Marianne Spier-Donati's account in Olga Tarcali, *Retour à Erfurt, 1935–1945: récit d'une jeunesse éclatée* (Paris: L'Harmattan, 2001). Hilde and Carl (referred to as Charles) Spier are listed as deportees on convoy 27, September 2, 1942, in Serge Klarsfeld, *Memorial to the Jews Deported from France, 1942–1944* (New York: Beate Klarsfeld Foundation, 1983),

241. The train left many male deportees capable of hard labor at Kosel before ending its journey at Auschwitz.

13. Fink interview, 3, CDJC, DLXI.

14. Exposé de Monsieur Donati, 1, CDJC, CCXVIII-22.

15. For an excellent description of this issue, see Daniel Carpi, *Between Mussolini and Hitler: The Jews and the Italian Authorities in France and Tunisia* (Hanover, NH: Brandeis University Press, 1994), 102–35.

16. For Lospinoso's statement, see the extract for his defense before the Commissione d'epurazione, 1946, from the Lospinoso papers and reproduced in Joseph Rochlitz, *The Righteous Enemy: Document Collection* (unpublished manuscript, Rome, 1988), 58. For Müller's report, see document 9 in Poliakov, *Jews under the Italian Occupation,* 73.

17. For German reports on Lospinoso, see docs. 10, 12, 13, 18, 22, and 24 in Poliakov, *Jews under the Italian Occupation,* 74–103.

18. Exposé de Monsieur Donati, 2, CDJC, CCXVIII-22; and extract for Lospinoso's defense in Rochlitz, *Righteous Enemy,* 58.

19. Père Marie-Benoît testimony at a conference at CDJC, March 10–12, 1979, in *La France et la question juive: 1940–1944,* ed. Georges Wellers, André Kaspi, and Serge Klarsfeld (Paris: Sylvie Messinger, 1981), 253.

20. Père Marie-Benoît interview with Ansky, CDJC, CCCLXXIII-25.

21. Testimony of Père Marie-Benoît in *Livre d'Or,* 308.

22. Carpi, *Between Mussolini and Hitler,* 136–41; and exposé de Monsieur Donati, 1, CDJC, CCXVIII-22.

23. Lospinoso to Sergio Piperno, February 8, 1962, b. 74 E, Unione delle Comunità Israelitiche Italiane (UCII). In this letter, Lospinoso claimed that soon after his arrival in Nice, Donati visited him to discuss the problems of the Jews.

24. Fink interview, 20, CDJC, DLXI,.

25. Exposé de Monsieur Donati, 3, CDJC, CCXVIII-22.

7. PÈRE MARIE-BENOÎT AND THE DONATI PLAN, JUNE TO SEPTEMBER 1943

1. Père Marie-Benoît to general minister, f. Marie-Benoît de Bourg d'Iré, doc. 3, Archivio Generale Cappuccini, Rome, G 94 – S IV (henceforth cited as Capuchin archives, Rome).

2. Ibid., docs. 4 and 5.

3. Interview with Ignace Fink, Fonds Annie Latour, n.d., but before 1970, 24 pp., 7 and 9, CDJC, DLXI.

4. Exposé de Monsieur Donati, 3, CDJC, CCXVIII-22. The total number of foreign Jews in Italy in July 1943 was probably about eighty-eight hundred. See Michele Sarfatti, *The Jews in Mussolini's Italy from Equality to Persecution*, trans. John and Anne C. Tedeschi (Madison: University of Wisconsin Press, 2006), 136.

5. Testimony of Père Marie-Benoît in *Livre d'Or des Congrégations françaises: 1939–1945* (Paris, D.R.A.C., 1948), 309. Père Marie-Benoît already knew some of these Jewish leaders. For example, he wrote in his notebook that he met with Jules Isaac and his wife in Aix-en-Provence on August 5, 1942, the same day that he visited Les Milles and recorded "lamentable cases." See also Père Marie-Benoît, *Carnet*, ACF, Paris, 13 LM 76.

6. "Père Marie-Benoît d'après l'interview accordé à M. Ansky," n.d., but not long after the war, CDJC, CCCLXXIII-25.

7. Ibid.; and Père Marie-Benoît testimony at a conference at CDJC, March 10–12, 1979, in *La France et la question juive: 1940–1944*, ed. Georges Wellers, André Kaspi, and Serge Klarsfeld (Paris: Sylvie Messinger, 1981), 254. On Donat de Welle's petition to Micara, see document by Père Marie-Benoît, no title, n.d., but after 1975,

f. 1: La Résistance: Récits, ACF, Paris, 13 LM 84. Père Donat de Welle is often cited as Donat (or Donato, in Italian) a Welle or da Welle, but in his correspondence he signed his name as Donat de Welle. Père Marie-Benoît referred to him in that way.

8. Père Marie-Benoît interview with Ansky, CDJC, CCCLXXIII-25. He wrote much the same thing in *Livre d'Or*, 309.

9. Père Marie-Benoît's dossier to Pope Pius XII is published in *Actes et Documents du Saint Siège relatifs à la seconde guerre mondiale* (ADSS), ed. Pierre Blet, Robert A. Graham, Angelo Martini, and Burkhart Schneider (Vatican City: Libreria Editrice Vaticana, 1975), vol. 9, doc. 264, July 15, 1943, 393–97. According to the editors of the ADSS, the official list of papal audiences for July 16, 1943, referred only to Père Donato da Welle [*sic*] "and others," without actually naming Père Marie-Benoît (9: 401, n. 1). The report of audiences in the Vatican daily newspaper *L'Osservatore Romano* the following day omitted the reference to "others." A copy of the dossier with its four requests (as distinct from the four appendixes) also exists in ACF, Paris, 13 LM 84. Appendix B is included, but not the other three (see below).

10. ADSS, vol. 9, doc. 264, July 15, 1943, 396–97. The source of Père Marie-Benoît's statistics of Jews in supervised residence is unclear. The actual number was lower than he stated to the pope. The number of Jews in the entire Italian-occupied zone who would be in danger if the Germans took over was much higher, however, but Donati had not yet formulated a plan for them all.

11. Ibid., 395–96, editors' footnote 16. The editors raised the same question in their introduction to volume IX, adding that the appendix concerning camps in and deportations from France mentioned nothing about the real fate of Jewish deportees. They asked, "Is that all that the Jewish community [in France] knew? Was

it refusing to believe the reports that were arriving?" (42).

12. Père Marie-Benoît, "Mon action en faveur des juifs persecutés à la seconde guerre mondiale," 9 pp., 2–3, ACF, Paris, 13 LM 97; and untitled document, n.d., but after 1975, f. 1: La Résistance: Récits, in same archives, 13 LM 84. Copies of the correspondence between Père Marie-Benoît and Father Robert Graham may exist in the Graham archives, which are not accessible to most scholars.

13. Jacob Kaplan, *Justice pour la foi juive: Pierre Pierrard intérroge le Grand Rabin Kaplan* (Paris: Centurion, 1977), 87–90; and Jacob Kaplan, *N'oublie pas* (Paris: Stock, 1984), 10.

14. Protest of the Consistoire central des Israélites de France, August 25, 1942, 1–4, CDJC, CCXIII-15.

15. Georges Wellers, *L'Étoile jaune à l'heure de Vichy: De Drancy à Auschwitz* (Paris: Fayard, 1973), 231.

16. Fink interview, 12 and 16, CDJC, DLXI. Serge Klarsfeld, who interviewed Fink about forty years ago, confirmed this story in a communication with this author, November 12, 2010.

17. Wellers, *L'Étoile jaune*, 7 and 228.

18. Henri Krasucki testimony in [n.a.], *Jawischowitz, une annexe d'Auschwitz: 45 deportés 8 mineurs témoignent* (Paris: Amicale d'Auschwitz, 1985), 221.

19. Robert Debré, *L'Honneur de vivre: Témoignage* (n.p.: Hermann et Stock, 1974), 231–32.

20. Saul Friedlander, *Kurt Gerstein ou l'ambiguïté du bien* (Tournai, Belgium: Casterman, 1967), 141; and Jurgen Schafer and Kurt Gerstein, *Zeuge des Holocaust: Ein Leben zwischen Bibelfreisen und SS* (Bielefeld: Luther-Verlag, 1999), 167. See also Gerstein's postwar report on his wartime activities reproduced in full in Dieter Gräbner and Stefan Weszkalnys, *Der ungehörte Zeuge: Kurt Gerstein, Christ, SS-Offizier, Spion im Lager der Mörder*

(Saarbrucken, Germany: Conte Verlag, 2006), 141–51.

21. Guenter Lewy, *The Catholic Church and Nazi Germany* (New York. McGraw Hill, 1964), 288; and Guenter Lewy, "Pius XII, the Jews, and the German Catholic Church," *Commentary*, February 1964, 27.

22. Alfieri to Ciano, February 3, 1943, 580–83, in *I Documenti diplomatici italiani*, series 9: 1939–1943, vol. 9, Ministero degli Affari Esteri, Commissione per la pubblicazione dei documenti diplomatici.

23. ADSS, vol. 9, doc. 82, Preysing to Pius XII, March 6, 1943, 170.

24. Ibid., doc. 85, 177–78, footnote 6; doc. 152, 254–56; and doc. 174, 274.

25. Ibid., doc. 264, 392.

26. For more on Père Marie-Benoît's views on conversions, see chapter 11.

27. Père Marie-Benoît referred to this meeting in a handwritten letter to André Bart, a pseudonym for Joseph Bass, in Cannes on July 29, 1943. He did not mention Lopinot's name, but described him as a fellow Capuchin priest who was an assistant Vatican representative to a Jewish internment camp in Cosenza, in southern Italy. This could only have been Lopinot, and the camp, Ferramonti-Tarsia. See letter in CDJC, CDXLVI-6.

28. Testimony of Mirko Haler, Fondo Israel Kalk, 8, CDEC, VII-1; and Fr. Callistus a Geispolsheim (Lopinot), "De Apostolatu inter Hebraeos in publicae custodiae loco cui nomen v. 'Campo di Concentramento Ferramonti-Tarsia (Cosenza),'" in *Analecta Ordinis Fratrum Minorum Capuccinorum* 60 (1944): 70–75; and 61 (1945): 40–47 and 71.

29. Père Marie-Benoît to his "dear friend," unnamed but certainly Joseph Bass, CDJC, CDXLVI-7. The date on the document looks like February 20, 1946, but is almost certainly 1945. Père Marie-Benoît wrote that he had just received a letter from the recipient, written from Paris on January 16, 1945. He also stated that he

was giving lectures on the Old Testament every three weeks, an activity that ended in May 1945, as will be seen in chapter 11. It appears that someone in the archives inadvertently wrote the number 6 over the typed number 5 on the original document.

30. ADSS, vol. 9, doc. 281, Maglione to Cicognani, August 1, 1943, 417.

31. Ibid., doc. 307, Cicognani to Maglione, August 23, 1943, 442; and Maglione to Père Marie-Benoît, printed in full in the testimony of Père Marie-Benoît in *Livre d'Or*, 310–11.

32. ADSS, vol. 9, doc. 264, 393.

33. Père Marie-Benoît to André Bart (Joseph Bass), July 29, 1943, in CDJC, CDXLVI-6.

34. For a good look at the attitudes and initiatives of Italian diplomats and civil servants, see Daniel Carpi, *Between Mussolini and Hitler: The Jews and the Italian Authorities in France and Tunisia* (Hanover, NH: Brandeis University Press, 1994), 173–74.

35. ACF, Paris, 13 LM 84.

36. Père Marie-Benoît testimonies in *La France et la question juive*, 254, and *Livre d'Or*, 311. Harold Tittmann's formal name was Harold H. Tittman Jr.

37. Récit de Monsieur Donati, n.d., CDJC, CCXVIII-78.

38. Exposé de Monsieur Donati, 3–4, CDJC, CCXVIII-22.

39. ADSS, vol. 9, doc. 267, Notes du Père Marie-Benoît, 401–402. According to the editors, this document bears the date July 1943, and they supplied the day, the sixteenth. This is an error. To a note to a Capuchin superior dated September 9, 1943, Père Marie-Benoît attached, for his information, a copy of a message dictated by Donati for the Jewish committee in Lisbon (see text, below), which, he explained, had been written on September 6, and a copy of this above-cited memorandum written by him, to be delivered to the Vatican Secretariat of State. Père

Marie-Benoît told his superior he gave that memorandum to Monsignor Martin and to a personal friend of Monsignor Tardini *along with a copy of the Lisbon note*. Thus, Père Marie-Benoît's memorandum for the Vatican could not have been delivered before September 6. See Père Marie-Benoît to "Révérendissime Père," doc. 9, September 9, 1943; and typed copy of the actual memorandum, without date, addressee, or signature, doc. 10, in f. Marie-Benoît de Bourg d'Iré, Capuchin archives, Rome, G 94 – S IV. The content of the memorandum also dates it in late August or early September. Père Marie-Benoît wrote of moving some thirty thousand to fifty thousand Jews to North Africa, a plan that Donati did not conceive of until after the fall of Mussolini on July 25. Père Marie-Benoît also wrote, "Italian troops are progressively leaving France and the Germans are already in the neighborhood of Nice." The Italian army did not agree to withdraw from any part of their French zone of occupation until August 15, and actual withdrawal ensued only after August 25. Finally, the "accord in principle" that Père Marie-Benoît alluded to in the memorandum could not have occurred in July, since discussions with American and British diplomats did not begin until August 15. There was little progress before the end of that month.

40. ADSS, vol. 9, doc. 321, Notes du Père Marie-Benoît, September 1943, no day given, 465–67. Probably because Père Marie-Benoît sent the copy to the Vatican, the editors of ADSS implied erroneously that he was the author. For Père Marie-Benoît's statement that Donati dictated the note to him on September 6, and for an undated copy of the note itself, see testimony of Père Marie-Benoît in *Livre d'Or*, 312–14; and Père Marie-Benoît to "Révérendissime Père," doc. 9, September 9, 1943, and doc. 11 in f. Marie-Benoît de Bourg d'Iré, Capuchin archives, Rome,

G 94 – S IV. See also Père Marie-Benoît to his superior, résumé of his wartime activities, n.d., but after 1948, A C F, Paris, 13 LM 84. Père Marie-Benoît stated that at Donati's request he also wrote a personal letter to Gerard Rufus Isaacs, the second Marquess of Reading, in London, describing the Donati plan and asking him to urge his government to help. There is no copy of such a letter among Père Marie-Benoît's papers.

41. Léon Poliakov, *L'auberge des musiciens: Mémoires* (Paris: Mazarine, 1981), 124–25.

42. Serge Klarsfeld, *Vichy-Auschwitz: Le rôle de Vichy dans la solution finale de la question juive en France: 1943–1944* (Paris: Fayard, 1985), 124; and Serge Klarsfeld, *Memorial to the Jews Deported from France, 1942–1944* (New York: Beate Klarsfeld Foundation, 1983), 455–526.

43. Ignace Fink of the Comité Dubouchage later testified that the committee was not able to help its refugees much after September 1943, because it had no funds. See Fink interview, 9, CDJC, DLXI.

44. For this story, see Alberto Cavaglion, *Nella notte straniera: Gli ebrei di St.-Martin-Vésubie* (1981; Dronero, Italy: L'Arciere, 2003); and Susan Zuccotti, *Holocaust Odysseys: The Jews of Saint-Martin-Vésubie and Their Flight through France and Italy* (New Haven, CT: Yale University Press, 2007).

45. For the memoirs of one who made this journey, see Karl Elsberg, *Come sfuggimmo alla Gestapo e alle SS,* intro. Klaus Voigt (Aosta, Italy: Le Château edizioni, 1999).

46. Adriana Muncinelli, *Even: Pietruzza della memoria: Ebrei, 1938–1945* (Turin: Gruppo Abele, 1994), 161.

47. Cavaglion, *Nella notte straniera,* 132–58, lists those sent back to Nice and indicates those who returned.

48. Exposé de Monsieur Donati, 4–5, CDJC, CCXVIII-22.

49. Marianne Spier-Donati's account in Olga Tarcali, *Retour à Erfurt, 1935–1945: récit d'une jeunesse éclatée* (Paris: L'Harmattan, 2001), 87. Père Marie-Benoît later remembered meeting Marianne in Rome when Donati and he met with Tittmann and Osborne. Marianne, he wrote, waited at the exit. He did not provide an exact date. See Père Marie-Benoît to Stefan Schwamm, March 1, 1984, in Schwamm private archives, Frankfurt am Main.

50. Spier-Donati in Tarcali, *Retour à Erfurt,* 87–129; and Marianne Spier-Donati, interview with this author, Paris, June 9, 2010. In 1999, on the testimony of Marianne and Rolf Spier-Donati, Francesco Moraldo was honored as a Righteous among the Nations at Yad Vashem.

51. Récit de Monsieur Donati, CDJC, CCXVIII-78. Donati did not specify the name of the religious order or the nature of his contacts there.

8. EARLY RESCUE IN ROME, SEPTEMBER AND OCTOBER 1943

1. Original handwritten report, July 20, 1944, f. P. Marie-Benoît, Activités de Guerre, Documents, 1942–1974, A C F, Paris, 13 LM 84; "Report on the activity of the Delasem by Father Benedetto," July 20, 1944, printed in full in Renzo De Felice, *The Jews in Fascist Italy: A History,* trans. Robert L. Miller (1961; New York: Enigma Books, 2001), doc. 41, 756–58, 757; and Père Marie-Benoît to his "dear friend," unnamed but certainly Joseph Bass, February 20, 1945, CDJC, CDXLV I-7. Delasem is an acronym for Delegazione assistenza emigranti ebrei. In his *L'assistenza ai profughi ebrei in Italia (1933–1947)* (Rome: Carucci, 1983), Settimio Sorani implied that he knew Padre Benedetto before September 8, 1943, for he wrote that he recognized him and Angelo Donati on that day as they were leaving the Vatican (138). They told Sorani of their

efforts to take Jewish refugees by boat from France to North Africa via Italy. This is not inconsistent with Padre Benedetto's statement that Alatri actually told him of the plight of a large group of refugees a few days later. Less clear is Sorani's statement that Padre Benedetto came to tell him of his desire to help on September 10, before the Jews from Saint-Gervais could have reached Rome (140). Sorani must have inadvertently advanced the date by two or three days, for in his "Attività della 'Delasem' dopo l'8 settembre 1943," he stated that the visit occurred "around" September 12 (May 16, 1944, 12 pp., 7, b. 8-A-I, f. Delasem – Settimio Sorani, CDEC). Had it occurred before the thirteenth, Padre Benedetto would not have met the Jews from Saint-Gervais on his first encounter with refugees, which he expressly stated that he did.

2. Lionello Alatri; his wife, Evelina Chimichi; and his father-in-law, Eugenio Elia Chimichi, are listed among the Jewish deportees from Italy in Liliana Picciotto, *Il libro della memoria: Gli ebrei deportati dall'Italia (1943–1945)* (1991; Milan: Mursia, 2002), 102 and 188. For more on the Rome roundup, see below.

3. For the account of those sent to Nice by trucks, see interview with Ignace Fink, Fonds Annie Latour, 24 pp., 9, CDJC, DLXI.

4. Aron Kasztersztein and Udla Bronstein were married in an orthodox Jewish service but not a civil one. For more on Kasztersztein, see Stefan Schwamm, "Déclaration sur l'honneur" on behalf of Udla Bronstein, March 22, 1979, f. 2, ACF, Paris, 13 LM 85; and Père Marie-Benoît, testimony on behalf of Aron Kasztersztein, November 8, 1952, ACF, Paris, 13 LM 84. Père Marie-Benoît's document was written because Kasztersztein, who had lived in Rome with false papers during much of the German occupation, had returned from deportation and was having

difficulty establishing his true identity. The name Kasztersztein is often spelled Kasterstein.

5. Père Marie-Benoît, his list of recipients of letters, ACF, Paris, 13 LM 76.

6. For more on Schwamm, see Curriculum Vitae, 1984, f. Correspondance – Schwamm, ACF, Paris, 13 LM 79; and Schwamm private archives, Frankfurt am Main. Stefan Schwamm has sometimes been described as a non-Jew, but this is clearly an error. In his curriculum vitae in 1984, Schwamm identified himself as a descendant of the Khazars, a semi-nomadic Turkic people who, according to him, converted to Judaism around the eleventh century. His certificate of marriage to Gisela Sofie Lange in Vienna in 1934 describes him as *mosaisch,* and another document in his archives states that he officially left the Jewish Community in Vienna in 1953. Gisela was a Protestant, and Anita was baptized. But even Schwamm's contemporaries were sometimes confused on this point. Settimio Sorani, his close associate in Jewish rescue in Rome, apparently believed he was "a so-called Aryan" but of Jewish origin and a Christian convert, which makes little sense. See Sorani to Eloisa Ravenna, July 19, 1966, 5 pp., 4, b. 13-B, f. Roma, CDEC.

7. Hanna Rawicz Keselman, interview with this author, Teaneck, New Jersey, December 14, 2007. Unless otherwise noted, all information about Hanna Rawicz is from this interview.

8. Frieda Schnabel Semmelman, interview with this author, New York City, November 6, 2008. Clara lived in Antwerp after the war and died in 1959. On the resistance activities of the Mandels and the subsequent arrest of Franz, see also the formal written declarations of Georges Vavasseur (secretary general of Mouvement de libération nationale), July 31 and October 20, 1948; Bertha Baron (hiding in the house at the time of the arrest),

January 12, 1955; and Dr. Henri Granel (who treated Clara for her injuries), September 18, 1951, f. 2, A C F, Paris, 13 L M 85. Vavasseur and Baron referred to Mandel as Franz, but his sister-in-law, Frieda Schnabel Semmelman, remembers him as Benjamin. He was deported under the name Frantz (*sic*) Mandel on September 14, 1942, on convoy 32 to Auschwitz. He may have been among the able-bodied young men who disembarked at Kosel, before arrival at Auschwitz, for work in neighboring camps, or he may have died at Auschwitz. Israel Schnabel was deported on March 4, 1943, on convoy 50, to the death camps of Majdanek and Sobibor. See deportation lists in Serge Klarsfeld, *Memorial to the Jews Deported from France, 1942–1944* (New York: Beate Klarsfeld Foundation, 1983), 277 and 402.

9. Abraham Dresdner, interview with this author, Brooklyn, New York, December 15, 2008. All subsequent references to the Dresdners are from this interview.

10. Rabbi Cassuto and the Florentine Jews helping him were associated with Delasem, the local counterpart of the group with which Padre Benedetto worked in Rome. Delasem leaders in Florence asked Cardinal Dalla Costa for help. The cardinal in turn recruited the network of local priests. For more on this situation, see Susan Zuccotti, *Under His Very Windows: The Vatican and the Holocaust in Italy* (New Haven, CT: Yale University Press, 2000).

11. For the story of the train and the statistic of two hundred passengers, see Stefan Schwamm's report in his private archives, Frankfurt am Main, Germany; and Stefan Schwamm, "Riassunto dell'attività di Padre Benedetto Maria O.F.M. Cap. e dei suo [*sic*] collaboratori," December 20, 1945, 9 pp., Marie-Benoît file 201, Department of the Righteous, Yad Vashem. Copies of this document are also in b. 13-B, f. Roma, and b. 8-B – Opera di soccorso e di

assistenza ai perseguitati, C D E C. It was translated into French and published in *Le Monde juif,* September–December 1993, n. 149, 95–102.

12. Schwamm report, Schwamm archives.

13. Charles Delzell, *Mussolini's Enemies: The Italian Anti-Fascist Resistance* (Princeton, NJ: Princeton University Press, 1961), 277.

14. Settimio Sorani, "Attività della 'Delasem' dopo l'8 settembre 1943," 7. Much of this report is printed in Sorani, *L'assistenza ai profughi ebrei,* appendix 43, 291–98.

15. *Actes et Documents du Saint Siège relatifs à la seconde guerre mondiale* (A D S S), ed. Pierre Blet, Robert A. Graham, Angelo Martini, and Burkhart Schneider (Vatican City: Libreria Editrice Vaticana, 1965–1981), vol. 9, doc. 338, Notes of the Secretariat of State, September 18, 1943, 482–83. The editors of A D S S identify Monsignor Riberi at that time as a member of the Pontifical Commission for Refugee Assistance, but that commission was not formed until March 18, 1944. See Agostino Giovagnoli, "Chiesa, assistenza e società a Roma tra il 1943 e il 1945," in *L'Altro Dopoguerra: Roma e il Sud, 1943–1945,* ed. Nicola Gallerano (Milan: F. Angeli, 1985), 213–24. In 1943 Riberi was an official in the Congregation di Propaganda Fide. The A D S S editors also suggest that the Jewish lawyer may have been Ugo Foà, president of the Roman Jewish Community. However, since, according to the document, the lawyer was introduced to Monsignor Di Meglio by a member of the Swiss legation, with which Sorani was personally familiar, it seems equally likely that the lawyer was Schwamm.

16. Schwamm, "Riassunto dell'attività di Padre Benedetto Maria." See also testimony of Père Marie-Benoît, in *Livre d'Or des Congrégations françaises: 1939–1945* (Paris: D.R.A.C., 1948), 315.

17. Sorani, "Attività della 'Delasem' dopo l'8 settembre 1943," May 16, 1944, 12. Sorani's statistics are confusing, for on page 5 of the same report he declared that Delasem was helping four thousand people, a figure that was subsequently repeated frequently by him, Padre Benedetto, and others. On page 7 he declared that there were about one thousand Jewish refugees in Rome from France and Yugoslavia, a figure not wholly inconsistent with his data on page 12. In "Riassunto dell'attività di Padre Benedetto Maria," Schwamm wrote that his team of Padre Benedetto, Kasztersztein, Sorani, and himself was helping twelve hundred foreign Jews (6–7).

18. Samuel Berlin, interview with this author, Riverhead, New York, August 5, 2008.

19. For arrests and atrocities in Merano, Novara, and the area around Lago Maggiore, see Picciotto, *Il libro della memoria*, 44, 818–19, and 868. For more on Lago Maggiore, see *La strage dimenticata: Meina settembre 1943: Primo eccidio di ebrei in Italia,* intro. Roberto Morozzo della Rocca (Novara, Italy: Interlinea, 2003).

20. Cited in Michael Tagliacozzo, "La persecuzione degli ebrei a Roma," in *L'occupazione tedesca e gli ebrei di Roma: Documenti e fatti,* ed. Liliana Picciotto Fargion (Rome: Carucci, 1979), 152.

21. On the gold extortion, see especially Ugo Foà, "Relazione del Presidente della Comunità Israelitica di Roma Foà Ugo circa le misure razziali adottate in Roma dopo l'8 settembre a diretta opera delle Autorità tedesche di occupazione," written November 15, 1943, to be saved in case he did not survive. This report is in *Ottobre 1943: Cronaca di una infamia,* ed. Comunità Israelitica di Roma, pamphlet printed in 1961, 9–29. See also Fausto Coen, *16 ottobre 1943: La grande razzia degli ebrei di Roma* (Florence: La Giuntina, 1993); Giacomo Debenedetti, *16 ottobre 1943* (Rome: OET, 1945); Robert Katz, *Black Sabbath: A*

Journey through a Crime against Humanity (Toronto: Macmillan, 1969); Picciotto, *Il libro della memoria,* 811–18; Michael Tagliacozzo, "La Comunità di Roma sotto l'incubo della svastica: La grande razzia del 16 ottobre 1943," *Gli ebrei in Italia durante il fascism: Quaderni del Centro di Documentazione Ebraica Contemporanea* 3 (November 1963): 9–10; and Michael Tagliacozzo, in *L'occupazione tedesca e gli ebrei di Roma,* 149–71. In *L'assistenza ai profughi ebrei in Italia,* Sorani stated that leaders of the Roman Jewish Community, including Renzo Levi, the president of Delasem in Rome and Sorani's close associate, met with Vatican officials to request help if the amount of gold demanded by the Germans could not be collected (145). On September 27, Vatican officials made it known that the pope agreed to a loan in that event. The fifty kilograms of gold were raised from contributions of Roman Jews and non-Jews, however, and the loan was not needed.

22. Sorani, "Attività della 'Delasem' dopo l'8 settembre 1943," May 16, 1944, 6–7; and Sorani, *L'assistenza ai profughi ebrei in Italia,* 138, 147, and 149–50. In 1968 the International College of Saint Lawrence of Brindisi was moved to quiet, spacious grounds on the circumferential highway or ring road that encircles Rome. There is little evidence of the old buildings in the via Sicilia. Some external walls seem to have survived, but the interior has been converted into private residences and meeting rooms.

23. Padre Maria Benedetto, "Aide clandestine aux refugiés politiques et confessionnels: Affaires d'Italie," n.d., but written while he was still living at the Capuchin monastery in Rome, and therefore before October 1953, CDJC, CCCLXXIII-25. Padre Benedetto mentioned the six boxes of Delasem papers and his nickname, "Father of the Jews," in his testimony in *Livre d'Or,* 315 and 317.

24. For more on the Rome roundup, see Debenedetti, *16 ottobre 1943*; Katz, *Black Sabbath*; Picciotto, *Il libro della memoria,* 877–82; Tagliacozzo, in *Gli ebrei in Italia durante il fascismo and in L'occupazione tedesca e gli ebrei di Roma*; and Susan Zuccotti, *The Italians and the Holocaust: Persecution, Rescue, and Survival* (New York: Basic Books, 1987), 101–38. The number of deportees has sometimes been given as 1,007, but according to Picciotto, it is now recognized to be at least 1,023 (*Il libro della memoria,* 882).

25. Sorani, *L'assistenza ai profughi ebrei in Italia,* 148.

26. For more on Pius XII's role in hiding Jews in Church institutions in Rome, see chapter 9.

9. WITH STEFAN SCHWAMM IN ROME: SECURING DOCUMENTS FOR JEWISH RESCUE

1. Testimony of Père Marie-Benoît (Benedetto) in *Livre d'Or des Congrégations françaises: 1939–1945* (Paris: D.R.A.C., 1948), 316.

2. Settimio Sorani, *L'assistenza ai profughi ebrei in Italia (1933–1947)* (Rome: Carucci, 1983), 149; and Settimio Sorani, "Come sono riuscito ad imbrogliare la Gestapo," *Israel,* December 28, 1944, 3. Kotnik was released after an intervention by ecclesiastical authorities but had been so mistreated in prison that he died soon after the war.

3. Stefan Schwamm, "Riassunto dell'-attività di Padre Benedetto Maria O.F.M. Cap. e dei suo [*sic*] collaboratori," December 20, 1945, 9 pp.; Marie-Benoît file 201, Department of the Righteous, Yad Vashem; Sorani, *L'assistenza ai profughi ebrei in Italia,* 141–42; Padre Maria Benedetto, n.d., b.7.A.73, "Aide clandestine aux refugiés politiques et confessionnels: Affaires d'Italie," CDJC, CCCLXXIII-25; and testimony of Père Marie-Benoît in *Livre d'Or,* 319.

4. After the liberation of Rome, Padre Benedetto made formal declarations regarding the goodwill and help provided by Luigi Charrier (sometimes written Charric or Chiarrier, on May 18, 1946), Cherubini (on February 5, 1945), and Emilia Bettini (May 18, 1946). Charrier and Bettini were apparently being considered for an honor for their record during the German occupation; Cherubini was being investigated by a commission conducting purges of former fascists. In his declaration for Bettini, Padre Benedetto wrote that many employees at the office of rationing were cooperative (f. 2, ACF, Paris, 13 LM 85).

5. The story of CAP is told in Schwamm, "Riassunto dell'attività di Padre Benedetto Maria"; Sorani, *L'assistenza ai profughi ebrei in Italia,* 141–42; and Padre Benedetto, "Aide clandestine aux refugiés" and his testimony in *Livre d'Or,* 319–20. The fact that Padre Benedetto was president of CAP does not imply that he was ever acting director of Delasem in Rome. Sorani retained that position throughout the German occupation. The incident concerning CAP documents and Dionisi may be connected to *Actes et Documents du Saint Siège relatifs à la seconde guerre mondiale* (ADSS), ed. Pierre Blet, Robert A. Graham, Angelo Martini, and Burkhart Schneider (Vatican City: Libreria Editrice Vaticana, 1965–1981), vol. 9, doc. 412, Père Marie-Benoît to Monsignor Montini, November 5, 1943, 544. In this document, the Capuchin priest wrote to ask for a personal recommendation from the Holy See. The editors of ADSS do not indicate the results of the request. According to doc. 412, however, Padre Benedetto was also hoping to persuade the German ambassador to the Holy See to endorse the CAP documents once he had a personal recommendation from the Vatican; doc. 415, Notes of the Secretariat of State, November 6, 1943, 549, indicates that Vatican officials, understanding that the effort was for foreign Jews, persuaded him that this was too dangerous.

6. ADSS, vol. 9, doc. 433, Notes of don Salvatore Asta, November 19, 1943, 568–69, and the editors' interpretation in the introduction, 59.

7. Testimony of Père Marie-Benoît (Benedetto) in *Livre d'Or*, 315; and documents by Père Marie-Benoît in ACF, Paris: "Mon action en faveur des juifs persecutés à la seconde guerre mondiale," 9 pp., 3, 13 LM 97; f. 1: La Résistance: Récits, untitled document, n.d., but after 1975, 13 LM 84; and f. 2, Dichiarazione [for Alberto De Dominicis], June 15, 1944, 13 LM 85. This latter declaration was apparently written because De Dominicis was under official investigation after the liberation of Rome.

8. ADSS, vol. 9, Note of Dell'Acqua, attached to doc. 433, November 20, 1943, 568–69.

9. Ibid., doc. 487, Notes of the Secretariat of State, December 29, 1943, 631–32.

10. Ibid., footnote 4, annotation by Dell'Acqua, 632. Strangely, when Dell'Acqua's notes were published in ADSS, Padre Benedetto denied he had ever met or spoken with him. Perhaps Dell'Acqua had sent an assistant. See Père Marie-Benoît, "Mon action en faveur des juifs persecutés à la seconde guerre mondiale," 8.

11. Ibid., vol. 9, doc. 390, Tacchi Venturi to Maglione, October 25, 1943, and attached note from Dell'Acqua, October 27, 1943, 525–26; and doc. 405, Notes of Monsignor Montini, November 1, 1943, 538. For what was known about the fate of deported Jews at the Vatican before the summer of 1943, see chapter 7; for more about knowledge after that date, see Susan Zuccotti, *Under His Very Windows: The Vatican and the Holocaust in Italy* (New Haven, CT: Yale University Press, 2000), 93–112.

12. *Summi Pontificatus* was discussed in chapters 3 and 5. For the other papal speeches and articles, see *L'Osservatore Romano*, December 25, 1942, 2; June 3, 1943, 1; October 25–26 and 29, 1943, 1; and

December 3 and 4, 1943, 1. The articles in October were the only times that the pope included the word "religion" in his expressions of concern for war victims. The articles in December were unique in using the word "Jews" but objected only to Italian policies, not to German ones. When Jews in Italy continued to be arrested and deported and Vatican objections were ignored, there was no follow-up.

13. For more on this subject, see Andrea Riccardi, *L'Inverno più lungo, 1943–44: Pio XII, gli ebrei e i nazisti a Roma* (Rome-Bari: Laterza, 2008); Zuccotti, *Under His Very Windows*, 171–326; and Susan Zuccotti, "Pius XII and the Rescue of Jews in Italy: Evidence of a Papal Directive," in Joshua D. Zimmerman, ed., *Jews in Italy under Fascist and Nazi Rule* (New York: Cambridge University Press, 2005), 287–307. For examples of more recent testimony regarding Rome, see Grazia Loparco, "Gli ebrei negli istituti religiosi a Roma (1943–1944): Dall'arrivo alla partenza," *Rivista di Storia della Chiesa in Italia*, anno LVIII, n. 1, January-June 2004, 107–210; Pina Baglioni, "Il Santo Padre ordina . . . ," *30Giorni* 7/8 (July-August 2006): 32–46; and *Memoriale delle Religiose Agostiniane Ven. Monastero dei SS. Quattro Coronati*, Roma, pages for 1943.

14. ADSS, vol. 9, doc. 482, attached note of an official at the Vatican Secretariat of State, December 22, 1943, 626. See a similar admonition in vol. X, doc. 32, Notes of the Secretariat of State, January 31, 1944, 105.

15. Diario delle consulte di *Civiltà Cattolica*, document dated January 1, 1944, Archivio della *Civiltà Cattolica*, cited by Giovanni Sale S.I., "Roma 1943: Occupazione nazista e deportazione degli ebrei romani," *La Civiltà Cattolica*, anno 154, vol. 4, December 6, 2003, 417–29, 426.

16. Diario, "Appendice," 17–18, b.7.A.73, Archivio del Seminario Lombardo, Rome.

17. ADSS, vol. 10, doc. 53, Anichini to Pius XII, February 13, 1944, and attached

note by Tardini, 127–29. The total number of fugitives in Vatican City in February 1944 is unclear, but this document states that there were about fifty hidden in private apartments in the Canonica. Nearly all were men. Roughly twenty-four were non-Jews, and another seventeen were Catholics described as "non-Aryans," meaning they were Jews who had converted. The religious affiliations of the others were not mentioned.

18. Testimony of Père Marie Benoît in Livre d'Or, 316.

19. Schwamm, "Riassunto dell'attività di Padre Benedetto Maria"; and testimony of Père Marie-Benoît (Benedetto) in Livre d'Or, 320. Sorani, L'assistenza ai profughi ebrei in Italia, also referred to Dr. Angelo De Fiore, head of the office for foreigners at police headquarters, who hid files and scrambled names to prevent more zealous policemen from finding them (144). In his testimony in Livre d'Or, Padre Benedetto called De Fiore his very good friend and wrote that without the goodwill and help from the central police headquarters, his rescue group would not have been able to endure (322).

20. Schwamm, "Riassunto dell'attività di Padre Benedetto Maria."

21. Ibid. Sam Waagenaar wrote a more elaborate version of Chauvet's withdrawal of protection in his The Pope's Jews (La Salle, IL: Open Court, 1974), 399–401. According to Waagenaar, the trouble started when the Italian Ministry of the Interior was informed that there were more than four hundred refugees from France in Rome and asked the Swiss consulate for a list of their names so that they could be repatriated. Waagenaar interviewed Padre Benedetto at length and is generally reliable, but I have confined my account to Schwamm's testimony.

22. Sedonie Templer Shytoltz (Sharon), interview, Haifa, Israel, February 27, 2008. See also Albert M. Sharon, Walking to

Valdieri (New York: MS Finian, 2003). Don Viale was honored as a Righteous among the Nations at Yad Vashem in 2000.

23. For the story of these coordinated efforts, see Zuccotti, Under His Very Windows.

24. Eliyahu Löwenwirth was deported from Fossoli to Bergen-Belsen on May 16, 1944. Transferred ultimately to a work camp near Dachau, he died there, probably of typhus, on February 11, 1945. For his deportation from Italy, see Liliana Picciotto Fargion, Il libro della memoria: Gli ebrei deportati dall'Italia (1943–1945) (1991; Milan: Mursia, 2002), 417.

25. Miriam Löwenwirth Reuveni, Dedication, unpublished English translation of her memoirs titled Hakdasha, written in Hebrew with Miriam Dubi-Gazan (Raanana, Israel: Docostory, 2002); also translated into Italian as Dedicazione (Aosta, Italy: Le Château, 2005); and interviews with this author in Nice and Cuneo, September 8 and 9, 2003, and in Haifa, February 26 and 27, 2008. For more about Miriam Löwenwirth, see Susan Zuccotti, Holocaust Odysseys: The Jews of Saint-Martin-Vesubie and Their Flight through France and Italy (New Haven, CT: Yale University Press, 2007).

26. Charles Roman, interviews with this author, Teaneck, New Jersey, July 22 and December 15, 2003, and much additional conversation. All subsequent information about Charles Roman is from these interviews. For more about Charles Roman, see Zuccotti, Holocaust Odysseys.

27. See Serge Klarsfeld, Memorial to the Jews Deported from France, 1942–1944 (New York: Beate Klarsfeld Foundation, 1983), 399. Leopold Gerhard is referred to as Adler Gerhard on the deportation list, but his identity is confirmed by his place and year of birth: Dukla, Czechoslovakia, 1907. He was deported from Drancy in convoy 50 on March 4, 1943, to the death camps of Majdanek and Sobibor. Only

four men from this convoy survived. Leopold Gerhard was not one of them.

28. Serena Szabo Gerhard's story was told by Jacques Samson, who was with her for part of her time in Valdieri and Rome, interview with this author, Menerbes, France, September 15, 2003. For more about Gerhard and Samson, see Zuccotti, *Holocaust Odysseys*. See also Jacky Gerhard, *Récit – Début*, unpublished manuscript in possession of this author, May 30, 2003.

29. Testimony of Père Marie-Benoît in *Livre d'Or*, 324–25, and, for the date of the raid at the Salus, Père Marie-Benoît, *Carnet*, entry for March 1, 1944, ACF, Paris, 13 LM 76. See also Padre Benedetto to Cardinal Joseph Mindszenty, February 28, 1946, f. 2, ACF, Paris, 13 LM 85. In this letter Padre Benedetto described the courageous assistance that Szasz had given during the German occupation of Rome and asked the cardinal if he could obtain some sort of official recognition from the Hungarian government for him. There is no record of the outcome in Padre Benedetto's papers. At the time of the raid on the Salus, German–Hungarian relations had reached the breaking point. The Germans occupied Hungary on March 19, 1944.

30. Testimony of Père Marie-Benoît in *Livre d'Or*, 322; and, for the reference to De Gasperi, Père Marie-Benoît to his "dear friend," unnamed but certainly Joseph Bass, February 20, 1945, CDJC, CDXLVI-7. The Franciscan convent in question was the Istituto Clarisse Missionarie Francescane del Santissimo Sacramento at 33 via Vicenza, which hid as many as seventy-six Jews. Not all of these were Delasem's protégés. The convent is mentioned in a list of Church institutions in Rome that helped Jews, in Renzo De Felice, *The Jews in Fascist Italy*, trans. Robert L. Miller (1961; New York: Enigma Books, 2001), 751. Padre Benedetto mentioned visiting the convent after the German occupation in his *Carnet*, entry for June 25, 1944. For examples of

letters of denunciation sent to the general minister at the Capuchin monastery, most of which complained that Padre Benedetto should be caring for poor Christians rather than "rich" Jews, see f. P. Marie-Benoît, Activités de Guerre, Documents, 1942–1974, ACF, Paris, 13 LM 84.

10. WITH STEFAN SCHWAMM IN ROME: SECURING FUNDS FOR JEWISH RESCUE

1. The statistics and quotation are from Settimio Sorani, *L'assistenza ai profughi ebrei in Italia (1933–1947)* (Rome: Carucci, 1983), 150–51; and Settimio Sorani, "Attività della 'Delasem' dopo l'8 settembre 1943," May 16, 1944, b. 8-A-I, f. Delasem – Settimio Sorani, CDEC. According to Sorani, the exchange rate was 400 to 420 lire per dollar (*L'assistenza ai profughi ebrei in Italia*, 153). However, in part because it was illegal to exchange lire for dollars, this rate changed frequently and is so approximate as to be almost meaningless.

2. Harold H. Tittmann Jr., *Inside the Vatican of Pius XII: The Memoir of an American Diplomat during World War II*, ed. Harold H. Tittmann III (New York: Doubleday, 2004), 190.

3. Testimony of Père Marie-Benoît in *Livre d'Or des Congrégations françaises: 1939–1945* (Paris: D.R.A.C., 1948), 317. In a letter to Harold Tittmann on January 22, 1962, Sorani claimed that *he* first asked the diplomat to send an appeal to the Joint. See the letter in English translation in "1943–1945; 1961–1962: Reports on the Situation of Jews in Italy," file 716, collection 33/44, Archives of the American Jewish Joint Distribution Committee, New York. Probably Padre Benedetto and Sorani visited Tittmann together.

4. Testimony of Père Marie-Benoît in *Livre d'Or*, 317, and "Alcune precisazioni di Padre Benedetto," *Israel*, anno XLVI, n. 36, July 6, 1961, 5; and Sorani, *L'assistenza ai profughi ebrei in Italia*, 151–52. Valobra's

undated letter to Sorani, Fondo Lelio Vittorio Valobra, b. 6, f. 3, CDEC, is cited in Sandro Antonini, *Delasem: Storia della più grande organizzazione ebraica italiana di soccorso durante la seconda guerra mondiale* (Genoa: De Ferrari, 2000), 285.

5. Testimony of Père Marie-Benoît in *Livre d'Or*, 317–18; Père Marie-Benoît (Benedetto), *Carnet*, entries for February 1944, ACF, Paris, 13 LM 76; and Sorani, *L'assistenza ai profughi ebrei in Italia*, 153.

6. *Actes et Documents du Saint Siège relatifs à la seconde guerre mondiale* (ADSS), ed. Pierre Blet, Robert A. Graham, Angelo Martini, and Burkhart Schneider (Vatican City: Libreria Editrice Vaticana, 1965–1981), vol.10, note of Maglione attached to doc. 103, Notes of the Secretariat of State, March 16, 1944, 177–79.

7. Owen Chadwick, *Britain and the Vatican during the Second World War* (Cambridge, UK: Cambridge University Press, 1986), 295.

8. Stefan Schwamm, "Riassunto dell'attività di Padre Benedetto Maria O.F.M. Cap. e dei suo [sic] collaboratori," December 20, 1945, 9 pp., 7, Marie-Benoît file 201, Department of the Righteous, Yad Vashem. After the war, Padre Benedetto testified on Girardi's behalf, probably because he was under investigation as a Fascist sympathizer. See f. Dichiarazione, April 20, 1945, ACF, Paris, 13 LM 85.

9. Stefan Schwamm to Padre Benedetto, January 30, 1984, Schwamm private archives, Frankfurt am Main.

10. Schwamm, "Riassunto dell'attività di Padre Benedetto Maria"; and Père Marie-Benoît, *Carnet*, entries for June 21 and 23, 1944, and September 9, 1945. Schwamm was not at Dachau, as Sorani claimed in his *L'assistenza ai profughi ebrei in Italia*, 146.

11. The story of Padre Benedetto's and Schwamm's trip to Milan is best told by the priest in his testimony in *Livre d'Or*, 325–27; and in Padre Maria Benedetto, "Aide clandestine aux refugiés politiques

et confessionnels: Affaires d'Italie," n.d., but written while he was still living at the Capuchin monastery in Rome, and therefore before October 1953, CDIC, CCCLXXIII-25. The specific dates of the trip are recorded in his *Carnet*. Sorani's claim in "Attività della 'Delasem' dopo l'8 settembre 1943," May 16, 1944, that the money from Genoa reached him on April 20 is an error unless Padre Benedetto somehow sent the money he secured in Genoa on to Rome before he arrived there.

12. Sorani, *L'assistenza ai profughi ebrei in Italia*, 151–53, and "Attività della 'Delasem' dopo l'8 settembre 1943."

13. Robert Leiber, S.J., "Pio XII e gli ebrei di Roma 1943–1944," *La Civiltà Cattolica*, vol. 1, quad. 2657, February 25, 1961, 452.

14. Lelio Vittorio Valobra, Renzo Levi, and Settimio Sorani, "Risposta a *Civiltà Cattolica*," *Israel*, anno XLVI, n. 32, June 8, 1961, 1.

15. Padre Maria Benedetto, "Alcune precisazioni di Padre Benedetto," *Israel*, anno XLVI, n. 36, July 6, 1961, 5. Padre Benedetto originally addressed this letter, dated June 24, 1961, to "Ottimo e caro Avvocato" (probably Carlo Alberto Viterbo). A copy exists in f. 3: P. Marie-Benoît Péteul: Activités de guerre: Correspondance, ACF, Paris, 13 LM 84. For his report to Monsignor Riberi, see Padre Maria Benedetto, "Relazione sull'assistenza agli Ebrei cattolici in Roma," January 24, 1945, ACF, Paris, 13 LM 84. Handwritten on the typed document are the words "For His Excellency Mgr. Riberi." Until his appointment to the Pontifical Commission for Refugee Assistance in March 1944, Riberi's wartime role at the Vatican was unofficial and unclear. He was one of many prelates of the Church with prewar overseas assignments that could not be fulfilled because of the conflict. Because he was born in Monaco, was a native French speaker, and was about the same age as

Padre Benedetto, however, the two men may have been personal friends. Regarding funds: in addition to the declaration that Delasem distributed twenty-five million lire during the German occupation of Rome, Padre Benedetto also confirmed for Riberi that he had received ninety-eight thousand lire from him after the liberation of the city, to be distributed among Jewish converts to Catholicism. The receipt and distribution of this money after liberation are described in more detail in chapter 11. The claim that Delasem distributed twenty-five million lire in Rome during the occupation was first made by Delasem immediately after liberation in an appeal to the Jews of Rome for future financial contributions so that the organization could continue its charitable work. See a copy of the appeal in f. 1: La Résistance: Récits, ACF, Paris, 13 LM 84. This sum was almost certainly too high.

16. Padre Maria Benedetto, "Alcune precisazioni di Padre Benedetto."

17. Père Marie-Benoît (Benedetto), Carnet, entry for February 8, 1944.

18. Sorani, L'assistenza ai profughi ebrei in Italia, 146; "Attività della 'Delasem' dopo l'8 settembre 1943"; and Sorani to Eloisa Ravenna, July 19, 1966, b. 13-B, f. Roma, CDEC.

19. Chadwick, Britain and the Vatican, 287.

20. ADSS, vol. 9, Note of the Secretariat of State, January 9, 1944, attached to doc. 412, 544–45.

21. Père Marie-Benoît, "Mon action en faveur des juifs persecutés à la seconde guerre mondiale," 9 pp., ACF, Paris, 13 LM 97; and f. 1: La Résistance: Récits, untitled document, n.d., but after 1975, ACF, Paris, 13 LM 84.

22. Père Marie-Benoît, "Mon action en faveur des juifs persecutés à la seconde guerre mondiale," 9.

23. Sorani, L'assistenza ai profughi ebrei in Italia, 153.

24. Ibid., 142, and "Attività della 'Delasem' dopo l'8 settembre 1943."

25. Testimony of Padre Benedetto on behalf of Kasztersztein, July 10, 1958, ACF, Paris, 13 LM 85.

26. Liliana Picciotto Fargion, Il libro della memoria: Gli ebrei deportati dall'Italia (1943–1945) (1991; Milan: Mursia, 2002), 52–53, 58–59, and 366. The exact number of deportees on this convoy is uncertain. The number identified is 527. The date of arrest given for Kasztersztein, April 1, 1944, is an error.

27. Schwamm, "Riassunto dell'attività di Padre Benedetto."

28. Sorani, L'assistenza ai profughi ebrei in Italia, 145–46, and "Attività della 'Delasem' dopo l'8 settembre 1943"; and Padre Benedetto, "Aide clandestine aux refugiés."

29. This information is based on research by Hanna Rawicz Keselman. In her list of Jewish deportees from Italy in Il libro della memoria, Picciotto Fargion has an entry for Jean Jacques Rawicz and another for Alessandro Ravicz (525). These two were the same person. The date for Jean Jacques Rawicz's first arrest is incorrect. The date for his deportation is that of the convoy from which he escaped. The information about Alessandro Ravicz is correct but incomplete.

30. Marie Warszawski, L'arrestation, la déportation, Journal de Rome (Paris: Lachenal et Ritter/Gallimard, 1998). Probably because he was deported under a false name, Oser Warszawski is not listed in Picciotto Fargion, Il libro della memoria.

31. Testimony of Père Marie-Benoît in Livre d'Or, 321–23.

11. AFTER THE LIBERATION OF ROME

1. Père Marie-Benoît, Carnet, entry for June 4, 1944, ACF, Paris, 13 LM 76; and Settimio Sorani, L'assistenza ai profughi ebrei in Italia (1933–1947) (Rome: Carucci,

1983), 157. Padre Benedetto's reference to the Figliuoli is difficult to decipher. The spelling of the name here may be slightly incorrect.

2. Sorani, *L'assistenza ai profughi ebrei in Italia,* 158. *Tevà* is an Italian spelling of a Hebrew word referring to the slaughter of animals. During and immediately after the war, it was sometimes used to refer to the mass murders of Jews, before the terms "Holocaust" or "Shoah" came to be used. I am grateful to Judah Gribetz and Professor Ed Greenstein for this information.

3. Padre Maria Benedetto to "my dear friend," probably Joseph Bass, February 20, 1945, CDJC, CDXLVI-7; and testimony of Père Marie-Benoît in *Livre d'Or des Congrégations françaises: 1939–1945* (Paris: D.R.A.C., 1948), 328.

4. For the speech, see "Décorations," f. P. Marie-Benoît Péteul, promotion au grade d'officier de la Légion d'honneur, ACF, Paris, 13 LM 86. For Sorani's handwritten invitation to Padre Benedetto to attend the service, see f. P. Marie-Benoît, Activités de guerre, Documents, 1942–1974, ACF, Paris, 13 LM 84. For attribution of the legend to Toaff, see Monsignor Elio Venier, *Il clero romano durante la Resistenza: Colloqui con i protagonisti di venticinque anni fa* (Rome: Colombo, 1972), 87–88. In preparation for his book, Monsignor Venier interviewed Rabbi Toaff. The book was also published in the magazine*Rivista Diocesana di Roma,* no. 11–13, 1969, and no. 1–2, 1970.

5. Père Marie-Benoît, *Carnet,* June 22, 1944. Padre Benedetto also mentioned that ceremony in his letter to his "dear friend" on February 20, 1945. Events that Padre Benedetto attended in 1945 included a ceremony on September 23 for the reopening of the Jewish orphanage in Rome and a reception at the Grand Hotel on November 5 for the American Jewish Joint Distribution Committee representative Reuben B. Resnik's departure for the United States. See *Carnet* entries for those dates.

6. Testimony of Père Marie-Benoît in *Livre d'Or,* 328–30. See also a beautiful handwritten letter of thanks to Rev. Père Donat de Welle by Clara Mandel, December 24, 1944, f. Marie-Benoît de Bourg d'Iré, doc. 12, Capuchin archives, Rome, G 94–S IV.

7. Padre Maria Benedetto, "Relazione sull'assistenza agli Ebrei cattolici in Roma, January 24, 1945, ACF, Paris, 13 LM 84. Handwritten on the typed document are the words "For His Excellency Mgr. Riberi."

8. Testimony of Père Marie-Benoît in *Livre d'Or,* 328.

9. Ibid. The date is from Père Marie-Benoît, *Carnet,* where he wrote on June 28, 1944, "We receive matzos to distribute."

10. Père Marie-Benoît, *Carnet,* entries for June 21 and 23 (for Schwamm, Ambord, and Riberi), July 19 (again for Riberi), and August 8 (for Kasztersztein), 1944.

11. Père Marie-Benoît, "Mon action en faveur des juifs persecutés à la seconde guerre mondiale," 9 pp., 3, ACF, Paris, 13 LM 97.

12. Padre Benedetto to Mgr. Riberi, January 24, 1945. For more on Weber, see Guenter Lewy, *The Catholic Church and Nazi Germany* (1964; Boulder, CO: Da Capo, 2000), 282–83.

13. Père Marie-Benoît, *Carnet,* entries in August 1944.

14. Padre Benedetto to Mgr. Riberi, January 24, 1945. In fact, Delasem did not announce that it could no longer help converted Jews until April 26, 1945. For a copy of that announcement, see "Avviso: Assistenza a Profughi battezzati," f. 1: Activités de guerre, ACF, Paris, 13 LM 84.

15. *Actes et Documents du Saint Siège relatifs à la seconde guerre mondiale* (ADSS), ed. Pierre Blet, Robert A. Graham, Angelo Martini, and Burkhart Schneider (Vatican City: Libreria Editrice Vaticana,

1965–1981), vol. 10, doc. 315, Padres Benedetto and Weber to Pius XII, September 2,
1944, 403–406.

16. Padre Benedetto to Mgr. Riberi,
January 24, 1945. That Padre Benedetto
was uncomfortable in the role of helper
specifically of Catholic Jews is also indicated in his letter to his "dear friend" on
February 20, 1945, when he wrote that he
had been "charged with assisting Catholic
Jews in the name of the Vatican, but in
a practical sense I also help many non-
Catholic Jews."

17. Padre Benedetto to Mgr. Riberi,
January 24, 1945.

18. Translated into French, "Amicizia
ebraico-cristiana" means Amitié Judéo-
Chrétienne, which was the name of an
ecumenical group of Jewish, Catholic, and
Protestant leaders created by Jules Isaac in
France in 1948. A similarly named group
existed in France during the war, dedicated to Jewish support and rescue. Jules
Isaac and Padre Benedetto were friends
and in regular contact during and after
the war. See Paule Berger Marx, Les Relations entre les Juifs et les catholiques dans la
France de l'après-guerre, 1945–1965 (Paris:
Éditions Parole et Silence, 2009), 125.

19. Padre Benedetto was apparently ill
and unable to go to the Seelisberg conference, but his friend and confrere in his
Rome monastery, the French Capuchin
priest Calliste Lopinot, attended. Seventy-
one years old in 1947, Lopinot was nearly
twenty years Padre Benedetto's senior.
For more on the Seelisberg conference,
see Christian M. Rutishauser, "The 1947
Seelisberg Conference: The Foundation
of the Jewish-Christian Dialogue," Studies in Christian-Jewish Relations 2, no.
2 (2008): 34–53; and Victoria Barnett,
"Seelisberg: An Appreciation," Studies in
Christian-Jewish Relations 2, no. 2 (2008):
54–57. Studies in Christian-Jewish Relations
is an e-journal of the Council of Centers
on Jewish-Christian Relations. Also see

Berger Marx, Les Relations entre les Juifs
et les catholiques dans la France de l'après-
guerre, 127–33, and appendix, 503–504.

20. For traditional Church guidelines
on the reading of scripture, see Pope Leo
XIII's encyclical Providentissimus Deus,
November 18, 1893, and, as those guidelines began to change, Pope Pius XII's
Divino Afflante Spiritu, September 30, 1943,
both available online.

21. Padre Maria Benedetto to an unidentified Vatican official, December 4,
1944, ACF, Paris, 13 LM 84.

22. Ibid.

23. The function of the Holy Office was
the preservation of authentic Catholic
teaching and the ferreting out of heresy
and error. In 1965, after the Second Vatican Council, it was renamed the Congregation for Doctrine of the Faith, but its
original purpose did not change.

24. The decree, published in Acta Apos-
tolicae Sedis 20 (1928), 103, was also printed
in "Cronaca contemporanea," La Civiltà
Cattolica anno 79, 1928, vol. 2, April 21,
1928, 171. In an effort to avert public criticism of a Vatican decree abolishing an
organization that called for treating Jews
with greater respect, Pius XI asked that it
also condemn antisemitism. Thus, the decree reminded readers that "the Catholic
Church has always prayed for the Jewish
people, depositories, until the coming of
Jesus Christ, of the divine promise, regardless of their subsequent blindness, or
rather, precisely because of it. Moved by
that spirit of charity, the Apostolic See has
protected this same people against unjust
vexations, and just as it reproves all ha-
treds and animosities between people, so
it especially condemns hatred against the
people elected by God, a hatred that today
is vulgarly called 'antisemitism.'"

25. For more on the Friends of Israel,
the petition for changes in the liturgy, and
Pius XI's role in the banning, see Hubert
Wolf, Pope and Devil: The Vatican's Ar-

chives and the *Third Reich*, trans. Kenneth
Kronenberg (Cambridge, MA: Harvard
University Press, 2010), 81‑123; and Hu‑
bert Wolf, "The Good Friday Supplica‑
tion for the Jews and the Roman Curia
(1928–1975): A Case Example for Research
Prospects for the Twentieth Century,"
*The Roman Inquisition, the Index, and the
Jews: Contexts, Sources, and Perspectives,*
ed. Stephan Wendehort (Leiden, The
Netherlands: Koninklijke Brill NV, 2004),
235–57. Wolf's information is based on his
study of documents from the pontificate
of Pius XI (1922–1939), recently released
by the Vatican Secret Archives in Rome.

26. "Il Pericolo giudaico e gli 'Amici
d'Israele,'" *La Civiltà Cattolica,* anno 79,
1928, vol. 2, May 19, 1928, 344. For Pius
XI's request to Padre Rosa, see Wolf, *Pope
and Devil,* 116.

27. Padre Benedetto to an unidentified
Vatican official, December 4, 1944.

28. In June 1948, during the papacy of
Pius XII, it was explained that *perfidis*
might be understood as meaning "unbe‑
lieving" rather than "perfidious" or "faith‑
less," a clarification that did not necessarily
please many Jewish spokesmen. Pius XII
authorized another alteration in 1956,
when he instructed that the reference
should be accompanied by kneeling and
silent private prayer as the Friends of Israel
had requested almost thirty years before.

29. Declaration of the Second Vatican
Council, "Nostra Aetate," October 28,
1965, no. 4, readily available online.

30. Padre Maria Benedetto to an un‑
identified Vatican official, July 7, 1945,
ACF, Paris, 13 LM 84.

31. Ibid.

32. Padre Benedetto had taken a differ‑
ent tack in November 1952, when he went
to Rome's central synagogue at the time
of a memorial service for Chaim Weiz‑
mann, the first president of the State of
Israel, who had just died. At that time he
did not enter the building, but delivered

his condolences outside. See *Carnet,* en‑
try for November 17, 1952. In fact, Canon
1258 of the 1917 Code of Canon Law states,
"It is not licit for the faithful by any man‑
ner to assist actively or to have a part in
the sacred [rites] of non‑Catholics" and
"Passive or merely material presence can
be tolerated for the sake of honor or civil
office, for grave reasons approved by the
Bishop in case of doubt, at the funerals,
weddings, and similar solemnities of non‑
Catholics, provided danger of perversion
and scandal is absent." See Edward N.
Peters, *The 1917 Pio‑Benedictine Code of
Canon Law in English Translation with
Extensive Scholarly Apparatus* (San Fran‑
cisco: Ignatius Press, 2001), 426–27. I
am grateful to Kevin Spicer, C.S.C., for
directing me to this source.

33. Père Marie‑Benoît, "Amitié Judéo‑
Chrétienne," *Bulletin Provincial des Frères
Mineurs Capucins de la Province de Paris,*
1960, 6.

34. Sorani to Eloisa Ravenna, July 19,
1966, 5 pp., 3, b. 13‑B, f. Roma, CDEC.

35. For discussion of this point, see
Kevin Spicer, "Selective Resistance: The
German Catholic Church's Response to
National Socialism," in *Confronting the
Holocaust: A Mandate for the 21st Century,*
part 2, ed. Stephen C. Feinstein, Karen
Schierman, and Marcia Sachs Littell, *Stud‑
ies in the Shoah,* vol. 20 (Lanham, MD:
University Press of America, 1998), 71–88.
Spicer stresses that not all priests and
practicing Catholics before the war shared
this view.

36. See drafts of this lecture in f. 1: Père
Marie‑Benoît: Amitié Judéo‑Chrétienne,
ACF, Paris, 13 LM 85.

37. Miriam Löwenwirth Reuveni, *Dedi‑
cation,* unpublished English translation of
her memoirs titled *Hakdasha,* written in
Hebrew with Miriam Dubi‑Gazan (Raa‑
nana, Israel: Docostory, 2002); also trans‑
lated into Italian as *Dedicazione* (Aosta,
Italy: Le Château, 2005); interviews with

this author in Nice and Cuneo, September 8 and 9, 2003, and in Haifa, February 26 and 27, 2008; and letter to this author, June 20, 2011.

38. For this exchange, see "L'Amicizia cristiano-ebraica," *L'Osservatore Romano*, October 6, 1946, 2; and handwritten copy of the Jewish leaders' response, published in *Israel*, October 9, 1946, and a typed copy of Padre Benedetto, letter to the editor, published in *Israel*, October 28, 1946, ACF, Paris, 13 LM 82.

39. Père Marie-Benoît, "Le Concile Vatican II et les Juifs," *Études franciscaines: Revue publiée par les Frères Mineurs Capucins* 18, no. 45 (1968): 54–63.

40. For details, see Robert G. Weisbord and Wallace P. Sillanpoa, *The Chief Rabbi, the Pope, and the Holocaust: An Era in Vatican-Jewish Relations* (New Brunswick, NJ: Transaction, 1992). For more on Zolli's position, see his memoirs written under the name of Eugenio Zolli, *Before the Dawn: Autobiographical Reflections* (New York: Sheed and Ward, 1954). For the case against him, see Louis I. Newman, *A "Chief Rabbi" of Rome Becomes a Catholic: A Study in Fright and Spite* (New York: Renascence Press, 1945).

41. Père Marie-Benoît, "Amitié Judéo-Chrétienne," *Bulletin Provincial*, 1960, 4.

42. For the exchange of letters between Sorani, Padre Benedetto, and the Jesuit priest Gozzelino Birolo, see Correspondance 1934–1990, ACF, Paris, 13 LM 78.

43. Years later Sorani remembered that he had visited as many convents and monasteries as possible in Rome after the war, asking for any Jewish children who might be there. In many cases, when he was told that there were none, he believed the reason was that they had been baptized and were therefore no longer considered to be "Jewish children." He was able to recover more than three hundred children, however. See Sorani, report to Ravenna, July 19, 1966, 3.

44. For more on this issue, see Michael R. Marrus, "The Vatican and the Custody of Jewish Child Survivors after the Holocaust," *Holocaust and Genocide Studies* 21, no. 3 (2007): 378–403.

12. THE FINAL DECADES

1. Padre Maria Benedetto to "Ottimo e caro Avvocato" (Carlo Alberto Viterbo), August 3, 1971, f. 3: "P. Marie-Benoît Péteul: Activités de guerre: Correspondance 1945–1972," ACF, Paris, 13 LM 84.

2. Examples of early works include Philip Friedman, *Their Brothers' Keepers* (New York: Crown, 1957); Kurt Grossmann, *Die unbesungenen Helden* (Berlin: Grunewald, 1957), 298–310; Rev. John A. O'Brien, "The Incredible Father Benoit [sic] – 'Rescuer of the Jews,'" *Pageant* 20, no. 5, November 1964, 130–37; James Rorty, "Father Benoit [sic]: 'Ambassador of the Jews': An Untold Chapter of the Underground," *Commentary*, December 1946, 507–13; Elio Venier, *Il clero romano durante la resistenza* (Rome: Colombo, 1972), 87–97; and Sam Waagenaar, *The Pope's Jews* (La Salle, IL: Open Court, 1974). The Grossmann chapter is largely a reprint of Rorty.

3. Padre Benedetto to "Ottimo e caro Avvocato," August 3, 1971.

4. Photocopies of the citations and medals are in "Décorations," f. P. Marie-Benoît Péteul, promotion au grade d'officier de la Légion d'honneur, ACF, Paris, 13 LM 86. For more on the ceremony honoring him as a chevalier of the Legion of Honor, see also *La Croix*, April 22, 1948.

5. For the ceremony of April 27, 1958, see "Manifestation du souvenir: 27 avril 1958," f. 2: Activités de guerre, ACF, Paris, 13 LM 84. Unable to attend the ceremony, Padre Benedetto was represented by Fernande Leboucher. Also honored at this time were Père Pierre Chaillet, Abbé Alexandre Glasberg, and Pastor Paul Vergara. The tribute by President Johnson is print-

ed in O'Brien, "Incredible Father Benoit,"
135. For the Légion d'Honneur event, see
"Décorations," ACF, Paris, 13 LM 86. For
more on the award of Righteous among
the Nations, see chapter 5.

6. The Capuchin order might conceiv-
ably have granted Padre Benedetto the use
of community funds to make such a trip if
he had requested it. There is no evidence
that he did.

7. Padre Benedetto was teaching near
Tours when he received the invitation
to visit Israel. The Capuchin provincial
minister in Paris wrote to the general
minister in Rome on June 27, 1958, asking
permission for Padre Benedetto to make
the trip. See the letter, f. Marie-Benoît de
Bourg d'Iré, doc. 23, in Capuchin archives,
Rome, G 94 – S IV.

8. Padre Benedetto to "Ottimo e caro
Avvocato," August 3, 1971. Enzo Sereni
founded the Kibbutz Givat Brenner in the
late 1920s. Padre Benedetto probably visited the Kibbutz Enzo Sereni, founded by
survivors from Buchenwald in 1948, rather
than the Kibbutz Givat Brenner.

9. Padre Benedetto's letters to Rachel
Fallmann in Tel Aviv, August 27 and November 1, 1958, are in the possession of Rachel Fallmann. For the offer in 1968, see an
article by Miriam Honig in the *Jerusalem
Post*, weekend magazine *Family*, March 15,
1968, 15. The author attributed the offer to
managers of the Hellenic Mediterranean
Shipping Lines. For Padre Benedetto's
intentions in 1971, see his letter to "Ottimo
e caro Avvocato," August 3, 1971.

10. Padre Benedetto to Rachel Fallmann, August 19, 1966; letter in possession
of Rachel Fallmann.

11. Stefan Schwamm to Padre Benedetto, Jerusalem, October 8, 1967, f. Correspondance: Schwamm, ACF, Paris, 13 LM
79. Sam Waagenaar, a writer and historian
who knew him, also wrote, "Father Maria
Benedetto, as he once confessed to me,
would like to end his days in an Israeli kib-

butz." See his "An Unknown War Hero,"
America 131, no. 11, October 19, 1974,
210 12.

12. Padre Benedetto was not alone
among rescuers of Jews who developed a
great appreciation of Israel after the war.
At least fifty Polish rescuers are known
to have settled there. Others, like Oscar
Schindler, visited often. I am grateful to
Michael Phayer for pointing this out to
me. See also Eva Fogelman, *Conscience
and Courage: Rescuers of Jews during the
Holocaust* (New York: Doubleday, 1994),
288–97.

13. Provincial Minister Dieudonne de
S. Gemmes to General Minister Donat
de Welle in Rome, February 20, 1946, f.
Marie-Benoît de Bourg d'Iré, doc. 14,
Capuchin archives, Rome, G 94 – S IV.

14. General Minister Donat de Welle
to Provincial Minister Dieudonne de S.
Gemmes, March 30, 1946, f. Marie-Benoît
de Bourg d'Iré, doc. 16, and a new Capuchin general minister in Rome to the provincial minister in Paris, October 2, 1953,
doc. 17, in Capuchin archives, Rome, G
94 – S IV. A copy of the first letter may also
be found at ACF, Paris, 2 C 77. See also
Père Marie-Benoît, *Carnet*, first entry for
August 1952, ACF, Paris, 13 LM 76. When
Padre Benedetto went there in 1953, Campobasso was in a region known as Abruzzo
e Molise.

15. Letter, October 14, 1953, "Au sujet du
P. Marie-Benoît," ACF, Paris, 5 E 2–4.

16. The commemorative scrapbook remained among Padre Benedetto's personal
papers and is today at ACF, Paris. For the
dates of his trips to and from Campobasso
and his vacation in France, see *Carnet*, entries for October 13, 1953; April 15–19 and
August 5, 1955. According to his *Carnet*,
Padre Benedetto's first visit to his brothers
in Angers after the war was in July 1946.
There is a gap in the *Carnet* from 1947 to
1951 and no mention of Angers from 1952
to 1954, but he visited his brothers again

in August 1955 and much more frequently after his return to France in 1956.

17. Letters from the general minister in Rome to the provincial minister in Paris, September 2 and 6, 1955, A C F, Paris, 2 C 86. The general minister received a letter from Padre Benedetto's director in Campobasso, written on September 5, stating that he could not manage without him. See f. Marie-Benoît de Bourg d'Iré, s.f. Benedictus Maria, Capuchin archives, Rome, G 94 – S IV.

18. Provincial minister in Paris and general minister in Rome, exchange of letters, June 26 and 30, 1956, f. Marie-Benoît de Bourg d'Iré, docs. 19 and 20, Capuchin archives, Rome, G 94 – S IV. There is a copy of the June 30 letter in A C F, Paris, 2 C 87.

19. For a description of the search and final arrest, see David Cesarani, *Becoming Eichmann: Rethinking the Life, Crimes, and Trial of a "Desk Murderer"* (Cambridge, MA: Da Capo, 2007), 200–36; and Zvi Aharoni and Wilhelm Dietl, *Operation Eichmann: The Truth about the Pursuit, Capture, and Trial,* trans. Helmut Bögler (New York: John Wiley, 1997). Eichmann was the head of section IV-B-4 of the Reichssicherheitshauptamt (R S H A), the Reich Security Main Office of German security police. "Section IV" constituted the Gestapo, "B" was concerned with sects, and "4" was involved with the Jews.

20. "Qui è rinchiuso Eichmann," *L'Europeo,* March 12, 1961, 52–57. Wiesenthal repeated these claims in his memoirs, *The Murderers among Us* (New York: McGraw-Hill, 1967), 121, and added that Klimrod had said, "We know that two priests, Father Weber and Father Benedetti, helped him [Eichmann] while he was in Rome. We know the Capuchin monastery where he was hiding."

21. For the article, see Lamberto Furno, "Eichmann giunse a Roma con passaporto Nansen," *Vita,* March 30, 1961, 11–13. For more on Hudal's attitudes toward Nazism

before the war, see Peter Godman, *Hitler and the Vatican: Inside the Secret Archives that Reveal the New Story of the Nazis and the Church* (New York: Free Press, 2004).

22. For details on the working of Hudal's subcommittee of the Pontifical Commission for Refugee Assistance, see Gerald Steinacher, *Nazis on the Run: How Hitler's Henchmen Fled Justice* (New York: Oxford University Press, 2011), 110–14.

23. *Vita,* March 30, 1961, 12. Some of these words were also quoted in "S. Exc. Mgr Hudal estime possible qu'Eichmann ait été caché parmi les refugiés qu'il a aidés après la guerre, *La Croix,* clipped and filed among Père Marie-Benoît's papers, but with no evident date, in Presse, A C F, Paris, 13 L M 81.

24. For details and evidence on Hudal's involvement with war criminals, see Steinacher, *Nazis on the Run;* Michael Phayer, *Pius XII, the Holocaust, and the Cold War* (Bloomington: Indiana University Press, 2008); Uki Goñi, *The Real Odessa: Smuggling the Nazis to Perón's Argentina* (London: Granta Books, 2002); and Andrea Casazza, *La fuga dei nazisti: Mengele, Eichmann, Priebke, Pavelić da Genova all'impunità* (Genoa: Il melangolo, 2007). Stangl was at various times the commandant of the Sobibor and Treblinka extermination camps; Mengele was the physician at Auschwitz responsible for selections and human experiments; Priebke directed the massacre of 335 partisans and Jews at the Ardeatine Caves in Rome; Roschmann was commandant of the Riga ghetto; and Rauff was a senior SS police official and developer of mobile gas vans.

25. Alois C. Hudal, *Römische Tagebücher: Lebensbeichte eines alten Bischofs* (Graz: Leopold Stocker, 1976), 21.

26. Gitta Sereny, *Into that Darkness: An Examination of Conscience* (London: Deutsch, 1974), 318–21.

27. Capuchin statement, *Vita,* March 30, 1961, 13.

28. Cesarani, *Becoming Eichmann*, 209.

29. For more on Dömöter, see Goñi, *The Real Odessa*, 236. As evidence, Goñi cites correspondence between Hudal and Dömöter in the archives of the Comisión de Esclarecimiento de Actividades Nazis en la Argentina. For details on Eichmann's stay in Bolzano and journey to Genoa, see Steinacher, *Nazis on the Run*, 21–23, 51–53, and 97; Cesarani, *Becoming Eichmann*, 200–209; and Goñi, *Real Odessa*, 292–99.

30. For the request for clarification, see Père François Solano to Padre Benedetto, March 15, 1961, 13 LM 84; for Padre Benedetto's response to Solano, March 20, 1961, see Presse, 13 LM 81; both in ACF, Paris.

31. Père Marie-Benoît to Carlo Alberto Viterbo, April 9, 1961, in P. Marie-Benoît Péteul, Activités de guerre: Correspondance 1945–1972, ACF, Paris, 13 LM 84.

32. "Testimoniamo per Padre Benedetto," *Israel*, March 30, 1961, no page given on the clipping in Père Marie-Benoît's files, Coupures de Presse, ACF, Paris, 13 LM 82.

33. For discussion of this letter to the editor, see chapter 10.

34. Capuchin general minister in Rome to Père Marie-Benoît, June 27, 1964, f. Marie-Benoît de Bourg d'Iré, doc. 25, Capuchin archives, Rome, G 94 – S IV.

35. Père Marie-Benoît to Capuchin general minister, June 30, 1964, f. Marie-Benoît de Bourg d'Iré, doc. 26, Capuchin archives, Rome, G 94 – S IV. Père Marie-Benoît's report was printed in *Livre d'Or des Congrégations françaises: 1939–1945* (Paris: D.R.A.C., 1948), 305–31. Renzo De Felice's *Storia degli ebrei italiani sotto il fascism* exists as *The Jews in Fascist Italy*, trans. Robert L. Miller (New York: Enigma Books, 2001). The list of religious institutions and Père Marie-Benoît's report are printed in attached documents 40 and 41, 751–58.

36. Volume 9 is part of *Actes et Documents du Saint Siège relatifs à la seconde guerre mondiale* (ADSS), ed. Pierre Blet, Robert A. Graham, Angelo Martini, and Burkhart Schneider (Vatican City: Libreria Editrice Vaticana, 1965–1981). For Père Marie-Benoît on French Jewish leaders, see chapter 7; on fraudulent documents, see chapter 9; and on Delasem loans and the Joint, see chapter 10.

37. Père Marie-Benoît, "Mon action en faveur des juifs persecutés à la seconde guerre mondiale," no date, but after 1975, 9 pp., 9, ACF, Paris, 13 LM 97, for the first quote; and Padre Maria Benedetto, "Alcune precisazioni di Padre Benedetto," *Israel*, anno XLVI, n. 36, July 6, 1961, 5, for the second.

38. Père Marie-Benoît, "Mon action en faveur des juifs persecutés à la seconde guerre mondiale," 2.

39. Capuchin general minister to provincial minister in Paris, September 17, 1964, f. Marie-Benoît de Bourg d'Iré, doc. 27, Capuchin archives, Rome, G 94 – S IV.

40. Capuchin provincial minister to general minister in Rome, September 24, 1964, f. Marie-Benoît de Bourg d'Iré, doc. 29, Capuchin archives, Rome, G 94 – S IV. Père Marie-Benoît's writings for *Études franciscaines* in the 1960s and 1970s were complex, subtle, and profound, revealing his mastery of both secular and religious philosophers, including Plato, Augustine, Aquinas, Newton, and many others. An excellent appraisal of these writings may be found in Gérard Cholvy, *Marie-Benoît de Bourg d'Iré (1895–1990): Itinéraire d'un fils de Saint François Juste des Nations* (Paris: Éditions du Cerf, 2010).

41. Frère Dominique Mouly, interview with this author, Paris, October 13, 2009. Information on the walks in the Luxembourg Gardens is from Marie-Hélène de Bengy, archivist at ACF, Paris, interview with this author, June 9, 2009.

42. Père Marie-Benoît to Mireille Tenenbaum, April 24, 1971, Correspondance 1934–1990, ACF, Paris, 13 LM 78.

43. Schwamm to Père Marie-Benoît, June 2, 1987, 13 LM 78, and April 20, 1988,

13 LM 86, in ACF, Paris. Schwamm seems never to have written the book. The works of Rorty and Waagenaar are cited above, note 2.

44. Letter in Schwamm private archives, Frankfurt am Main.

EPILOGUE

1. Padre Maria Benedetto to "my dear friend," probably Joseph Bass, February 20, 1945, CDJC, CDXLVI-7.

2. Serge Klarsfeld, *Memorial to the Jews Deported from France, 1942–1944* (New York: Beate Klarsfeld Foundation, 1983), xvi. Of the seventy-five thousand Jews deported to the east, twenty-seven hundred survived.

3. Liliana Picciotto Fargion, *Il libro della memoria: Gli ebrei deportati dall'Italia (1943–1945)* (1991; Milan: Mursia, 2002), 27. Of the 6,806 Jews known to have been deported, 837 survived.